IMAGES
of America

JOHN APPERSON'S LAKE GEORGE

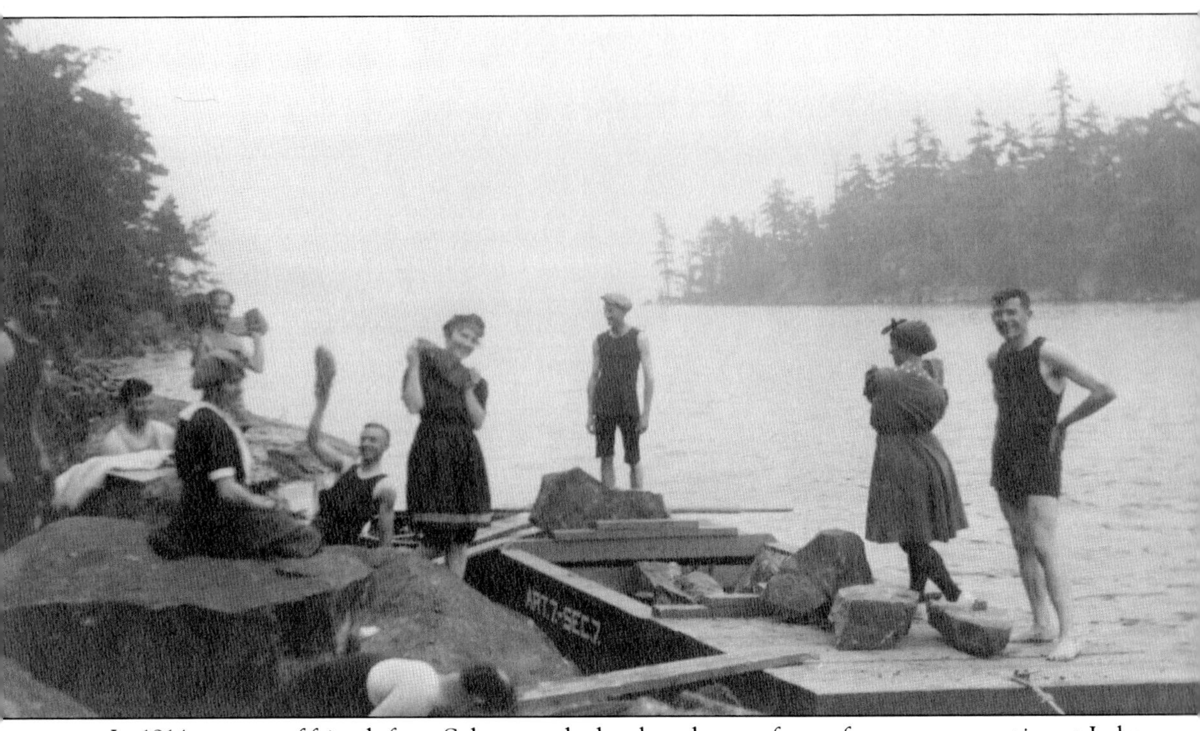

In 1914, a group of friends from Schenectady developed a new form of summer recreation at Lake George, combining camping and swimming with a rigorous restoration project, gathering and hauling rocks to protect the islands from erosion. (Courtesy of the Kelly Adirondack Research Center.)

On the Cover: John S. Apperson Jr., shown here delivering a boatload of rocks to one of the islands at Lake George, recruited hundreds of others to the cause, eventually saving about 50 islands from destruction. (Courtesy of the Kelly Adirondack Research Center.)

IMAGES
of America

JOHN APPERSON'S LAKE GEORGE

Ellen Apperson Brown

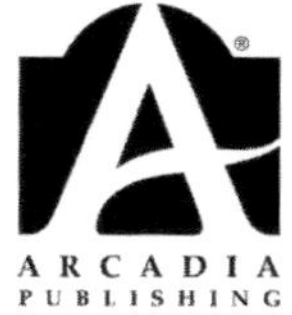

ISBN 978-1-4671-2476-8

Published by Arcadia Publishing
Charleston, South Carolina

Printed in the United States of America

Library of Congress Control Number: 2016947181

For all general information, please contact Arcadia Publishing:
Telephone 843-853-2070
Fax 843-853-0044
E-mail sales@arcadiapublishing.com
For customer service and orders:
Toll-Free 1-888-313-2665

Visit us on the Internet at www.arcadiapublishing.com

To James W. Apperson, my Uncle Jim, and to Douglas Langdon and William M. White, good neighbors and friends, for keeping up the good fight.

Contents

ACKNOWLEDGMENTS

I remember summer vacations at Uncle John's camp in Huddle Bay—of cooking over a wood stove, learning to paddle a canoe, and going for boat rides out to see Dome Island. About 20 years ago, I decided to find out what happened when my great uncle John S. Apperson Jr. first fell in love with Lake George. This project has led me on a fascinating journey visiting relatives, searching through archives in museums, and making frequent visits back to the lake.

One summer, friends took me up into the Narrows to meet John Newkirk, one of the original members of the Turtle Bay Association. On another visit, we went out to Dome Island to attend the annual meeting of the Dome Island Committee and to Crown Island, summer home of Roger Summerhayes, grandson of Irving Langmuir. In 1998, Bill White showed me his "playhouse" in Northwest Bay and invited me to spend a week or so in the Adirondack Research Library, making photocopies of letters from the Apperson collection.

It has been a challenge to work on an Apperson biography when most of the pertinent documents are stored in Schenectady, New York, far from my home. Fortunately, in 2011, when Union College took over responsibility for the Adirondack Research Library as a permanent loan from PROTECT the Adirondacks, my job got a little easier. They set up the Kelly Adirondack Research Center, obtained grant funding, and started processing the huge collection of materials. In June 2016, they invited me to spend several days in Schenectady, giving us a chance to look through hundreds of photographs together and choose our favorites for this book.

Special thanks go to Ted Caldwell, Bolton town historian, who graciously offered to serve as editor for this text, and several others, including Peter White, Doug Langdon, and my brother Tom Apperson, who helped me identify people and places. Several key organizations, including the Eastern New York chapter of the Nature Conservancy and the Lake George Land Conservancy, are helping me put Lake George into the bigger picture of New York's environmental history.

The photographs come from two main sources: the Kelly Adirondack Research Center (KARC) in Schenectady, or the author's personal collection (author's collection).

Introduction

In the early 1900s, Lake George was a popular summer destination for wealthy visitors from metropolitan areas in the northeast. These vacationers traveled by train to Glens Falls or Ticonderoga and continued their journey by steamboat to be deposited at hotels scattered up and down the lake—at the Sagamore in Bolton Landing, or at the Sherman House on French Point. However, when a new industrial city sprang up almost overnight in Schenectady, New York, scores of young professionals started coming to Lake George. They preferred "roughing it" instead of paying for a classy hotel. They liked the exotic sports being developed by some of their friends from General Electric (GE), such as skate sailing and skiing, and they enjoyed camping in the islands of the Narrows.

John S. Apperson Jr. first arrived in Schenectady in 1900, hoping to find a job in the exciting new field of electrical engineering. Once accepted into the training program at GE, he thrived in the fast-paced environment and advanced steadily up the management ladder, eventually becoming a senior engineer in the power and mining department.

Apperson enjoyed living in Schenectady, too, especially because of its proximity to so many lakes, rivers, and mountains—all just waiting to be explored. Apperson became an avid promoter of outdoor recreation and soon took an interest in New York's Forest Preserve. Back in 1895, New York voters had created both the Adirondack Park and a Forest Preserve, passing a constitutional amendment with a special "forever wild" clause prohibiting logging on state owned land within certain counties.

By 1907, Apperson had discovered Lake George and the joys of island camping. His affection for one island was triggered by an incident in late autumn 1908, when his canoe hit a log and overturned. He barely managed to make it to shore on West Dollar Island. Grateful to have survived, he made up his mind to try to protect the island, whose shores were rapidly eroding.

While working for a railroad in Virginia, Apperson had learned a technique called riprapping, which involved piling rocks underneath the train tracks to stabilize them. He decided to try the same strategy at West Dollar Island and began constructing rock walls along its perimeter, utilizing the labor of friends and volunteers.

At the Constitutional Convention of 1915, Apperson made friends with prominent lawyers and politicians, returning to Lake George with renewed confidence and determination. He soon began helping state officials remove squatters from state-owned islands. Because of his persistence, scores of buildings were torn down or relocated. Eventually, the islands became part of a state-run camping system, operated and maintained by the local forest ranger, Jay Taylor, and his crew.

As pressure mounted for the construction of new roads, the value of shoreline properties began to rise. Realtors and contractors encouraged the economic boom, as more families began building summer homes ranging from informal camps to elegant mansions. Several of the prominent local families took an interest in preserving the natural beauty of the lake's central section, including Tongue Mountain, Dome Island, and Paradise Bay. William K. Bixby, Mary Loines, and George

Foster Peabody began promoting the idea and formed the Bolton Improvement Association to prevent undesirable development. They were impressed with the energetic and determined young activist Apperson and welcomed him to the cause.

By 1918, state officials were taking over the island campgrounds. Since Apperson could no longer use the islands for his base of operations, he purchased a lot in Turtle Bay, situated on the eastern side of Tongue Mountain, and encouraged friends to buy neighboring parcels. Then, in Bolton Landing, he heard about the Lake View Hotel property in Huddle Bay that was up for sale. It was expensive, so he asked around in Schenectady and found two engineers willing to consider a joint purchase: G. Hall Roosevelt, brother of Eleanor Roosevelt, and William Dalton. Margaret and Hall Roosevelt assumed ownership of the annex, Ida and William Dalton took the middle portion, and John Apperson took the southern strip, with a huge boathouse and an icehouse that he remodeled into a two-story camp.

Eventually, the Roosevelts and the Daltons sold off their interests, forcing Apperson to find other potential buyers. One couple, Florence and Kilgore Christie, bought the annex, adding stability and gracious charm to the growing community. Irving Langmuir and his wife, Marion, bought property close by and persuaded Marion's sister, Dorothy Mersereau, as well as two prominent scientists, Katherine Blodgett and Edith Clark, to join them in "the Huddle." Over the years, Apperson invited his siblings, nieces, and nephews to come for extended summer visits, putting them up in his Main Camp, known as "Chilhowie" (after his home town in Virginia), or with Florence Christie in the annex, affectionately known as "Flonnykill."

During the 1930s, Apperson launched a nonprofit organization, the New York Forest Preserve Association (FPA), with several prominent friends as directors, including George Foster Peabody and Irving Langmuir. The group's first project was to pay for the publication of a pamphlet, "The Tragic Truth About Erosion," for the US Soil Conservation Service in Washington, DC. In the 1940s, Apperson launched another organization, the Lake George Protective Association, to address specific problems threatening the lake. During World War II, Apperson became a chief witness for the State of New York in a lawsuit against the International Paper Company, owners of the dam at Ticonderoga, protesting the destruction, or "trespass," of state property caused by high water levels.

Over several decades, Apperson tried to establish neighborhood associations in both Huddle Bay and Turtle Bay with restrictions against unsightly development. Perhaps his proudest accomplishment, however, was in finding an organization that could take over ownership of Dome Island, which he had purchased in 1939 with help from his good friend Irving Langmuir. It took nearly two decades to find a satisfactory solution, but he eventually donated the island to the newly formed Eastern New York chapter of the Nature Conservancy in 1956. Friends raised $20,000 as an endowment, and a committee was appointed to watch over the beautiful scenery in perpetuity.

Apperson had always planned to leave his property in Huddle Bay to his nephew and namesake, John Apperson III, but by the time of his death in 1963, the young family had moved to Charlotte, North Carolina. John Apperson III died in 1971, Apperson's other nephew, Jim Apperson, died in 1980, and the great-niece and great-nephews (Ellen, John, and Tom, all of whom lived far away and could not afford to own property in an expensive resort area), were forced to sell off the last parcel in 1996. Perhaps a new generation of young campers, hikers, and mountain climbers will find inspiration in John Apperson's prodigious accomplishments and follow his lead, saving their favorite wild places for generations to come.

One

Engineers at Play

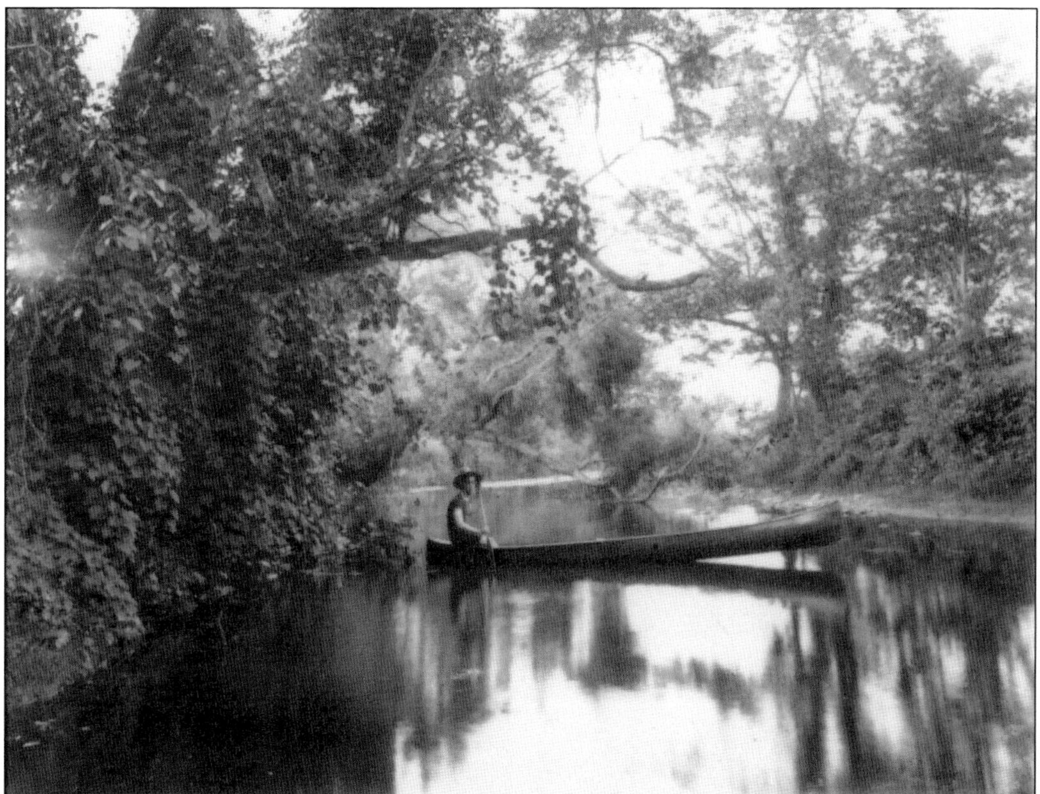

As Schenectady grew from a sleepy town into a booming industrial city, many of its young professionals hated being stuck indoors and were eager to escape to the countryside. John Apperson apparently borrowed a canoe one day and ventured onto the Mohawk River around 1903. (Courtesy of KARC.)

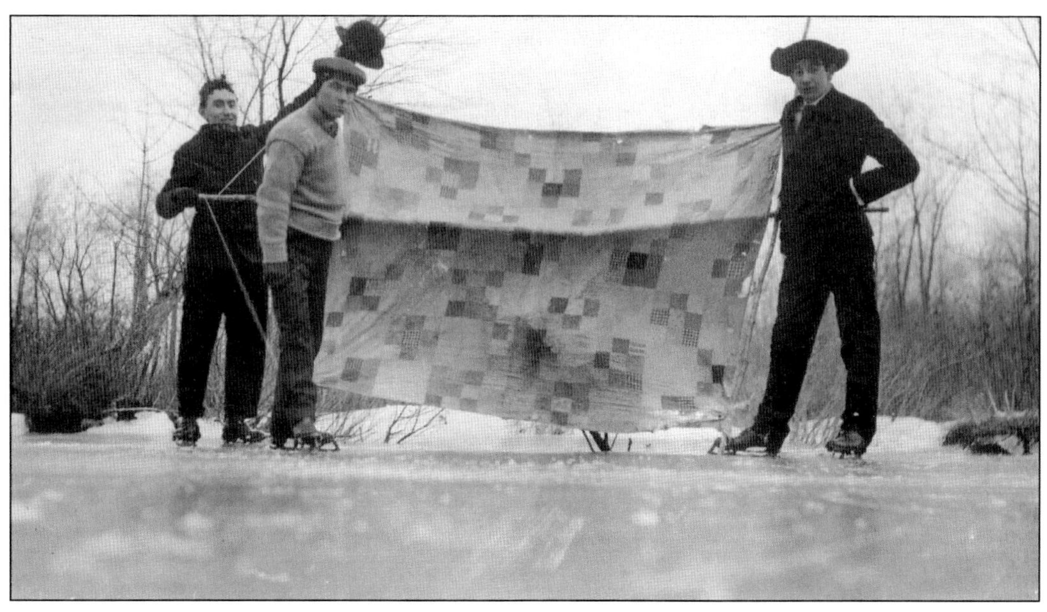

When skate sailing was first introduced in Schenectady, no one had the proper equipment. Above, John Apperson and his friends had to improvise, borrowing a quilt for a sail. Below, these young sailing enthusiasts eventually began manufacturing homemade sails and frames, as seen in this photograph of four men practicing the new sport on Ballston Lake. (Both, courtesy of KARC.)

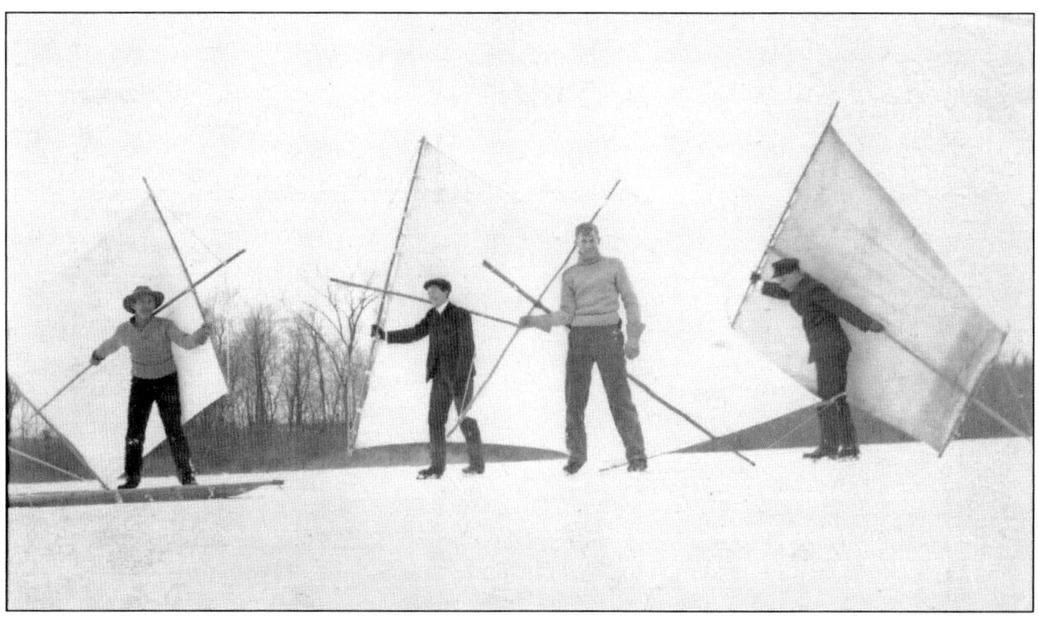

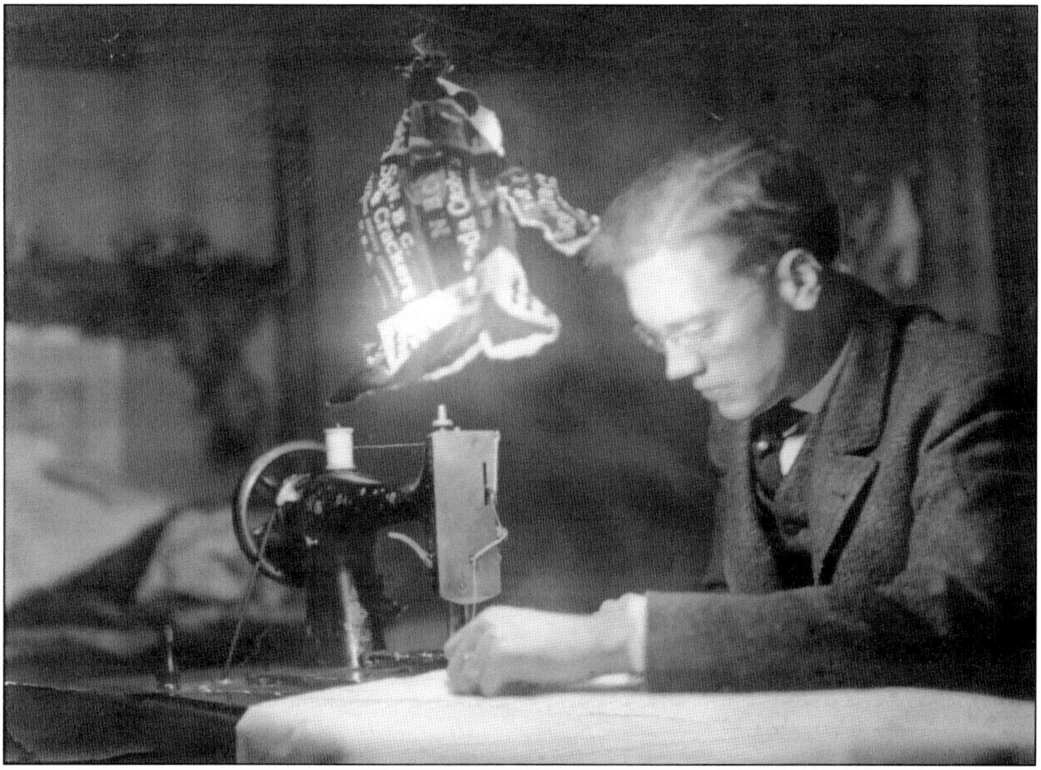

Apperson and his friends devoted much of their leisure time to preparing for their next excursion. They bought a sewing machine, ordered fabric, and began designing their own sails, as well as tents and sleeping bags. Robert E. Doherty solved the problem of glare from the light bulb in a creative way, wrapping a bag around it, yet leaving enough light for an excellent photograph. (Courtesy of KARC.)

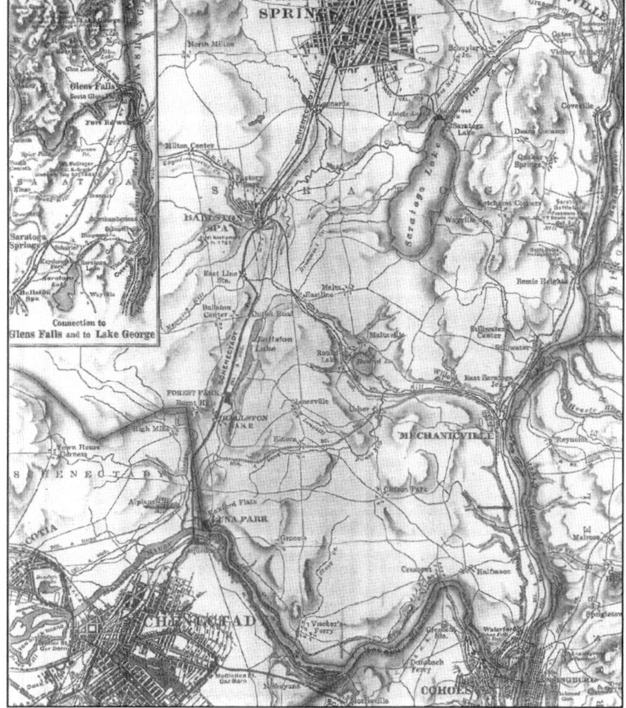

Ballston Lake, one of their favorite destinations, was just north of Schenectady and reachable by the Schenectady Railway. This map, found in the Apperson papers, dates to 1911. (Courtesy of KARC.)

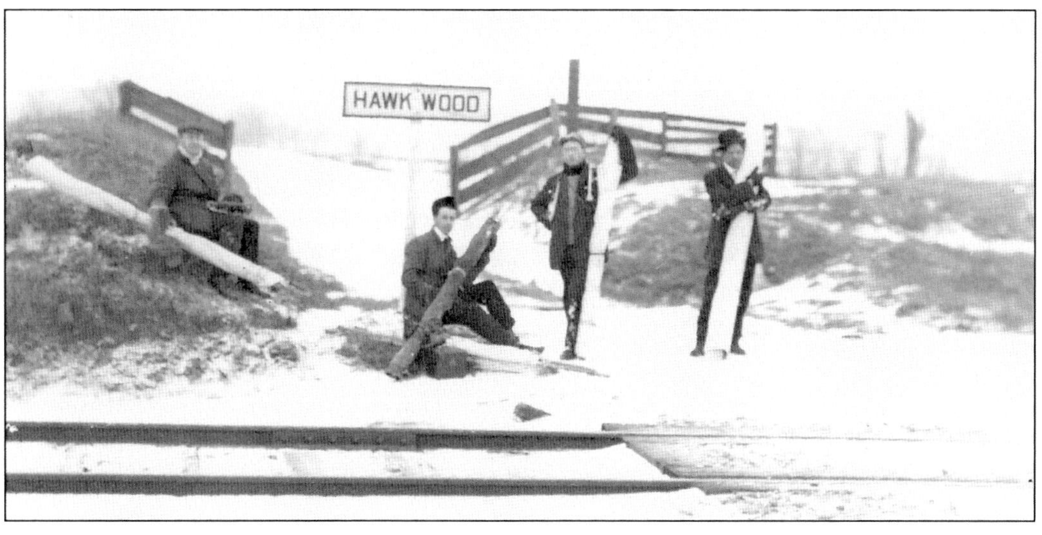

Above, four men wait to catch a ride to another favorite destination, Ballston Lake. By wrapping their sails around the frames and slinging their skates on their shoulders, they could easily carry all their sporting gear for a day trip. Below, perhaps on another occasion, other skating enthusiasts wait at the same train stop, including three women and a child. (Both, courtesy of KARC)

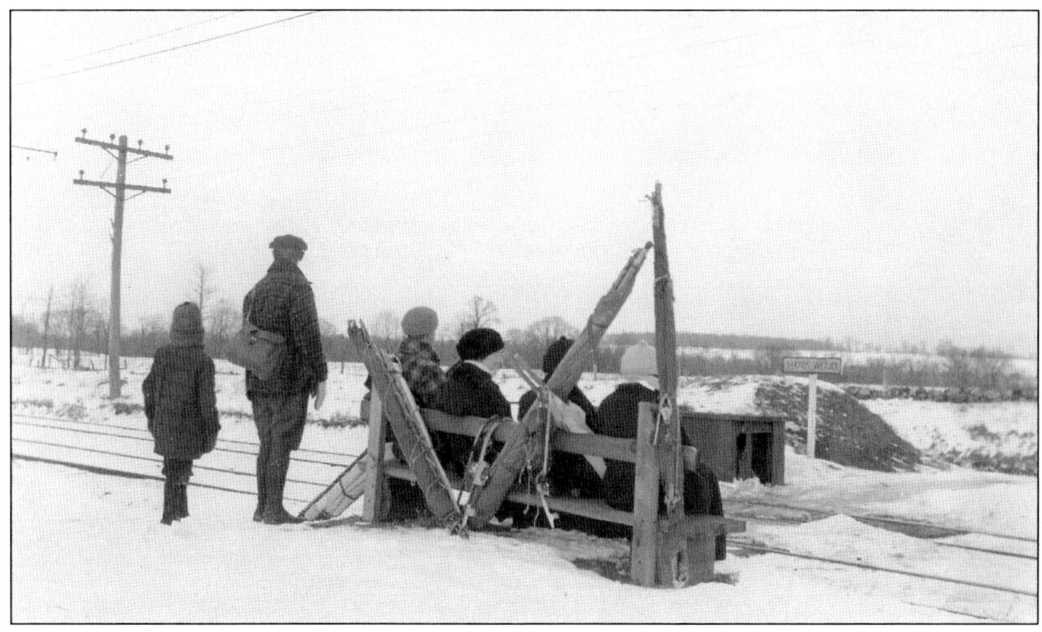

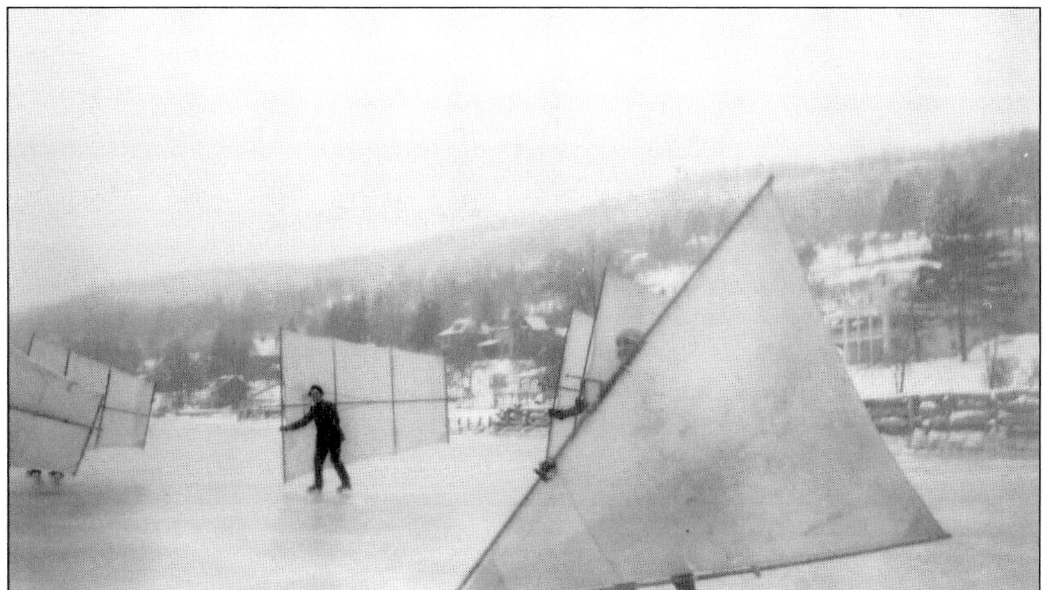

Skate sailing became a popular sport throughout the northeast. This photograph, marked on the back with the words "Tappan Zee," was apparently taken near New York City in 1911. (Courtesy of KARC.)

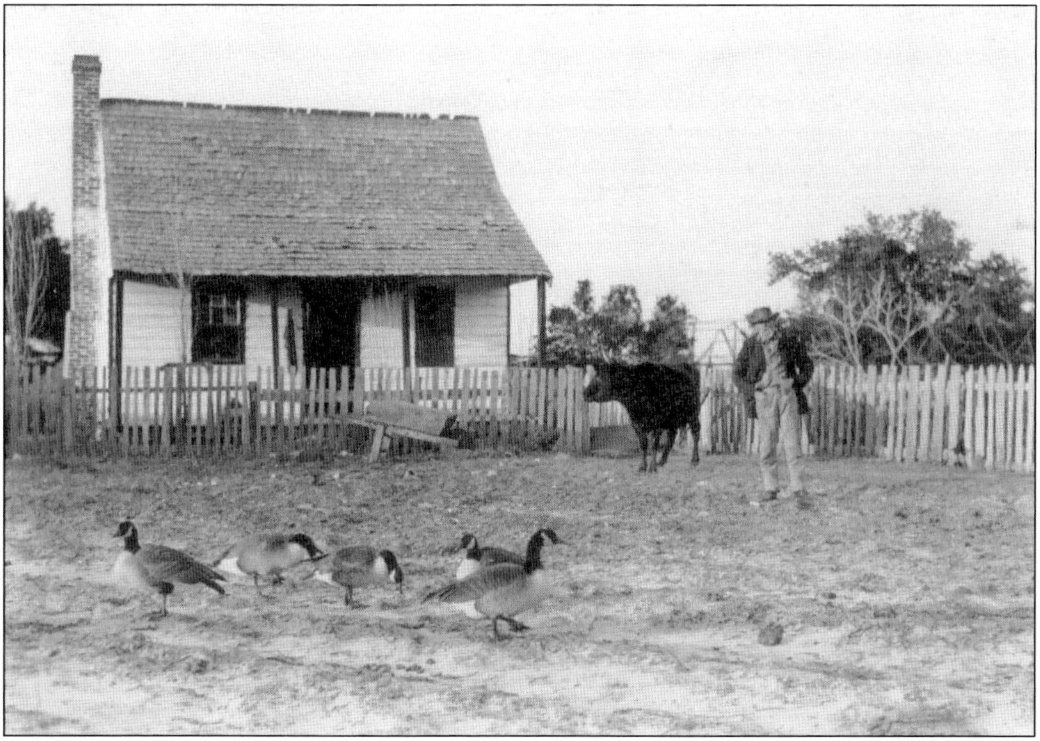

John Apperson took solo hikes into the Forest Preserve, making friends with some of the local people. He exchanged letters with Seth Wadsworth, discussing how to help Seth's father, Dan Wadsworth, and find him a suitable home. Here is Dan, comfortably situated in his new home, along with his cow and chickens. (Photograph by John Apperson, courtesy of KARC.)

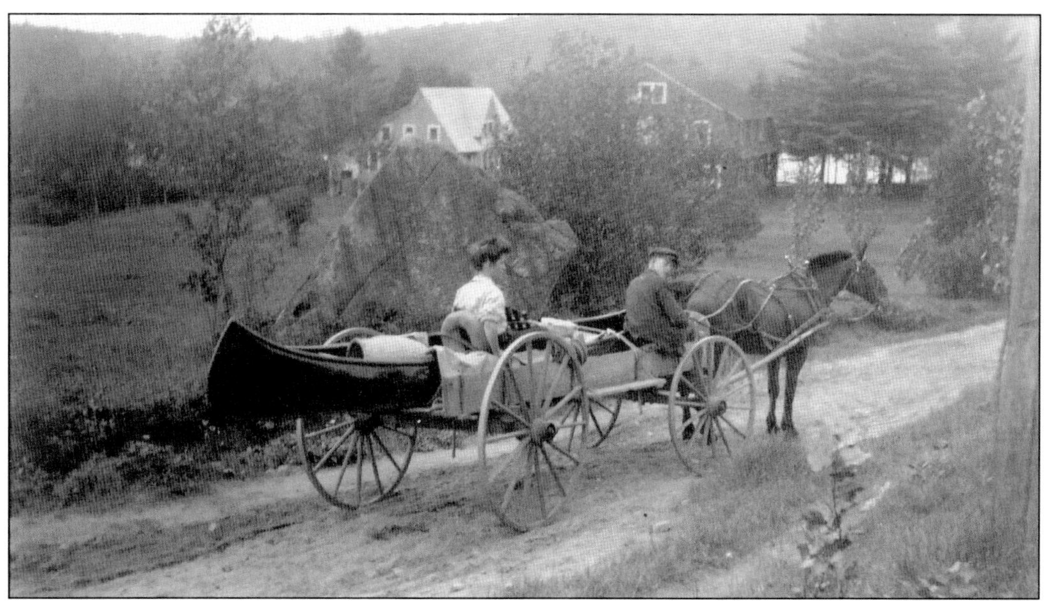

In the summer of 1906, John Apperson invited his sister Nancy to come along on a camping trip into the Fulton Chain. She rode in style in a horse-drawn buckboard. The photograph below offers a glimpse of the equipment and gear they carted into the wilderness, including pots and pans, a bottle of ketchup, tents, a hatchet, and even cushions to provide comfortable seats. The guide must have taken this photograph of his three clients, from left to right, Marc Hannah, John, and Nancy. (Both, author's collection.)

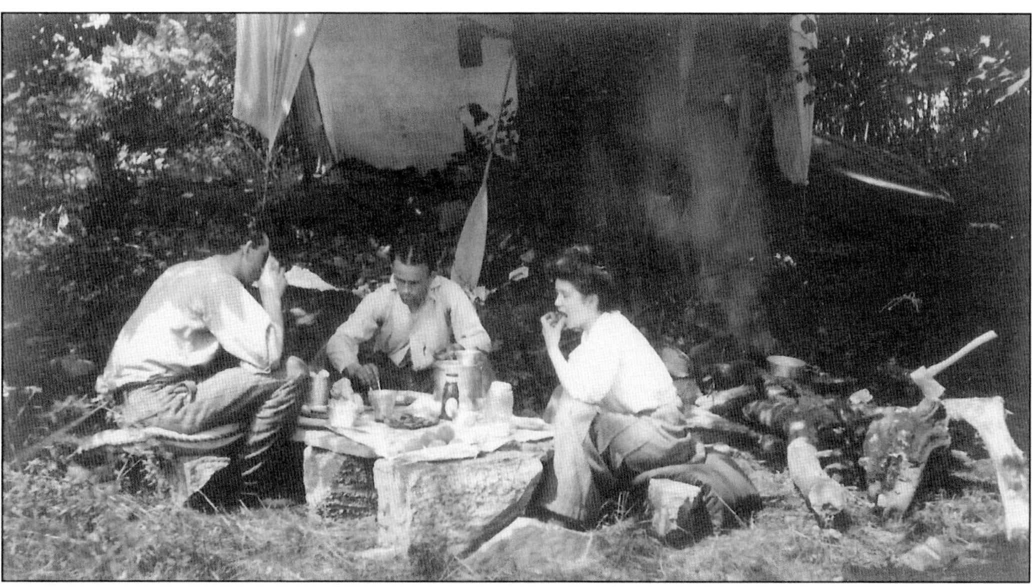

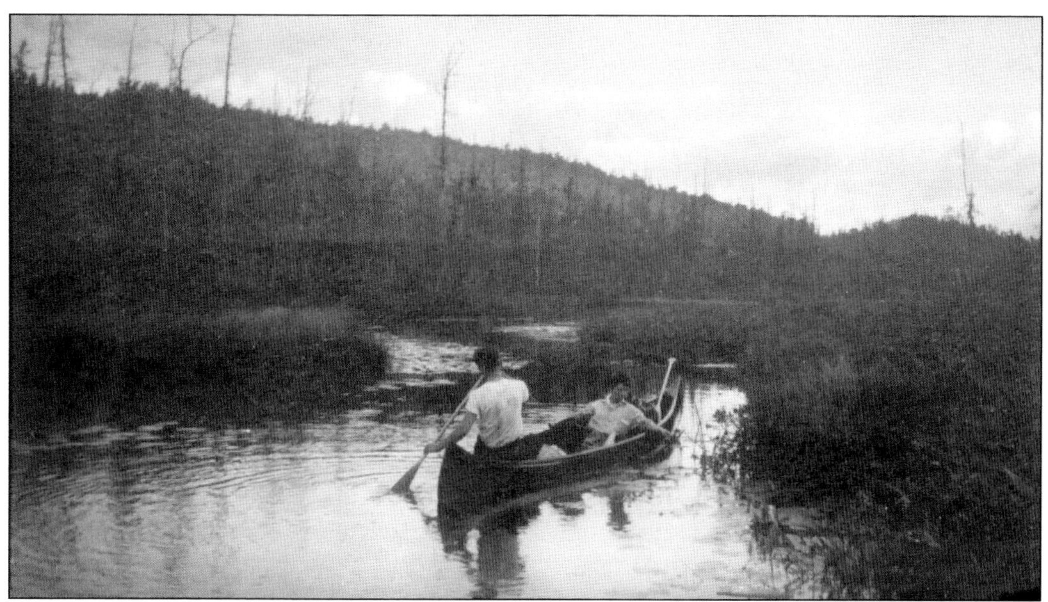

Marc Hannah, a cousin from Illinois, and Nancy Apperson, wearing city garb, seem to be enjoying a canoe trip through a swamp near the Raquette River. This photograph was probably taken by John Apperson riding in a second canoe. Below is a peaceful scene as the canoe approaches a dock. Although it is not known for certain who brought the camera along for the trip, someone certainly had a good eye for beauty, capturing the reflection of the canoe, the dock, and the lily pads in the water. (Both, author's collection.)

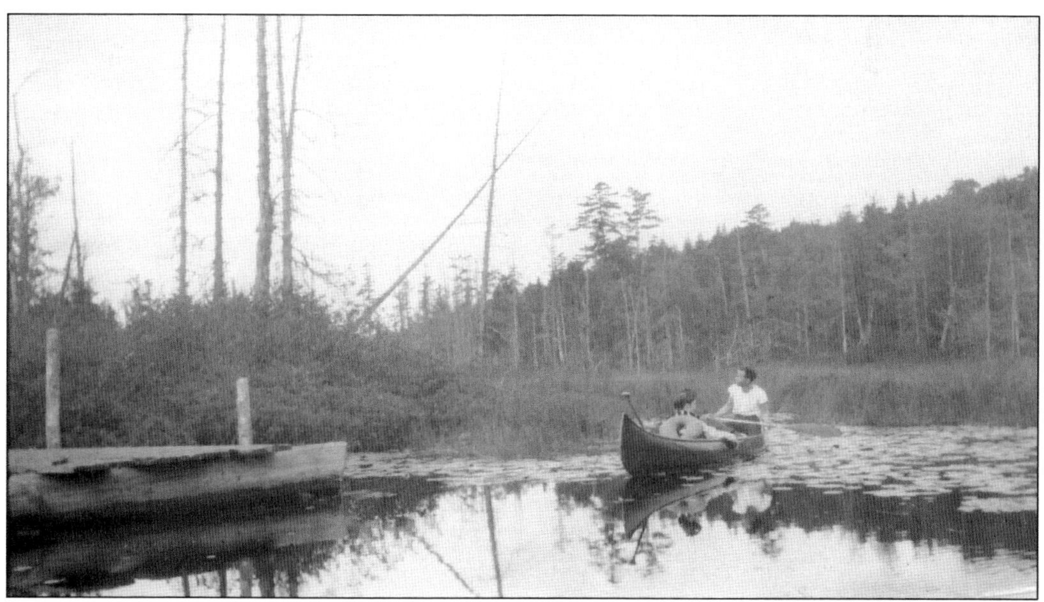

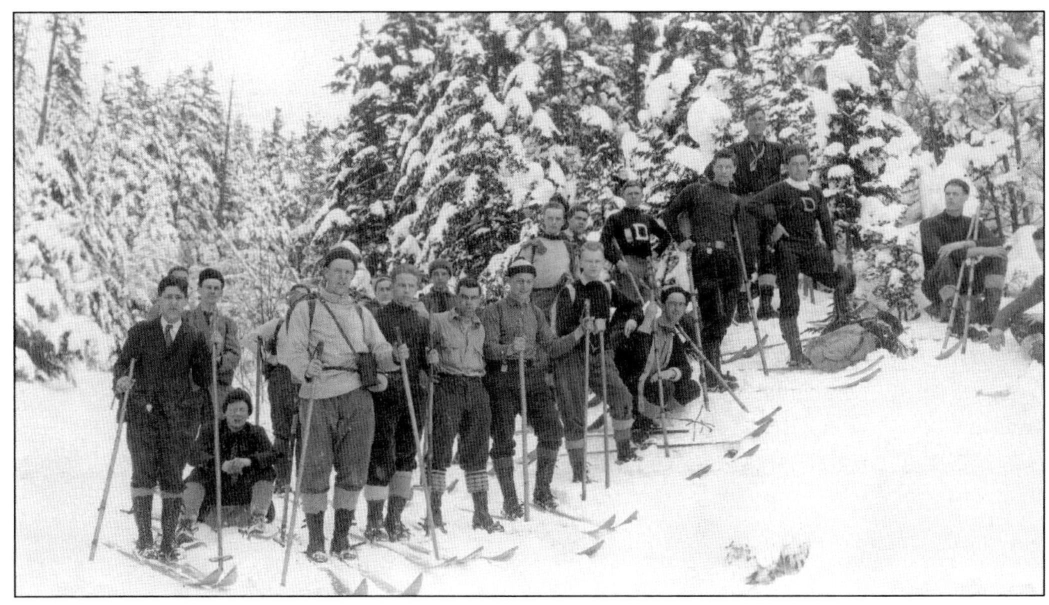

One of John Apperson's best friends, Irving Langmuir, had lived in Europe and learned to ski in the Alps. In 1914, the men arranged to go along on an outing with the Dartmouth Outdoor Club in the White Mountains. Below, Apperson and Langmuir encouraged these young college men to go camping and hiking in the winter and considered this a healthy alternative to competitive sports. Years later, when attempts were made to build ski resorts or toboggan runs in the Forest Preserve, Apperson opposed them, preferring to promote forms of recreation that did not disturb the wilderness. (Both, author's collection.)

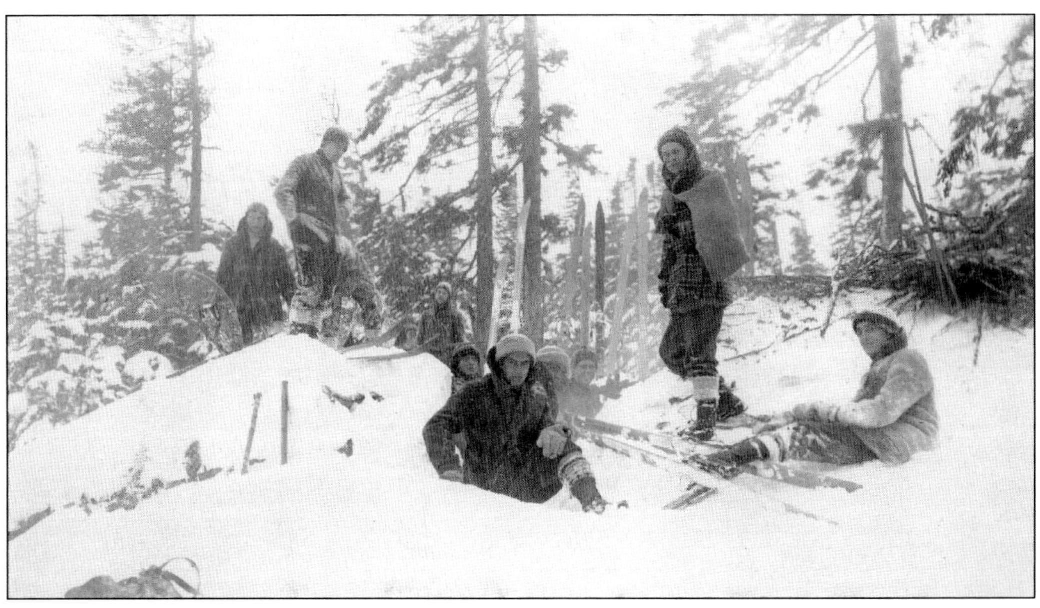

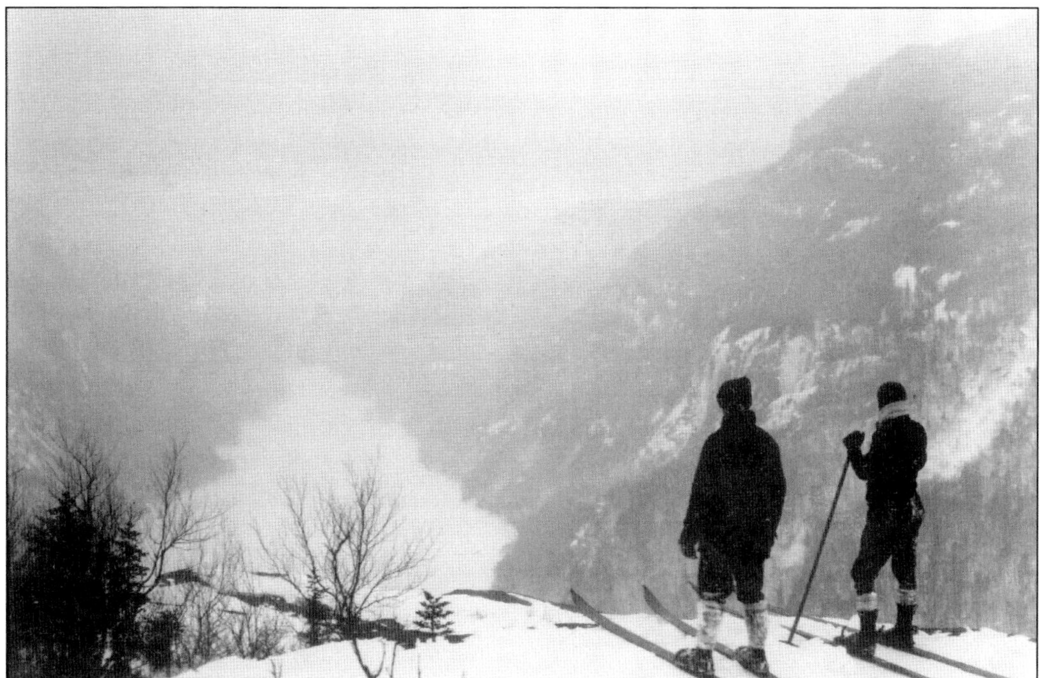

Cross-country skiing did not become a popular sport until much later in the 20th century, but in 1911, John Apperson and Irving Langmuir were pioneers. They strapped ropes around their skis to give them traction, grabbed a long stick (for a ski pole), and started climbing. Here they are on a wintry day, looking down on the Ausable Chasm. Apperson is at right. (Author's collection.)

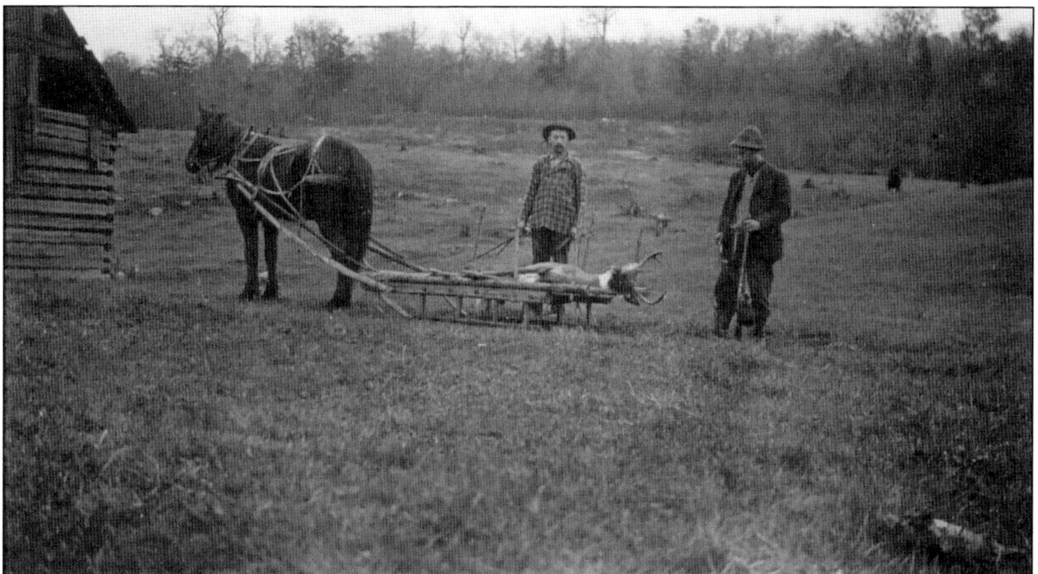

Apperson (right) did not limit himself to the continental United States, but also ventured into Canada for hunting and hiking. He apparently pursued one stag for several days and, after finally bagging him, brought back the antlers as a trophy. This may have been his last hunting trip in about 1910, as he began to take a greater interest in preserving the water, soil, and wildlife in New York's vast Forest Preserve. (Courtesy of KARC.)

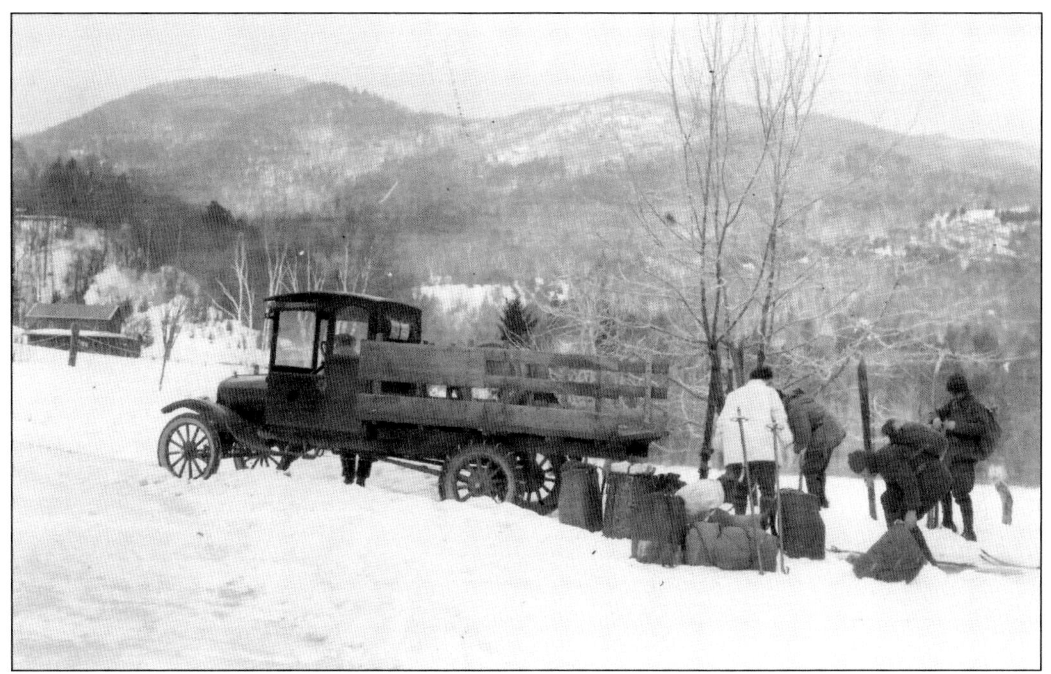

A successful excursion into the high peaks required months of careful planning: inviting dozens of friends, sending them lists of supplies and gear to take along, and then arranging for housing and transportation. This picture was taken in 1911 during an expedition to Mount Marcy. Below is their destination—at least for a few days of their trip—a clubhouse near the Ausable River. (Both, author's collection.)

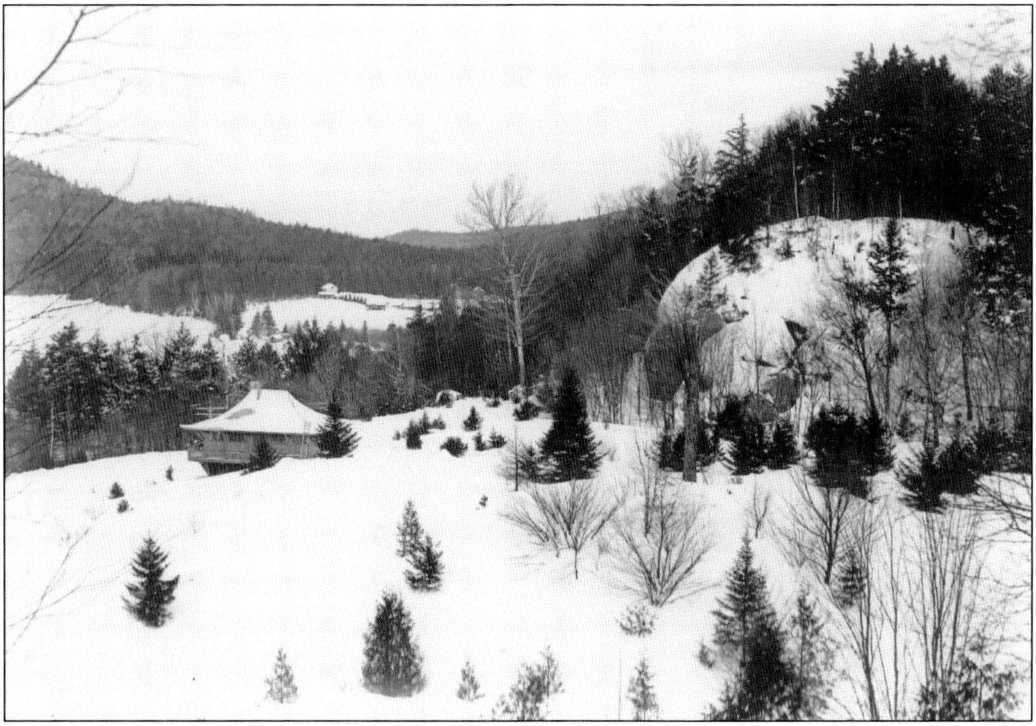

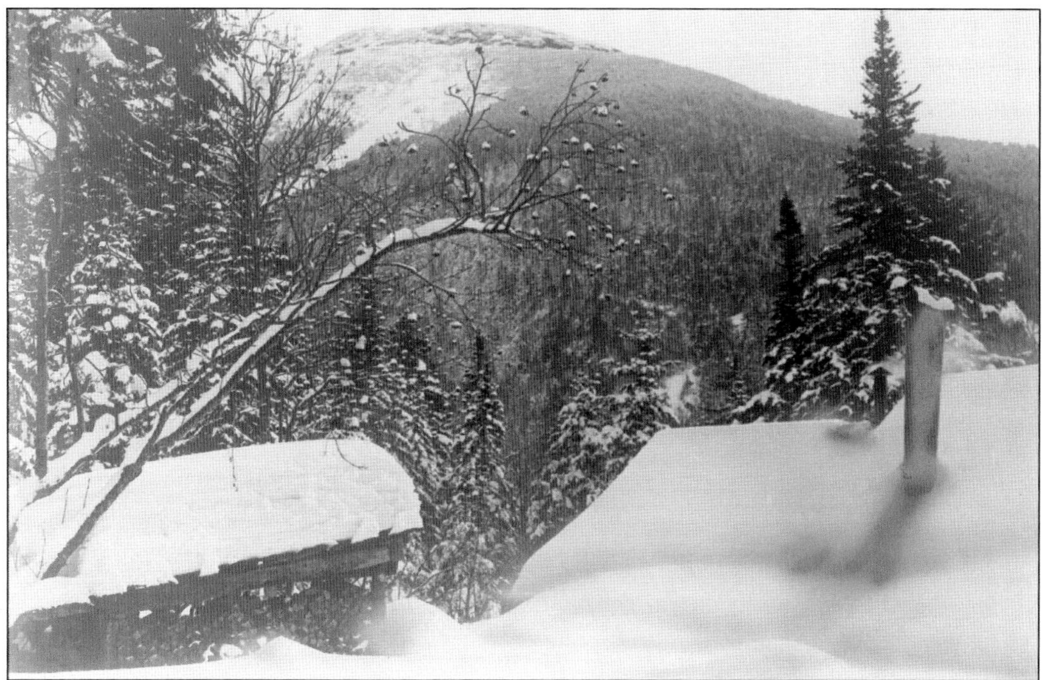

They encountered some serious snowfall exactly what these adventurous friends were hoping for. They enjoyed the challenge of facing the elements, with snow so deep it nearly hid these buildings from view. (Author's collection.)

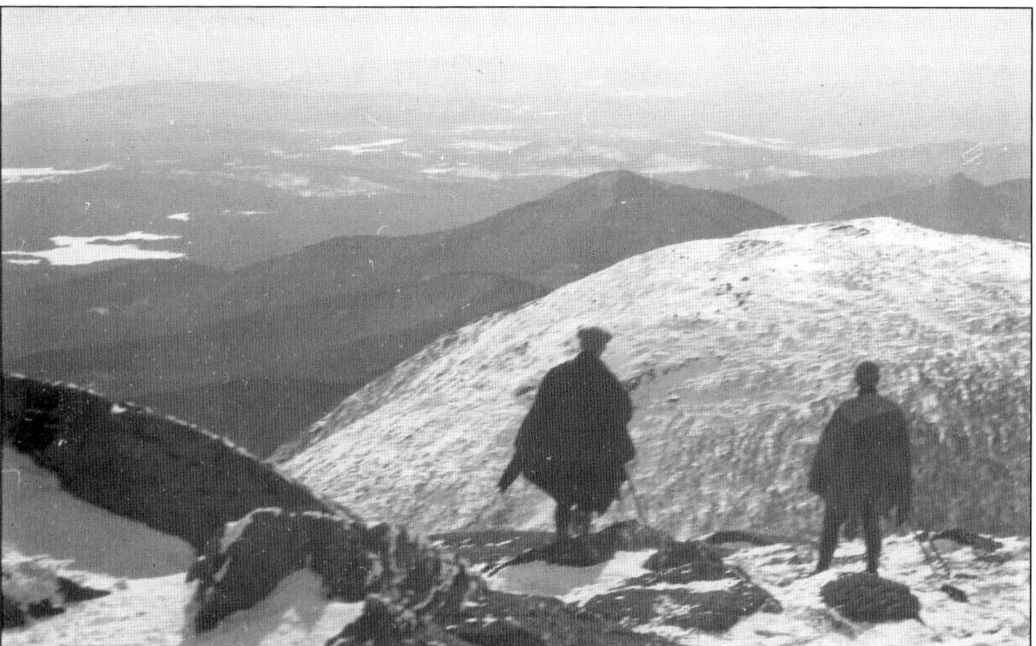

The most impressive and record-breaking accomplishment for these hearty outdoorsmen was to reach the summit of Mount Marcy, having climbed up most of the way on skis, in bitterly cold weather in 1911. John Apperson (right) and Irving Langmuir were the first known to do so. An unidentified photographer captured this scene on a glass plate. (Courtesy of KARC.)

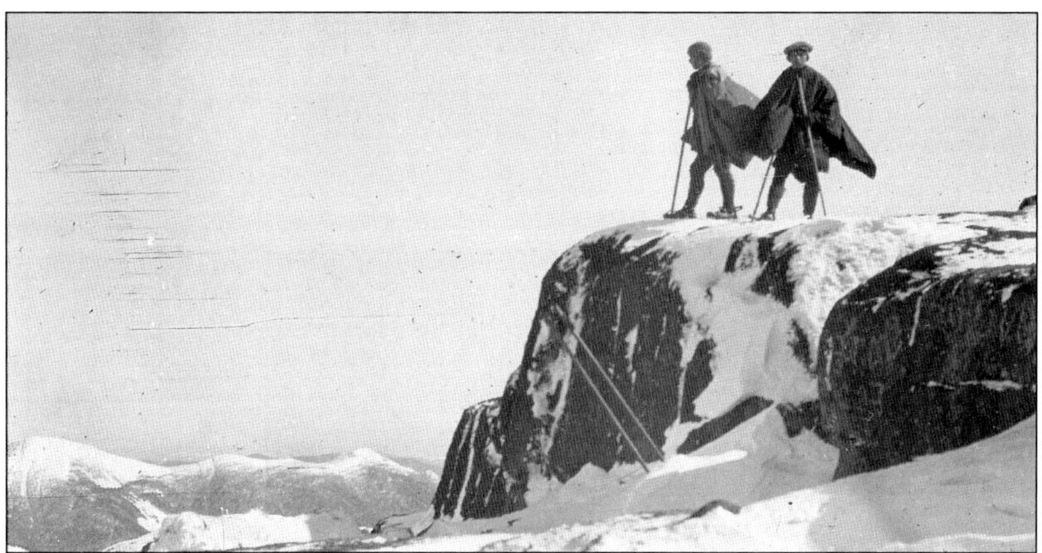

From another glass plate, and taken from another angle, this further documents the historic accomplishment as Apperson (left) and Langmuir stand on the summit of Mount Marcy. (Courtesy of KARC.)

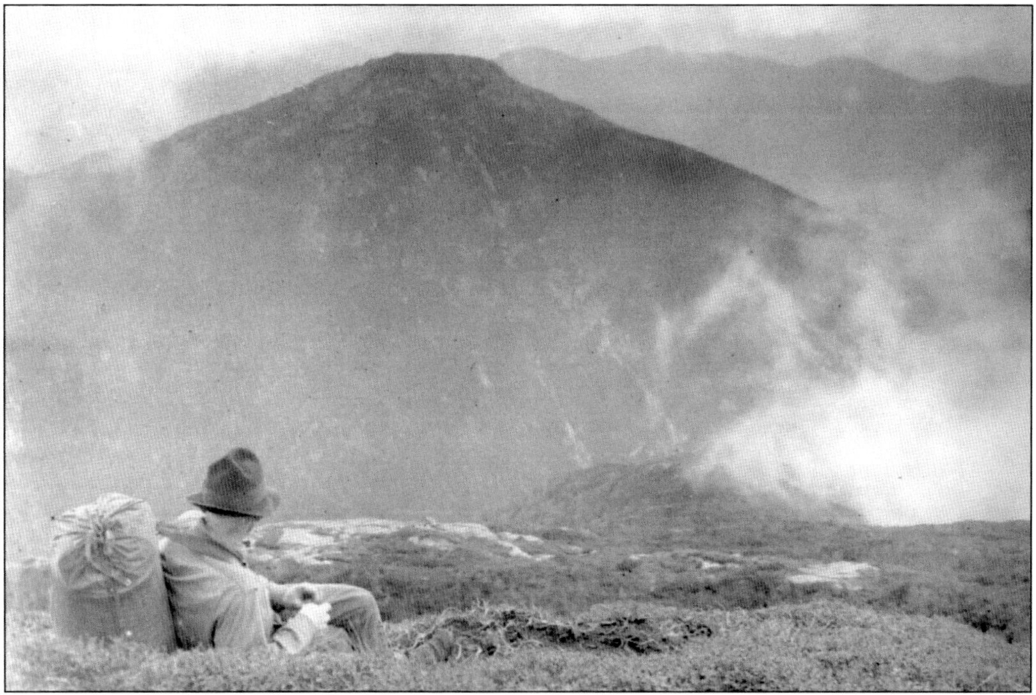

An unidentified hiker, on a later expedition into the high peaks of Saddleback and Tabletop Mountains, pauses to take in the view. Apperson was enthusiastic about taking state officials to see these fragile mountain slopes firsthand so that they could better understand the harm being done by logging and forest fires. He joined many of the big, influential clubs, such as the Association for the Protection of the Adirondacks and the Adirondack Mountain Club, hoping to encourage members to take a stand against logging of the high peaks and against legislation that threatened the "forever wild" clause of the New York constitution. (Courtesy of KARC.)

Two

Recreation at Lake George

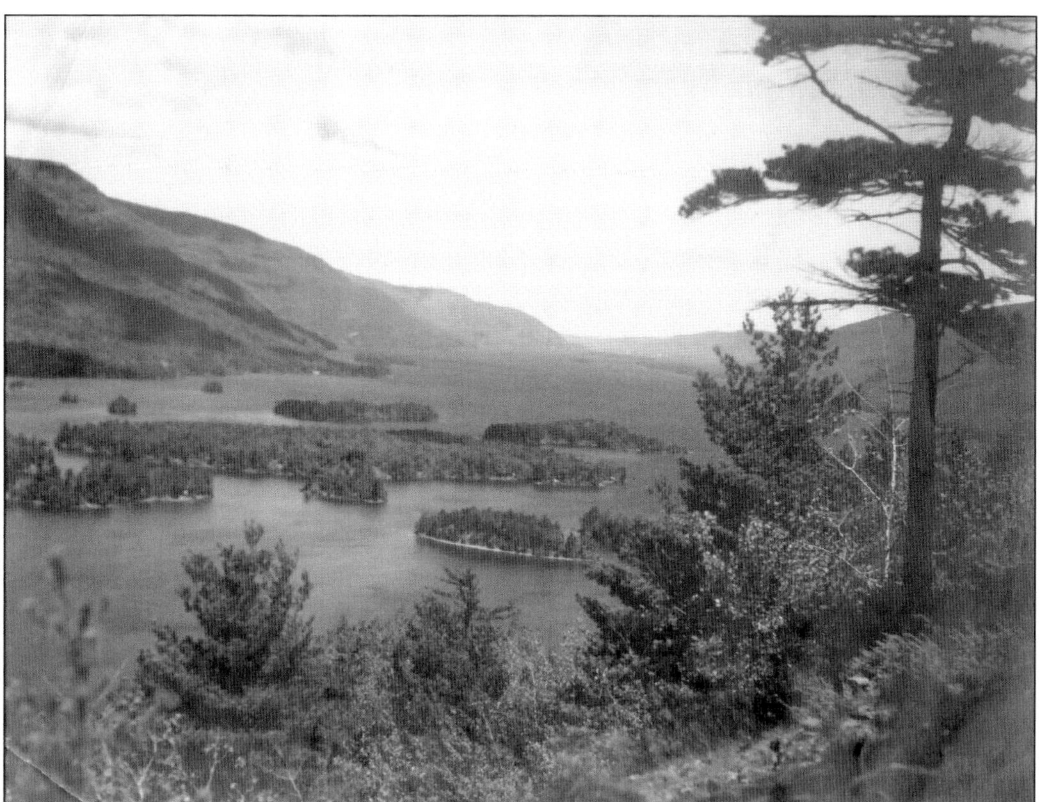

John Apperson probably came to Lake George by train between 1900 and 1907, getting off in Fort Ann and hiking into Shelving Rock, situated on the east side of the lake near the Narrows. This photograph captures the panorama that greeted him as he looked out to the countless islands and north toward French Point. He made up his mind to visit each of the islands, climb each of the mountains, and bring along as many friends as possible. He spent the next 50 years fighting to protect this central portion of the lake from high water, squatters, developers, road builders, and logging interests. (Author's collection.)

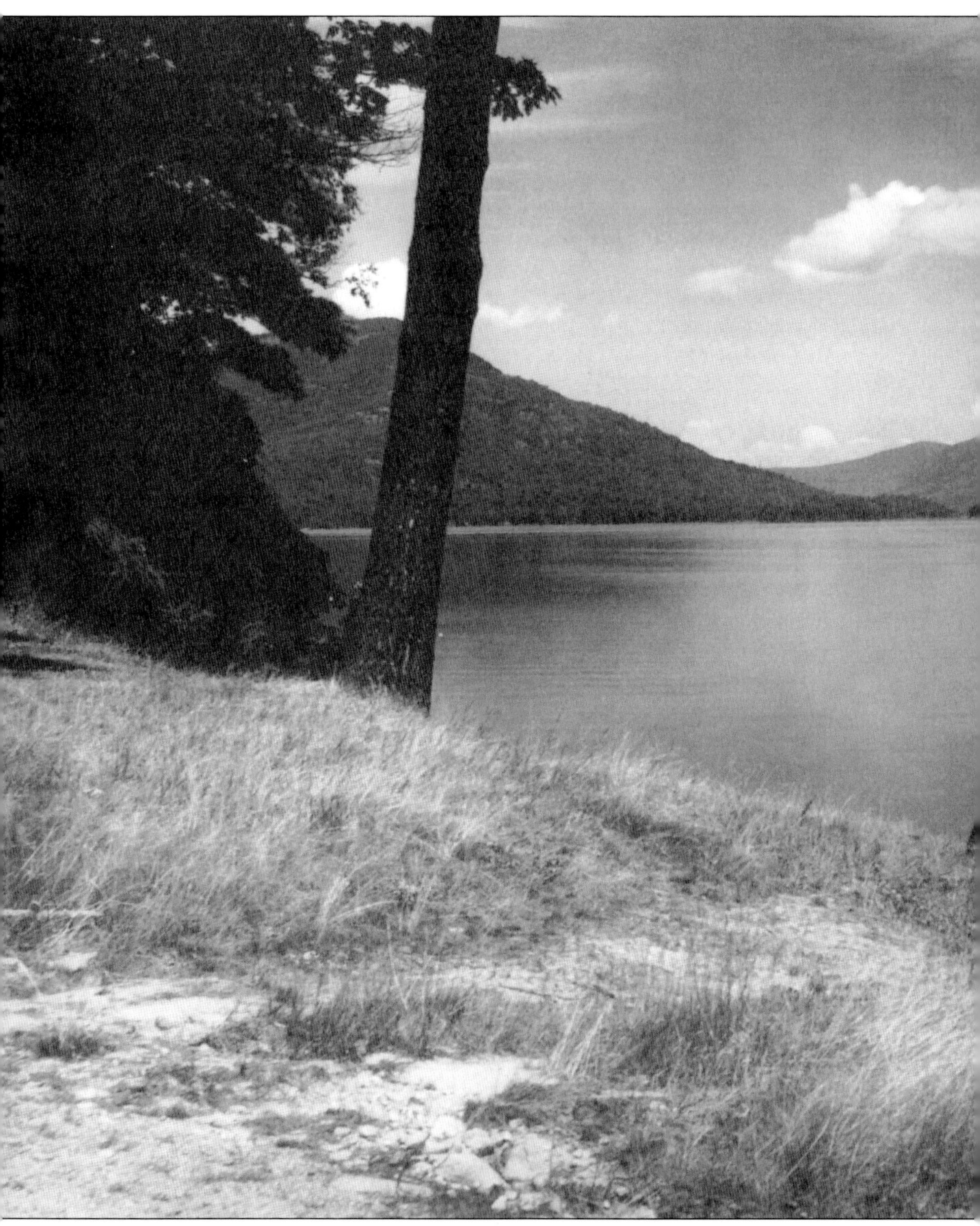

This photograph, probably taken from the Loines property in Northwest Bay in 1910, looks north into the Narrows and captures the serene, undeveloped scenery Apperson hoped to preserve. He

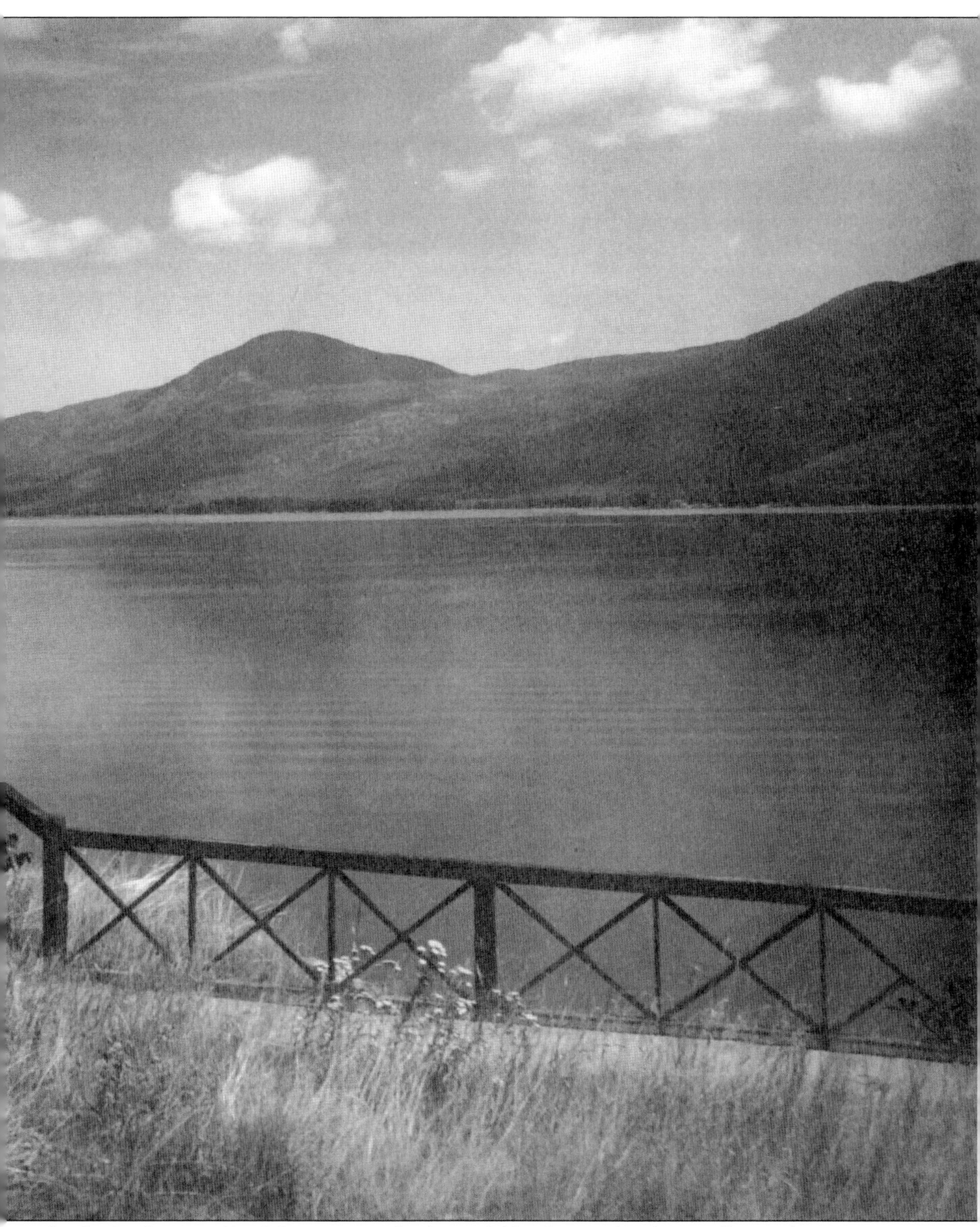

fought for the rest of his life to protect this beautiful landscape. (Author's collection.)

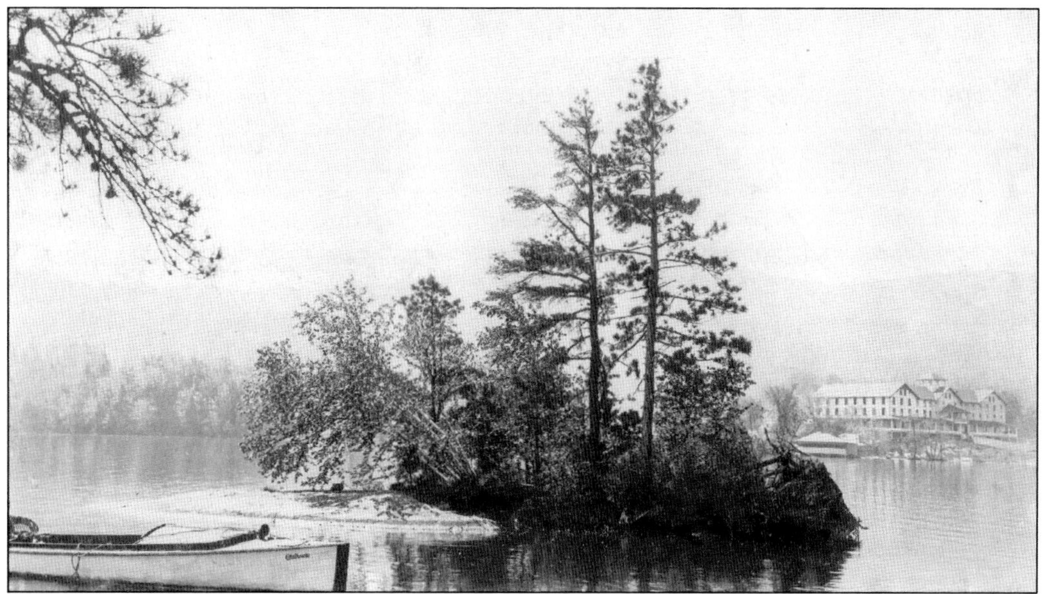

By 1914, John Apperson was using his camera to document problems of erosion, as shown on this island, where a tree has been toppled with its roots exposed. The boat in the foreground, *Chilhowie*, was named after Apperson's hometown in Virginia. Not long after this photograph was taken, the buildings at far right, part of the Sagamore Hotel, were destroyed by fire. (Author's collection.)

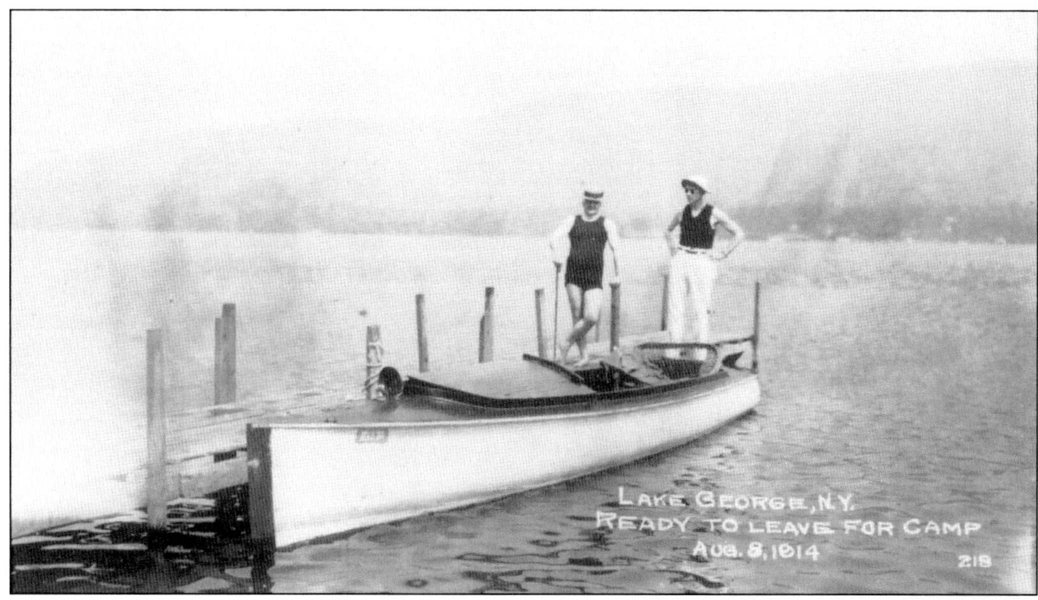

Having a reliable motorboat was crucial to all of John Apperson's plans. He kept camping gear stashed in various locations around the lake, and he offered others the use of his boat, as well as his canoe and his barge *ART. 7-SEC. 7*, to others. The man in the straw hat may have been David Rushmore, John Apperson's boss in the power and mining department, who became an eager participant in these recreational activities at Lake George. (Courtesy of KARC.)

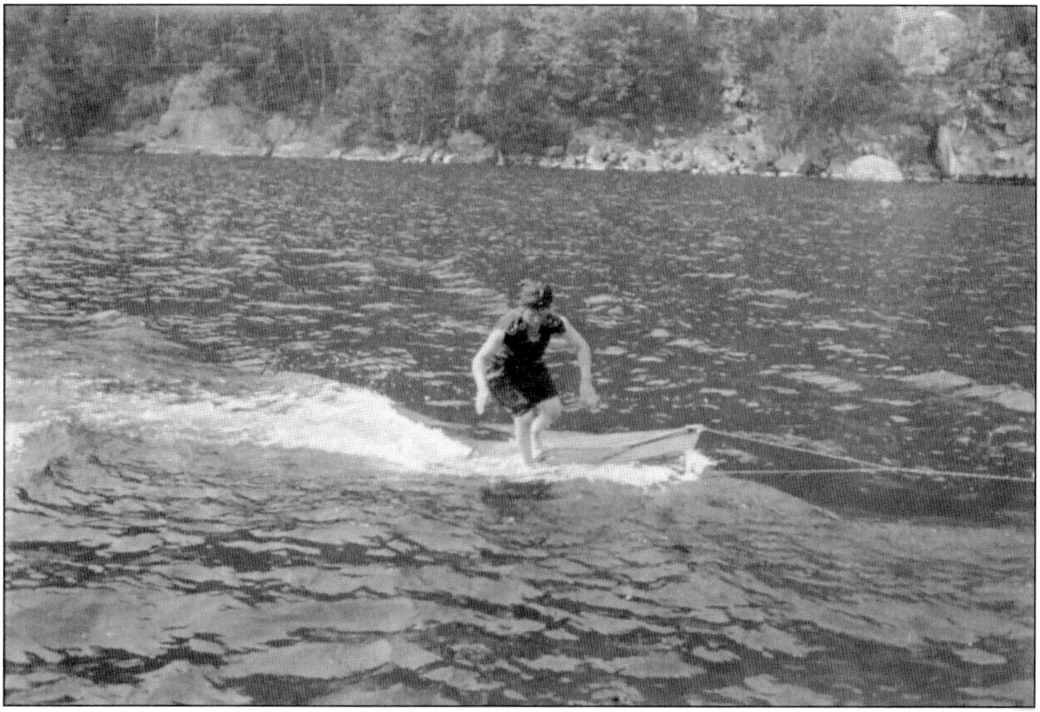

A precursor to water skiing, the sport of aquaplaning, or hydroplaning, was briefly popular at Lake George. Although no name is attached to the back of this print, this appears to be a young woman, perhaps from the camp sponsored by General Electric on French Point, around 1920. Below is another view. It must have been a challenge for the photographer to capture the action on film before the advent of high-speed photography. (Both, author's collection.)

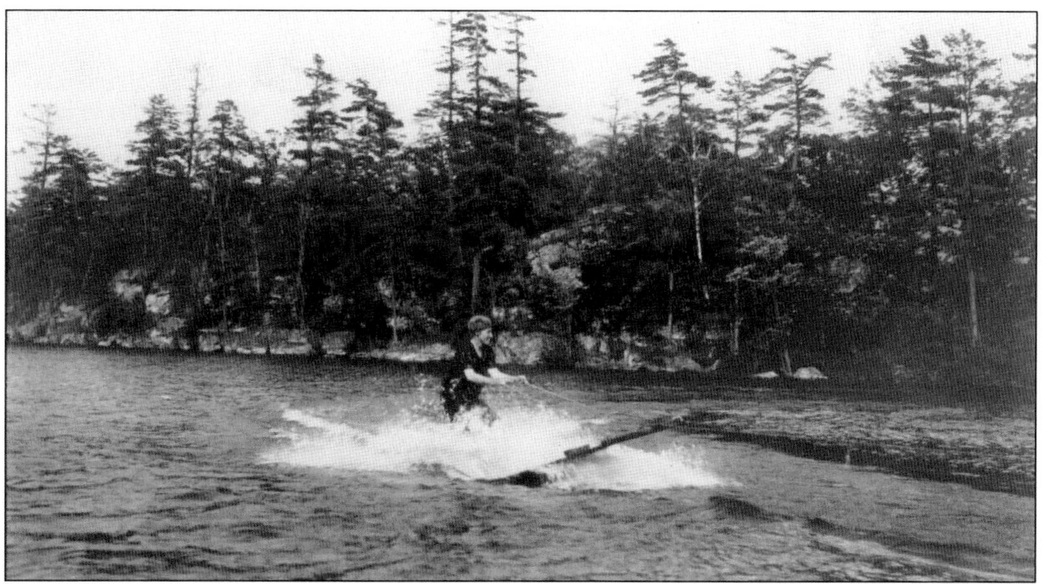

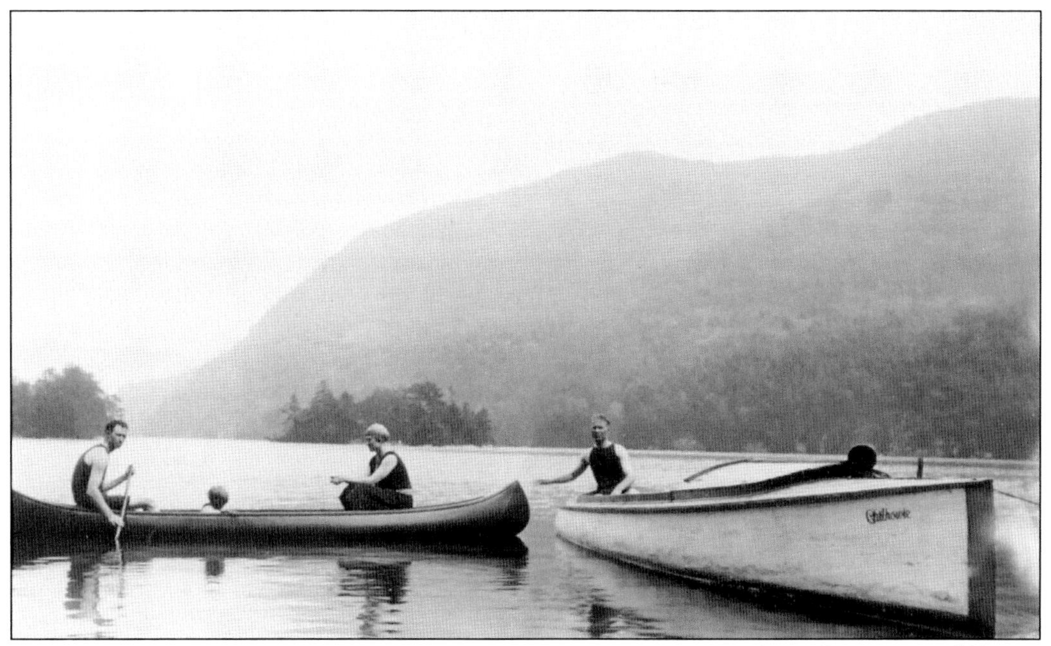

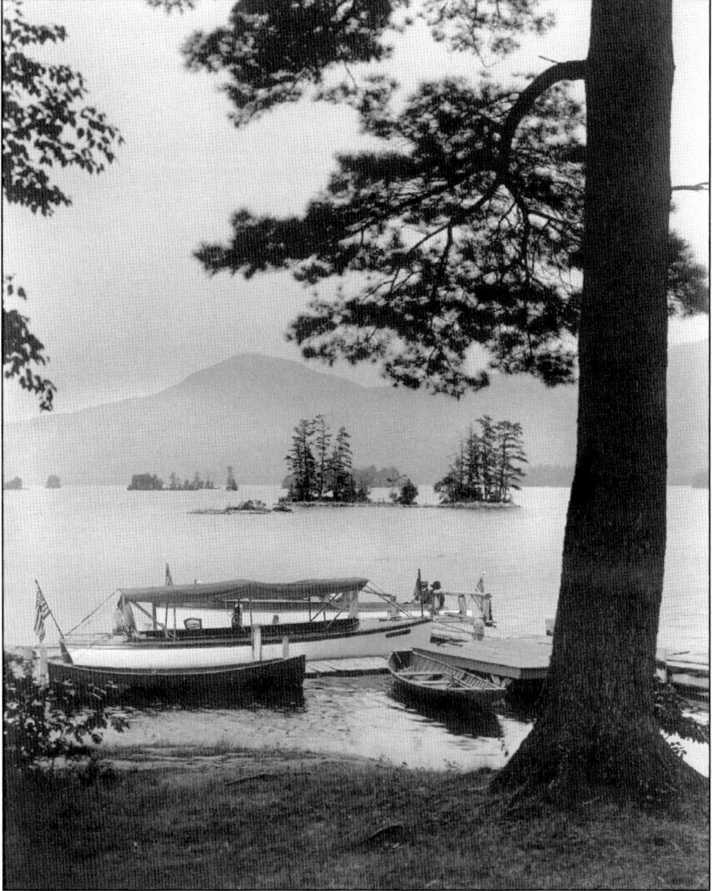

Over the years, as fellow engineers left Schenectady for jobs in other places, Apperson kept in touch with them and invited them back to the lake for summer vacations. This unidentified young family is enjoying the use of a canoe while Apperson sits in his motorboat *Chilhowie* close by. At left, this c. 1915 photograph illustrates the variety of wooden boats in use on Lake George. Here are two motorboats and two rowboats at a dock on the west side of the Narrows looking north toward Black Mountain. (Both, courtesy of KARC.)

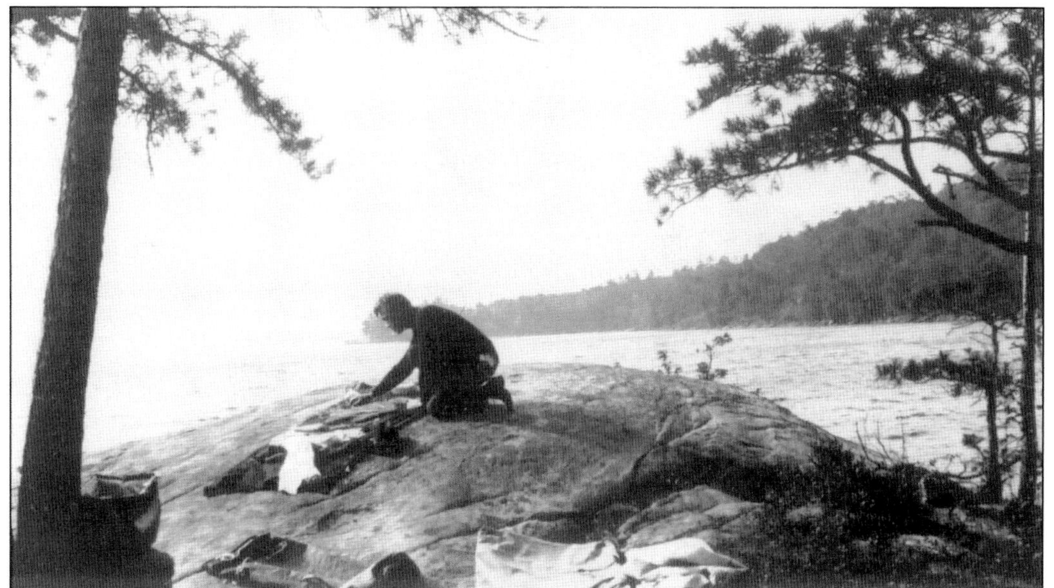

By 1908, Apperson had formed an attachment to the Dollar Islands and camped out there in all seasons. Here, he folds his sleeping bag, with French Point in the background. (Courtesy of KARC.)

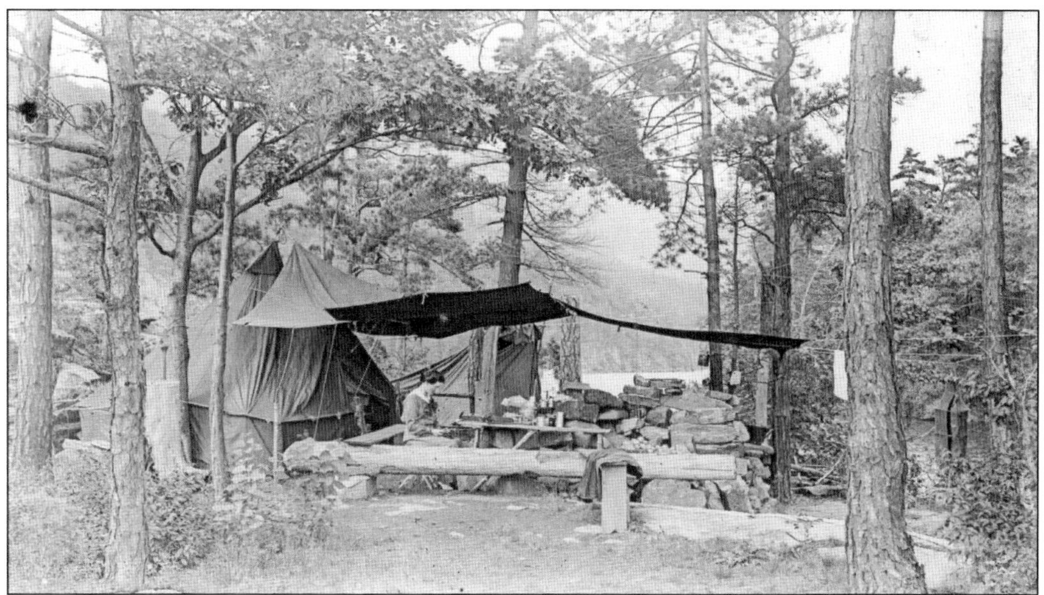

The campsite on West Dollar Island became rather elaborate, as seen here, with tables and benches arranged near a fireplace. The tents and tarpaulins have been carefully engineered too, stretched by ropes to cover the table and provide shade. The young woman is unidentified. (Author's collection.)

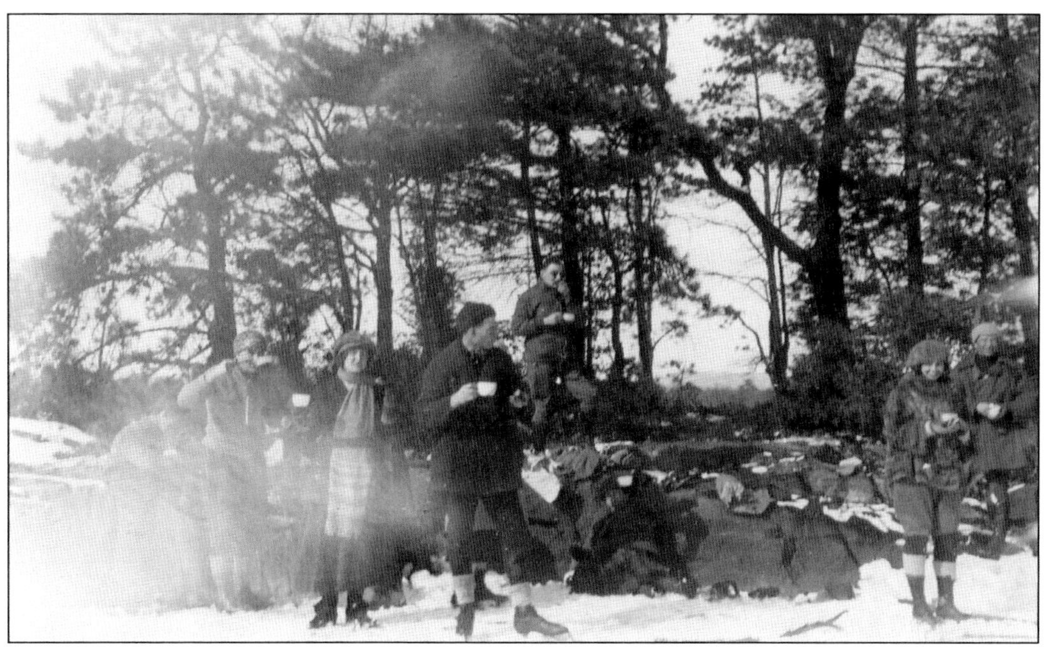

Wintertime excursions to Lake George apparently attracted a nice mix of men and women. The woman in the fur coat at right shows up in quite a few photographs, but her identity is still a mystery to the author. They all seem happy to be warming up with a hot drink, perhaps a cup of hot chocolate, after spending a few hours skating on the lake. Below, warm sweaters, scarves, mittens, and hats were a necessity, as were primitive cooking skills. It was a progressive age, and many of the women who participated were graduates of women's colleges such as Bryn Mawr, Smith, or Radcliffe. Eager to be independent and to have the right to vote, some of these women helped Apperson form an early preservation lobby, writing articles in newspapers and establishing conservation committees at their women's organizations. (Both, courtesy of KARC.)

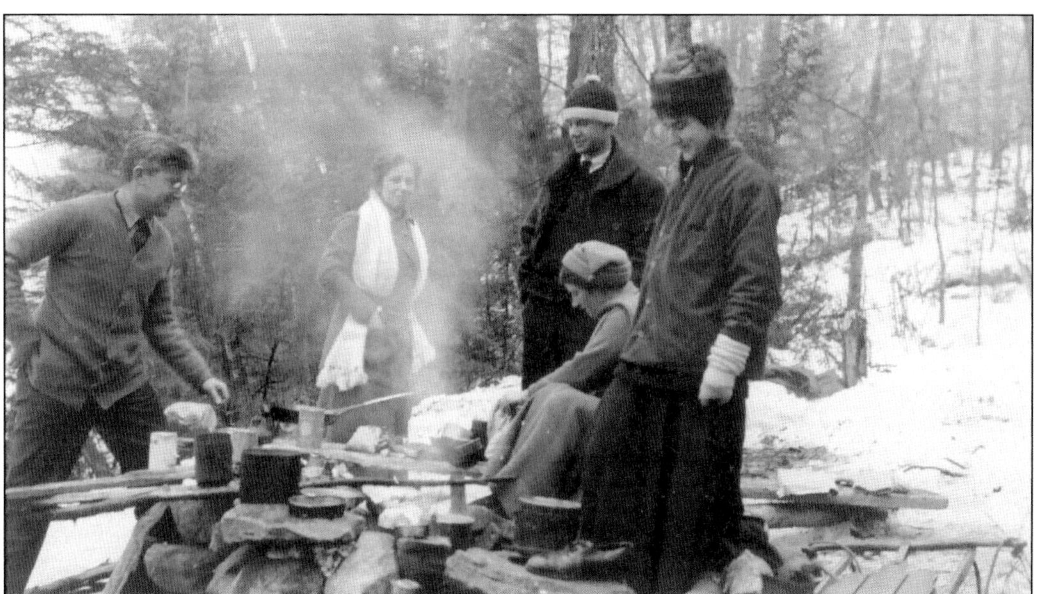

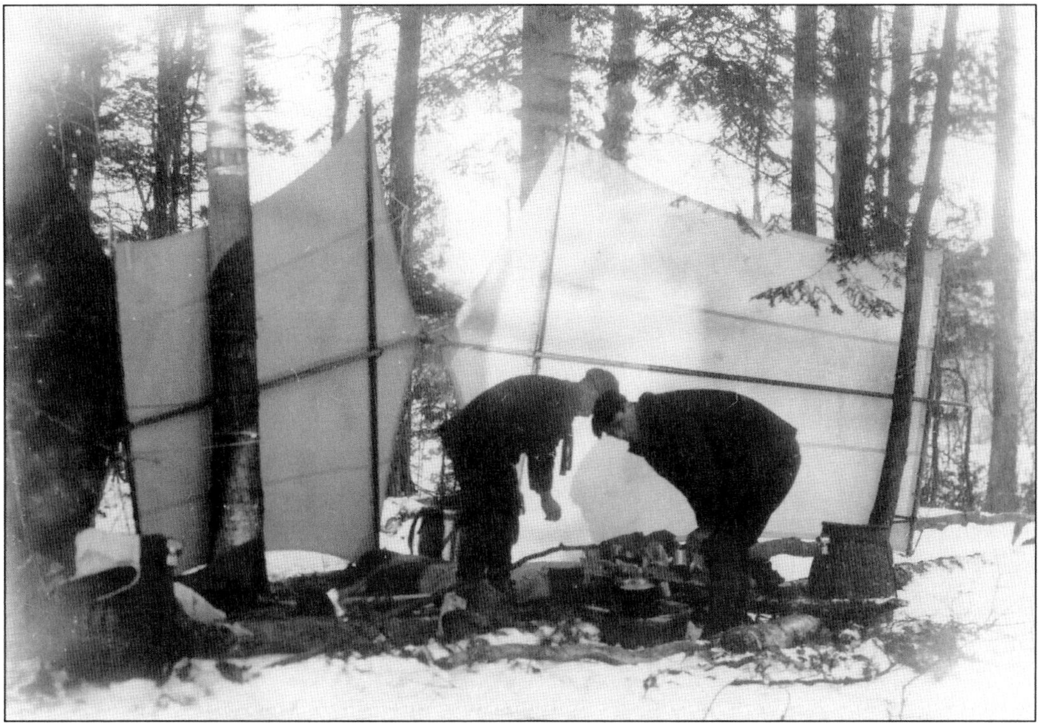

Skate sailing was one of the most popular activities during these wintertime camping trips. Here, two sails are positioned as a sort of windbreak. Apperson thought it would be wonderful if Lake George could be promoted for this sort of winter sport, and he kept busy making sails, teaching classes, and ordering the latest equipment. Apperson felt that winter sports should be promoted at Lake George using the state-owned islands at low cost. Each person could bring his own equipment (such as sails, skis and skates, and sleeping bags) and have a wonderful adventure in fresh air. Below, two white sails slide silently across the black ice with Tongue Mountain in the background in 1912. (Both, courtesy of KARC.)

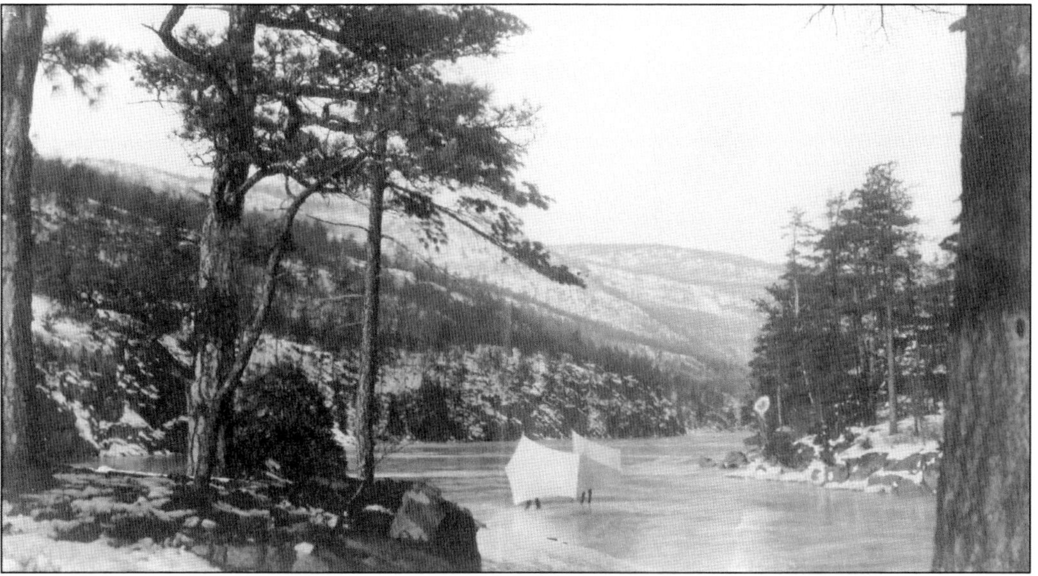

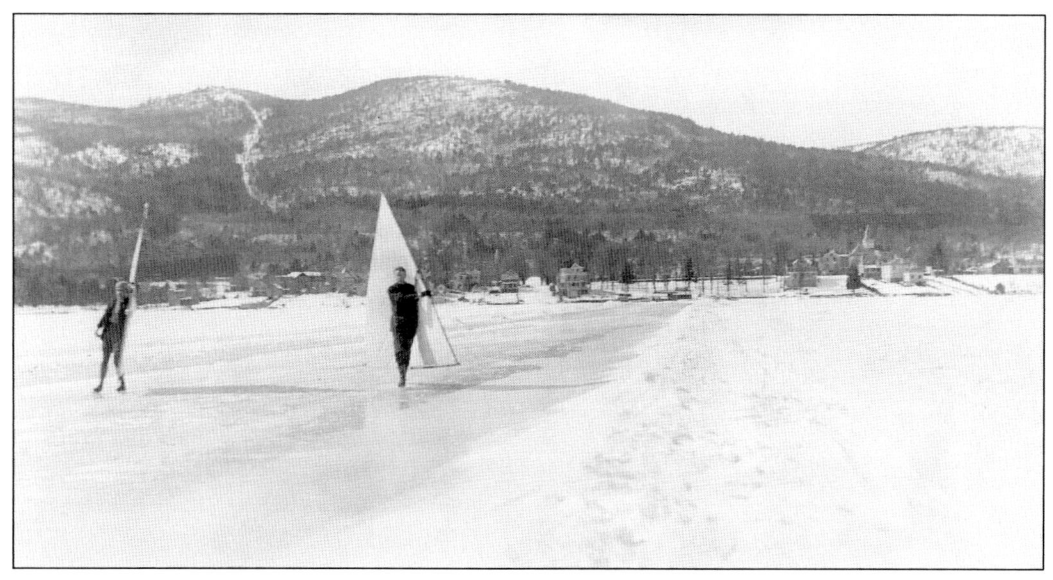

Apperson found other skate-sailing enthusiasts at the southern end of the lake near Lake George Village and joined them one wintry day. An inch or so of snow had fallen, so they had to sweep off the snow and clear a large, wide swath. Below, on another day in Lake George Village, before snow had fallen, there was plenty of black ice, which was ideal for skating. The two men in the foreground practice skating before picking up their sails. (Both, courtesy of KARC.)

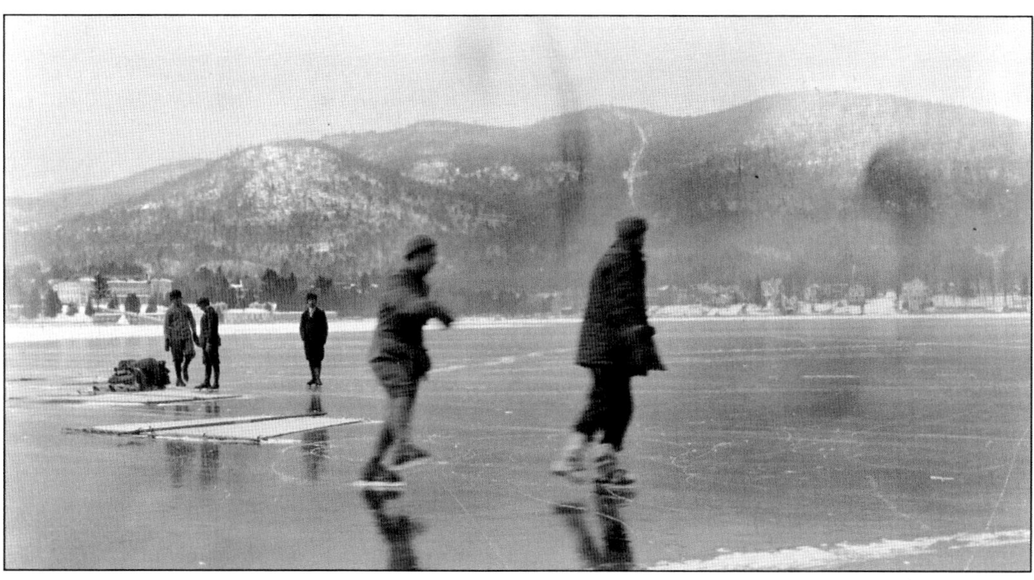

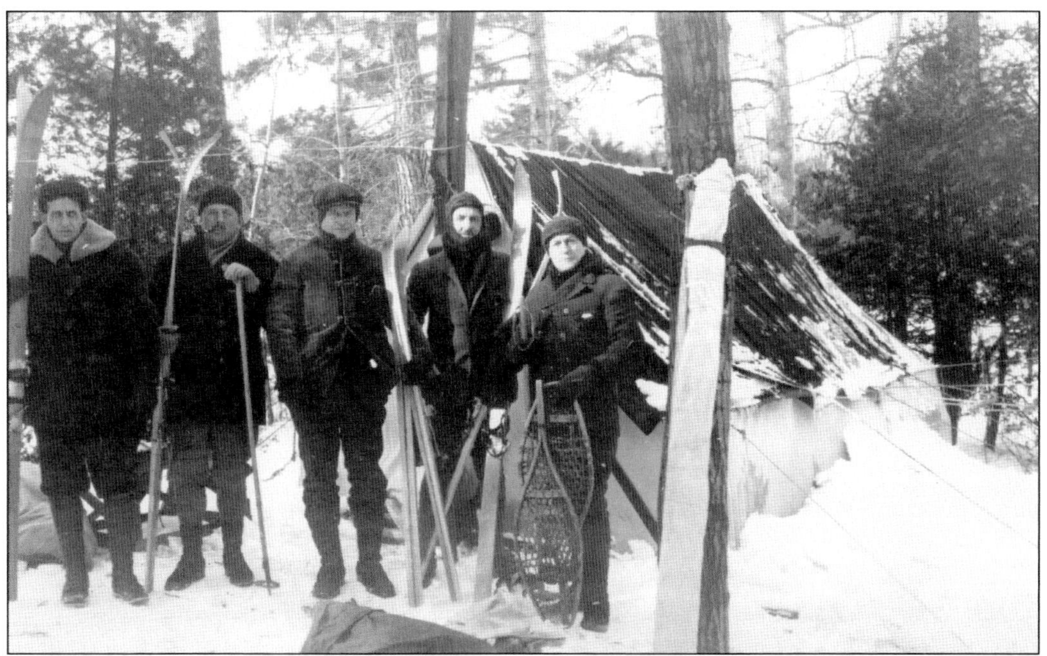

In 1918, before any commercial ski slopes were available, Apperson and friends tried skiing on the lake. If there was considerable snow on the ice, skating was not a good option, but skis were perfect. Apperson was apparently the first to invent the sport of ski-sailing. Many were skeptical, but these five men may have given it a try! Below are four men taking a lunch break, seated on a snow bank. They were dressed well for the sport, with many layers, and had brought along some tasty food. Their ski poles are made of wood, and were longer than the downhill ski poles that came into vogue a few decades later. (Both, courtesy of KARC.)

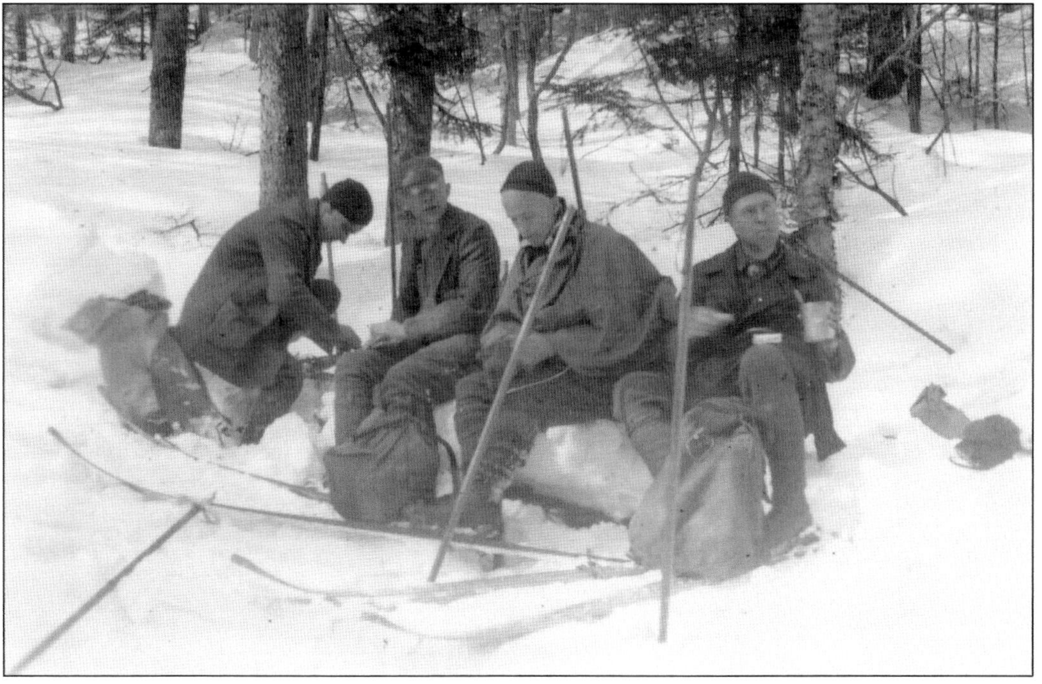

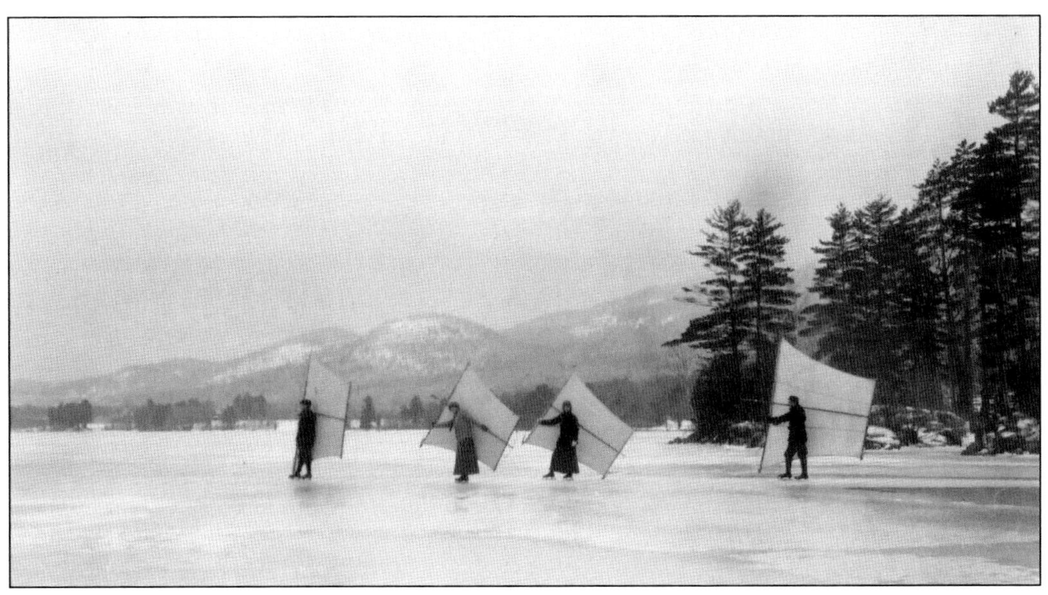

According to pamphlets published by the New York State Conservation Commission, Apperson offered classes for skate sailing at Lake George, attracting as many as a dozen students at a time. The photograph above was used by the commission to promote outdoor recreation. As seen below, the sailing classes were open to women too. Notice the two women on the left. (Both, courtesy of KARC)

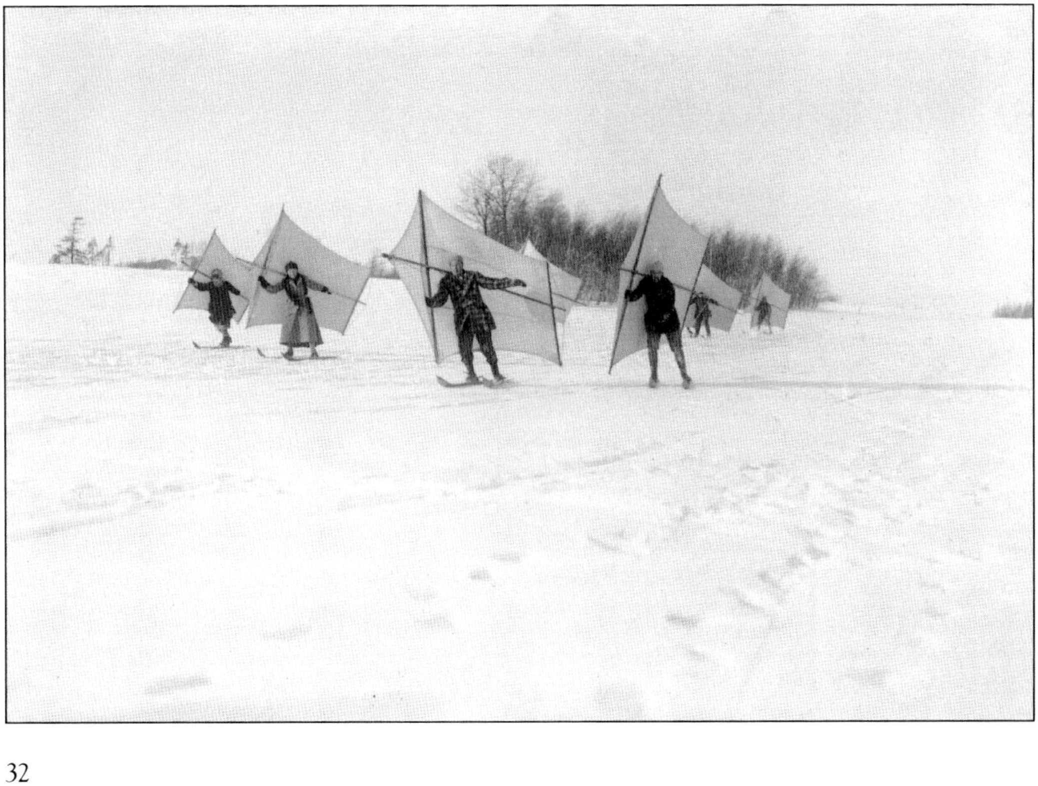

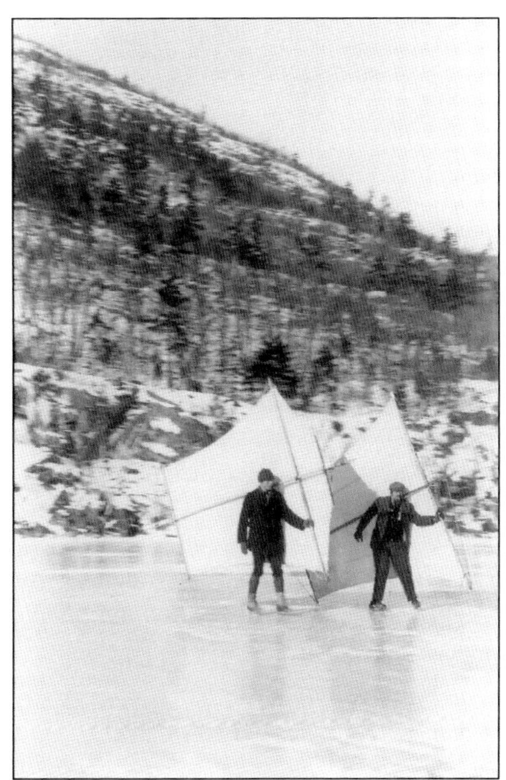

At right, participants in a sailing class enjoy the benefit of a huge icy playground, letting the wind take them miles away. One of these sailors seems to be just barely able to control his skates. Below, one of the skaters has ventured as far as Roger's Rock, which was covered in ice. (Both, courtesy of KARC.)

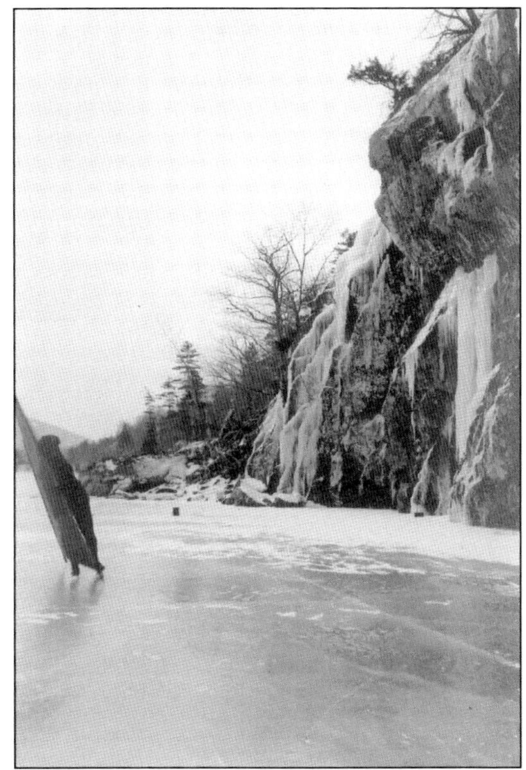

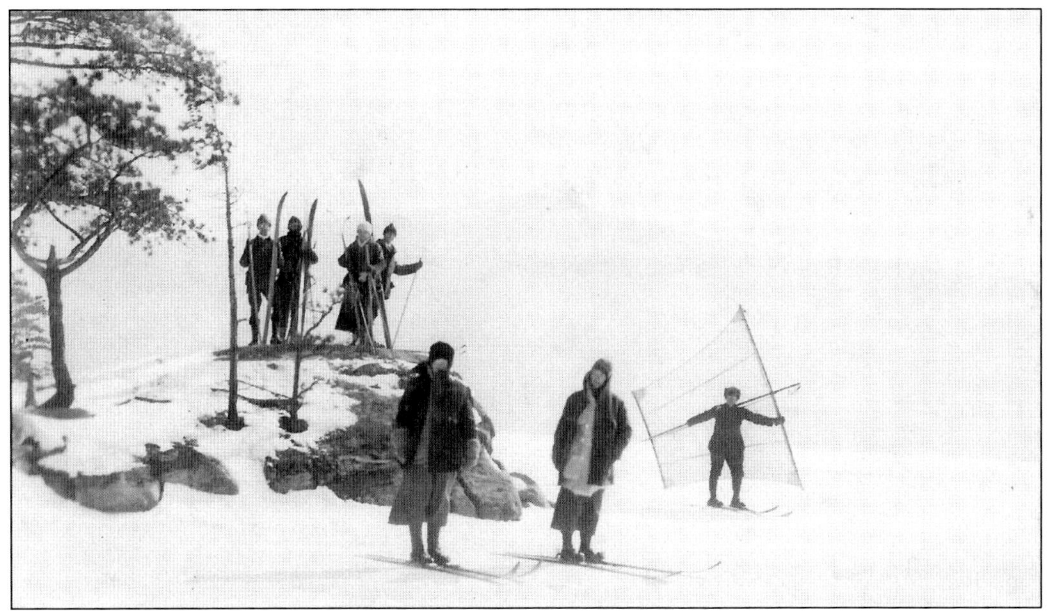

By the 1920s, these activities attracted the attention of many young people whose families had summer homes in the area, and they started coming up to Lake George to enjoy the winter sports. Apperson made new friends that way, some of whom he later recruited to help with his preservation projects. (Author's collection.)

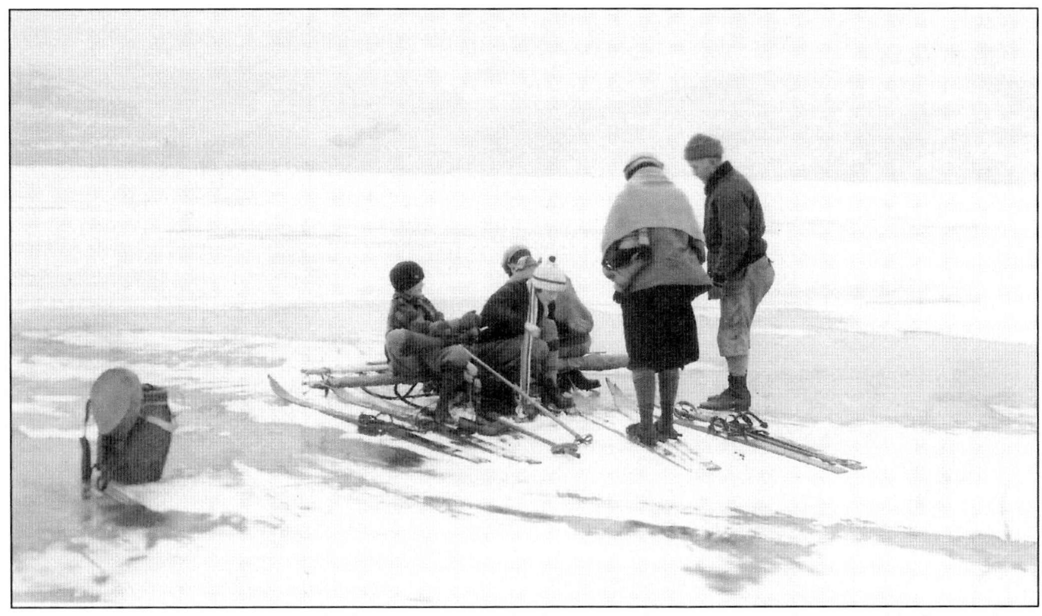

Apperson became friends with the Loines family from Northwest Bay and enjoyed helping them try out all these exciting new sports. Here, Apperson (right) watches while Barbara and Margot Loines try on their skates in 1923. The woman with her back to the camera was Sylvia Loines, and the man seated on the sled was Ted Dreier, an engineer at GE who later married Barbara Dreier. (Author's collection.)

Three

PROBLEMS IN PARADISE

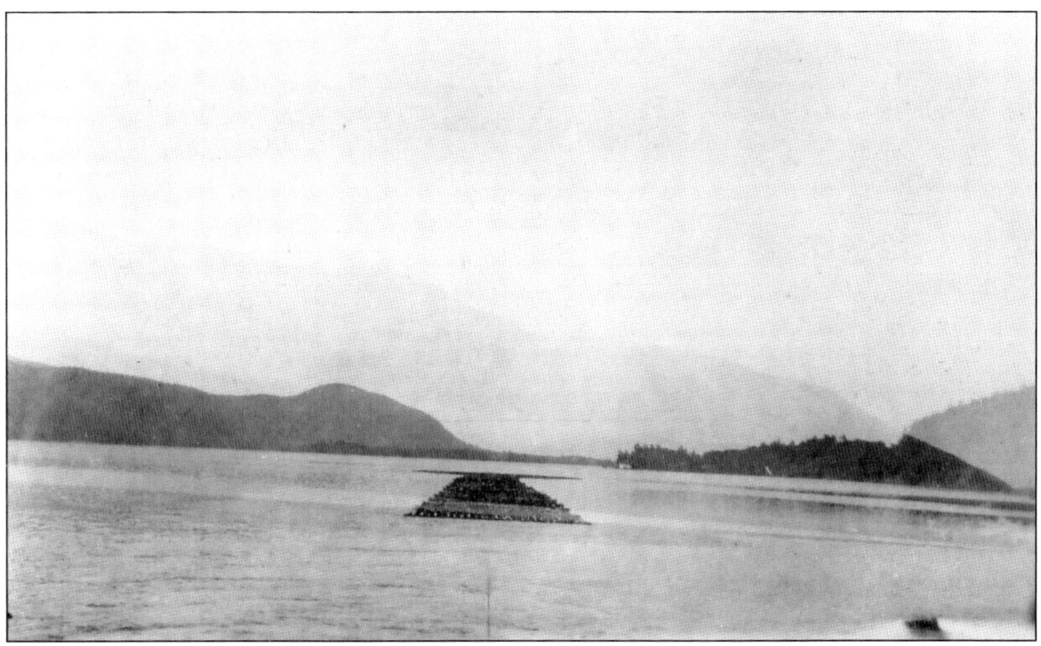

One of the earliest images Apperson captured, on an early glass plate, was of logs being rafted down the lake. It is unclear whether he deliberately made a double exposure, but the outline of a mountain can be seen in the background, as if to say, "Look what the loggers are doing to destroy this beautiful scenery." (Courtesy of KARC.)

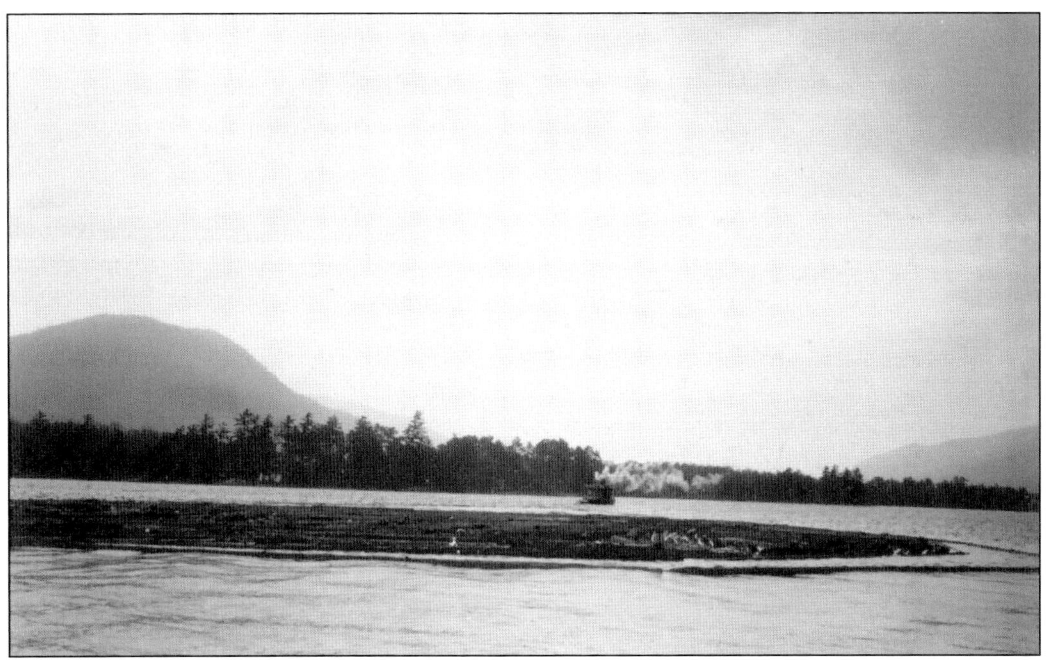

This similar scene shows a small tugboat pushing or pulling a huge raft of logs at the northern end of the lake. Apperson had already seen the harm done by logging in Virginia, and this evidence of logging and the use of Lake George as a commercial waterway must have stirred up his concern. (Courtesy of KARC.)

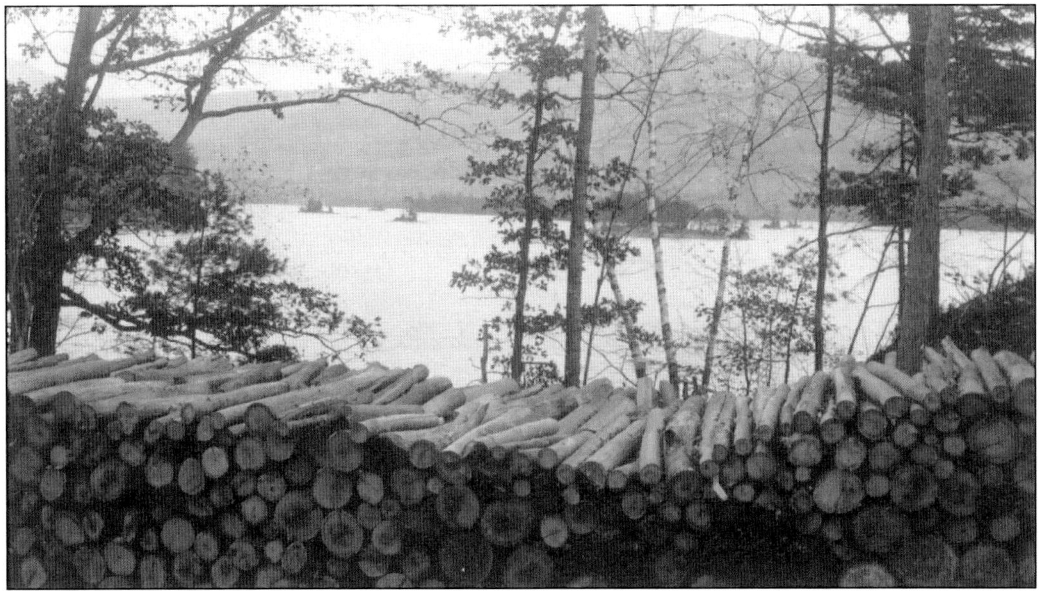

It was not long before Apperson found another disturbing sight of freshly cut lumber stacked and ready to be floated to the lumber mill. He wondered whether there was any way to prevent the lumber companies from destroying these forests and decided to get answers. In 1918, he purchased a lot near where this picture was taken in Turtle Bay. (Courtesy of KARC.)

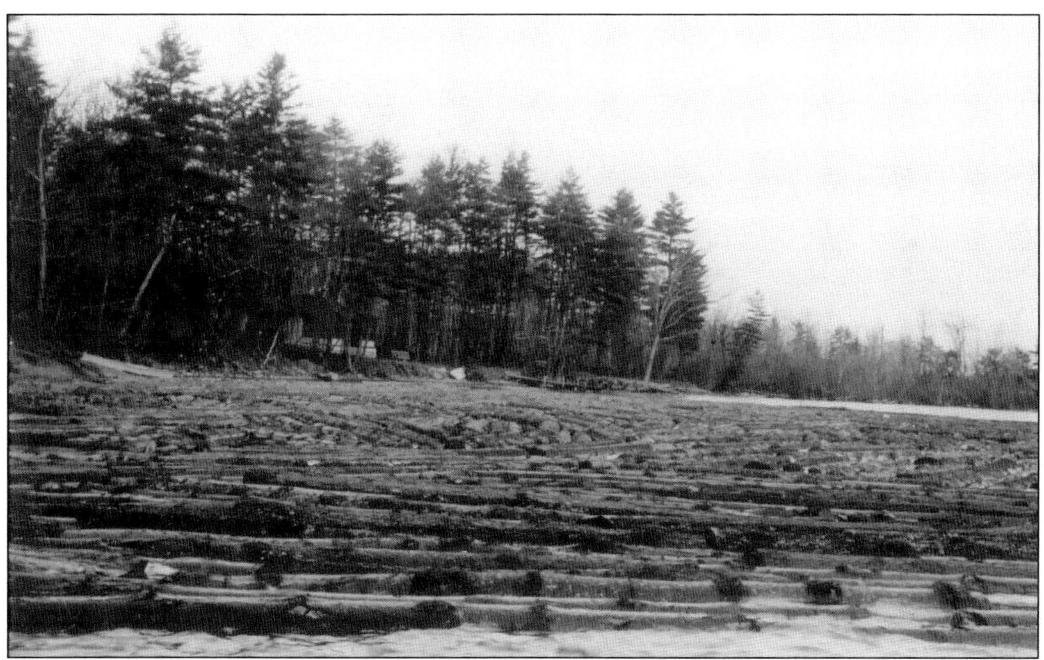

There could be no question in Apperson's mind that commercial interests had no right to block the lake with so many logs, making it completely unnavigable. The lumber companies tried to move the logs during the off-season, knowing that summer tourists would object. John Apperson, with his promotion of winter sports, began to put new pressure on this commercial operation. Below, logs surround an island and continue to obstruct traffic year-round. In 1908, Apperson's canoe hit one of these logs and overturned, so he had strong feelings about this nuisance and hazard. (Both, courtesy of KARC.)

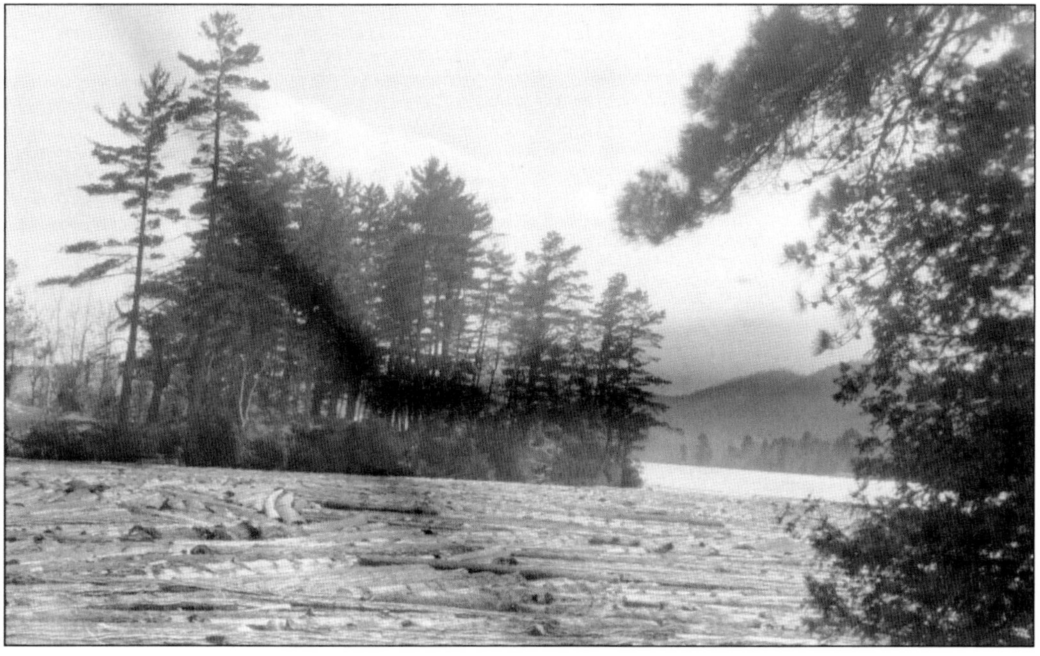

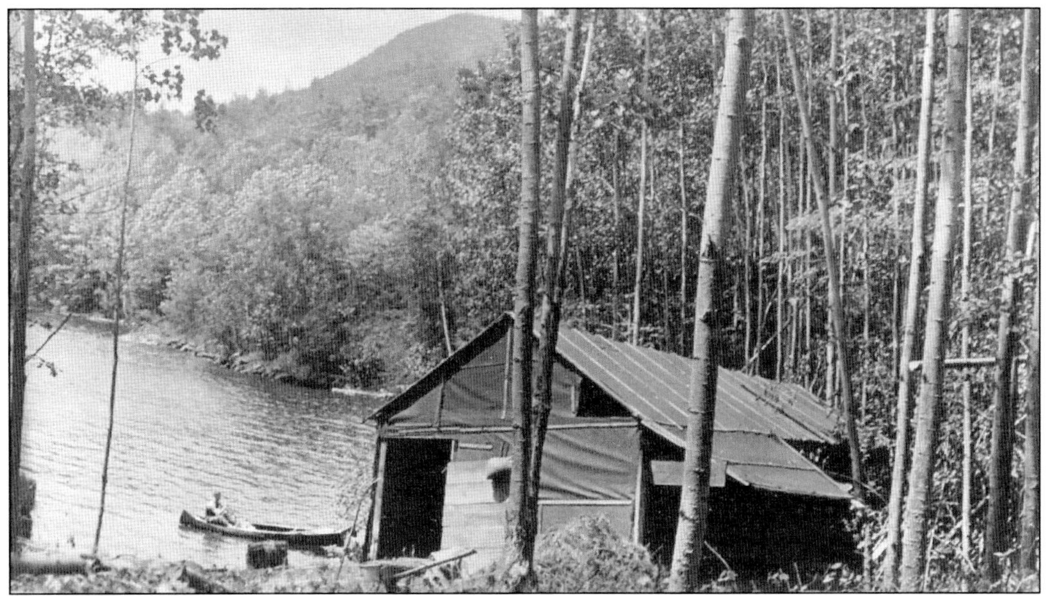

Apperson found others who shared his concerns, and they traveled around the lake, taking photographs of all the trouble spots, such as this lumber camp. They were convinced that a photograph could speak louder than words. The photograph below, with the sign in the middle saying "state lands," seems to be making two points: that state lands should not be suffering from erosion (there is no soil left on the rock) and ramshackle buildings do not belong there. Apperson may have been recording the presence of a squatter's cabin. In fact, this shack may be one that he eventually had moved off the property to return the land to a natural state. (Both, courtesy of KARC.)

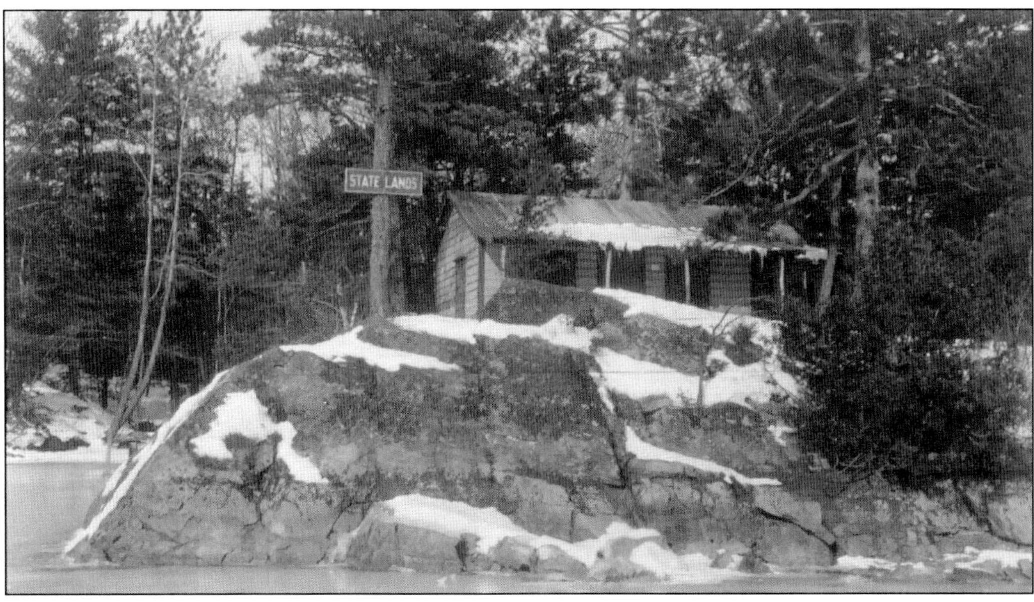

Apperson became a whistle blower on the lumber industry, taking pictures of illegal logging in remote locations throughout the Forest Preserve. Logging was threatening the forests throughout the entire Lake George watershed and on Black Mountain and Tongue Mountain, but it was not the sort of problem one could confront head-on. Apperson tried to push and prod state officials to enforce the laws, with mixed success. (Author's collection.)

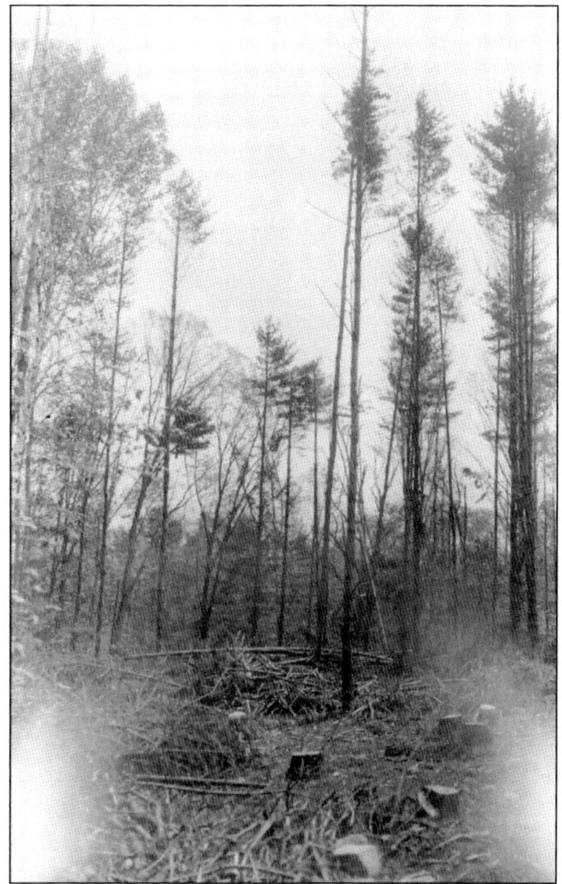

This photograph captures two of Apperson's concerns: logs in the lake and high water flooding the docks. The earliest strategy he developed to address the problem of high water was to build rock walls around the perimeter of state islands, a process called riprapping. (Courtesy of KARC.)

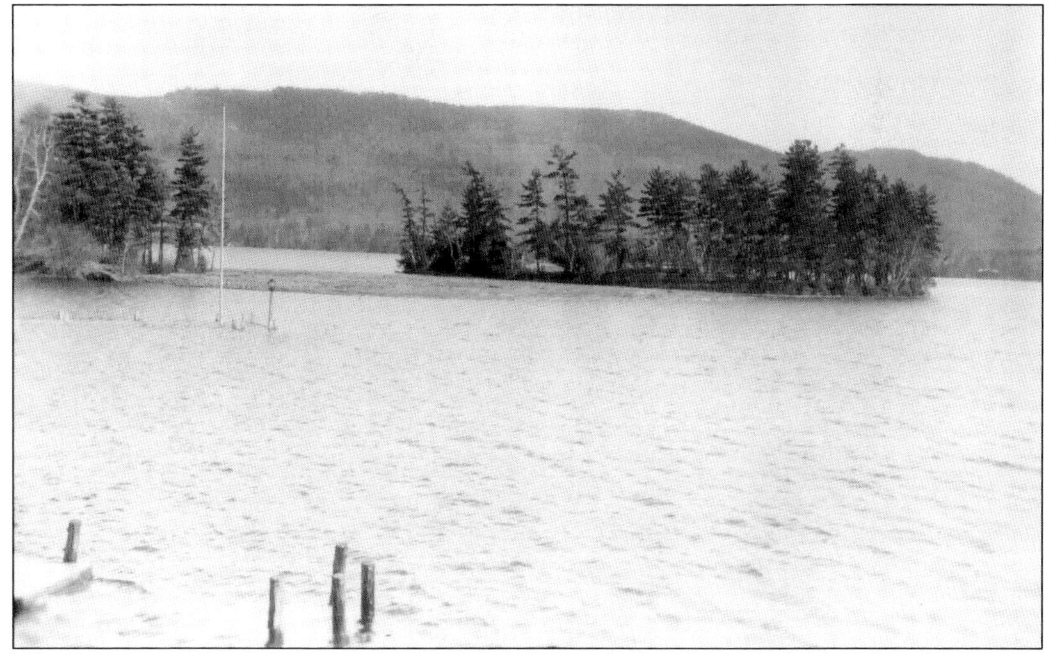

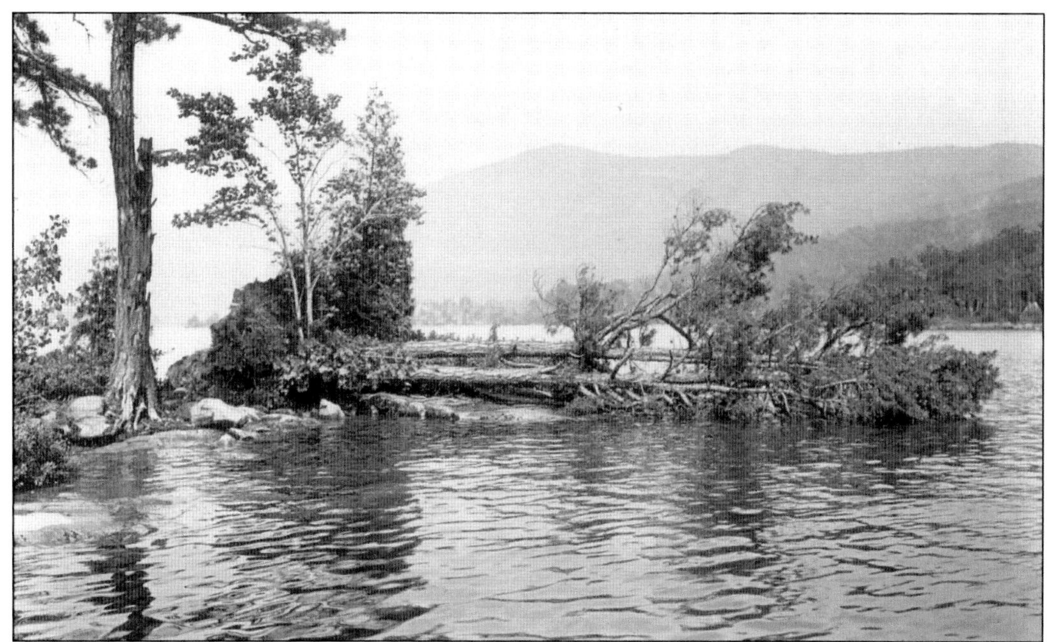

For several decades, Apperson recorded and collected evidence of high water, caused by the flashboards installed by the International Paper Company at Ticonderoga. Officers of the Lake George Association disputed his claims. Photographs like this one, with an island underwater and a huge tree lying on its side, provided a very effective weapon for the fight. Below, this photograph shows the destruction on Pudding Island, with the soil disappearing and the trees falling. Ten years later, Apperson used this photograph in a pamphlet, as part of his long-running legal battle called the Lake George Trespass Case. (Both, courtesy of KARC.)

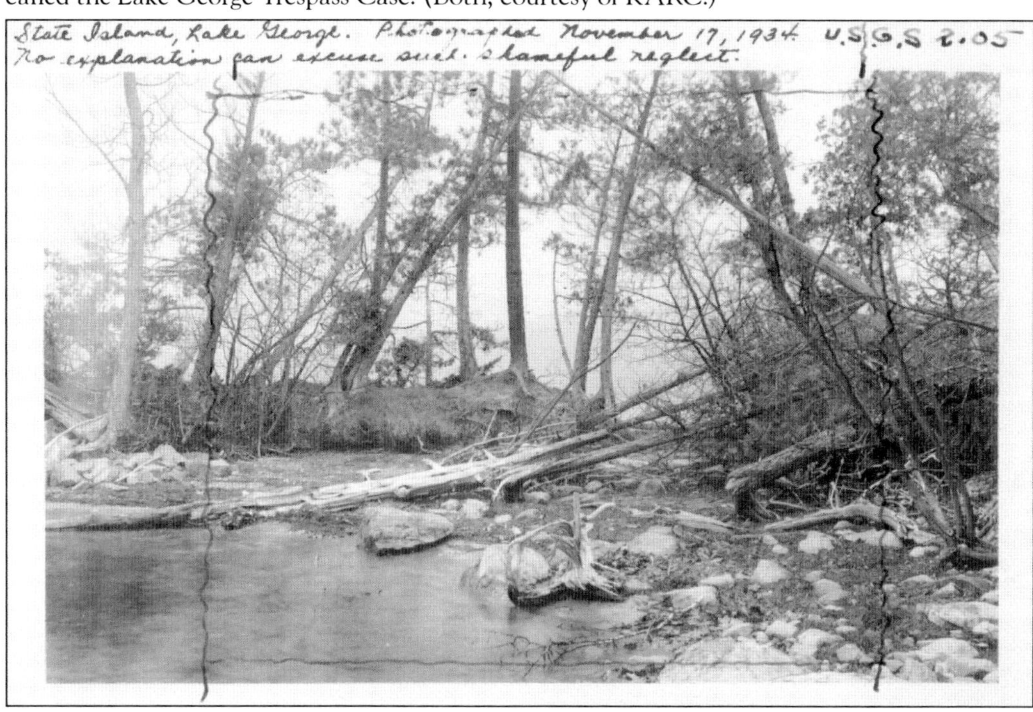

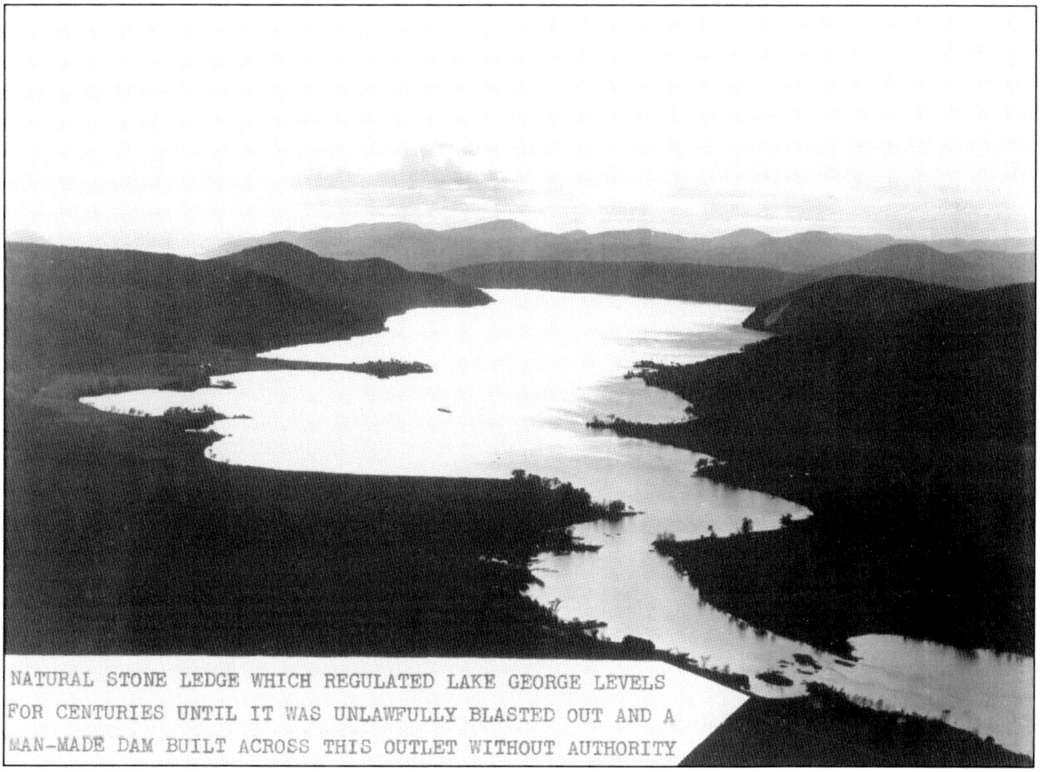

NATURAL STONE LEDGE WHICH REGULATED LAKE GEORGE LEVELS
FOR CENTURIES UNTIL IT WAS UNLAWFULLY BLASTED OUT AND A
MAN-MADE DAM BUILT ACROSS THIS OUTLET WITHOUT AUTHORITY

Above, Apperson and his supporters believed that the natural stone bridge at the northern outlet of the lake should be restored and the offending man-made dam be removed, or at least more carefully regulated. It became a hotly contested battle. In his ongoing efforts to convince the public that there was an erosion problem, Apperson kept looking for dramatic photographs to illustrate how high the water had reached, such as the one at right showing the erosion of all the soil from around the base of this forlorn tree. (Both, courtesy of KARC.)

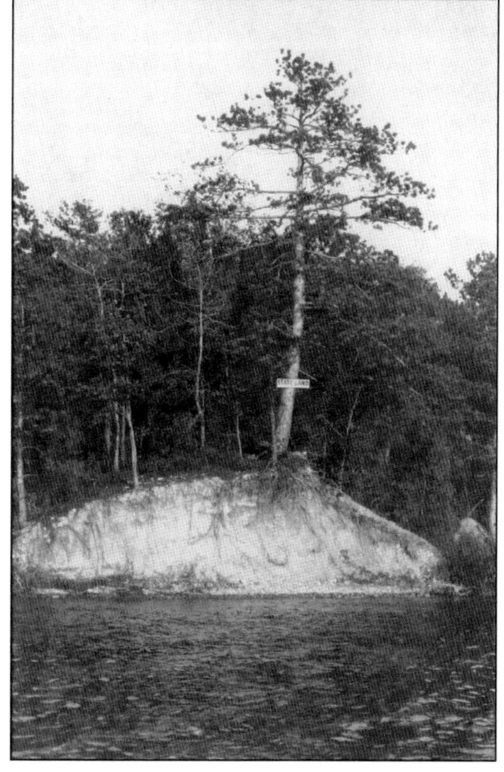

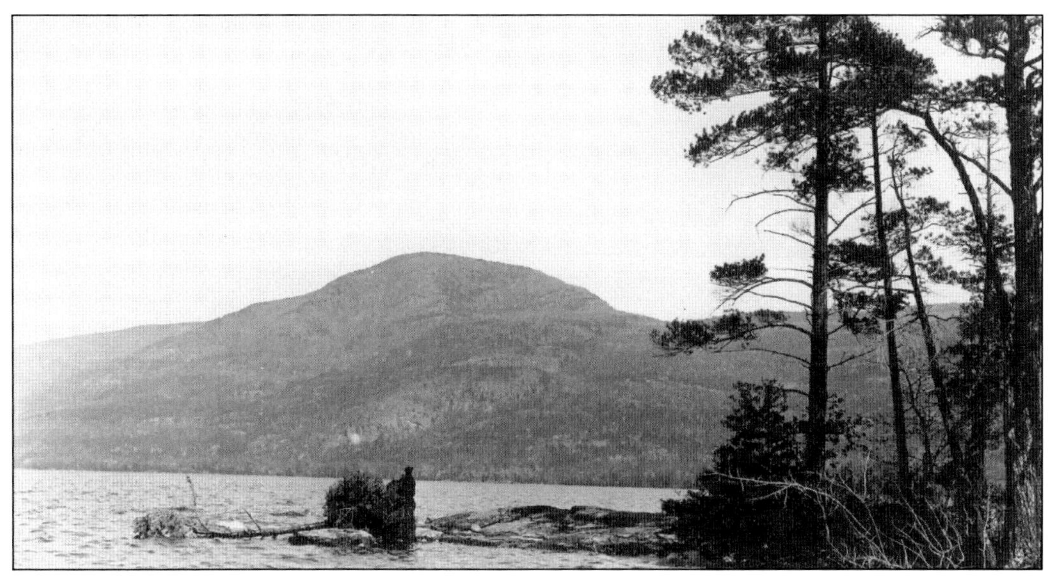

Photographs like the one above convinced many shore owners that something was wrong with the operations of the dam, but the officers of the Lake George Association still turned a blind eye to the evidence and blamed unusual weather conditions for the harm. These arguments went back and forth for many years and were taken up in hearings and in a protracted legal battle. Below is another heartbreaking example of an island disappearing. State officials ignored Apperson's persistent calls for action. (Both, courtesy of KARC.)

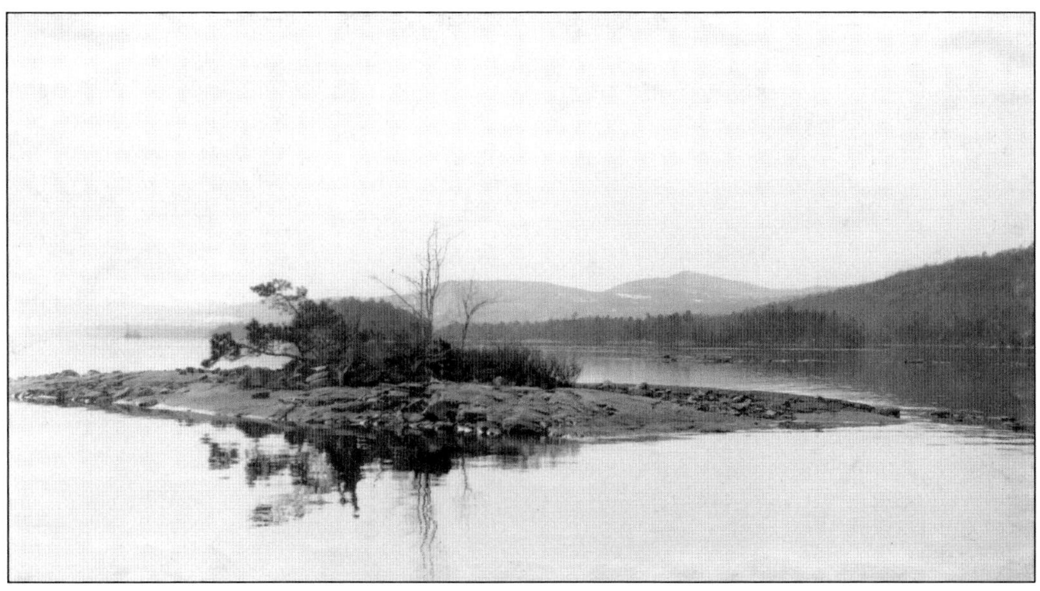

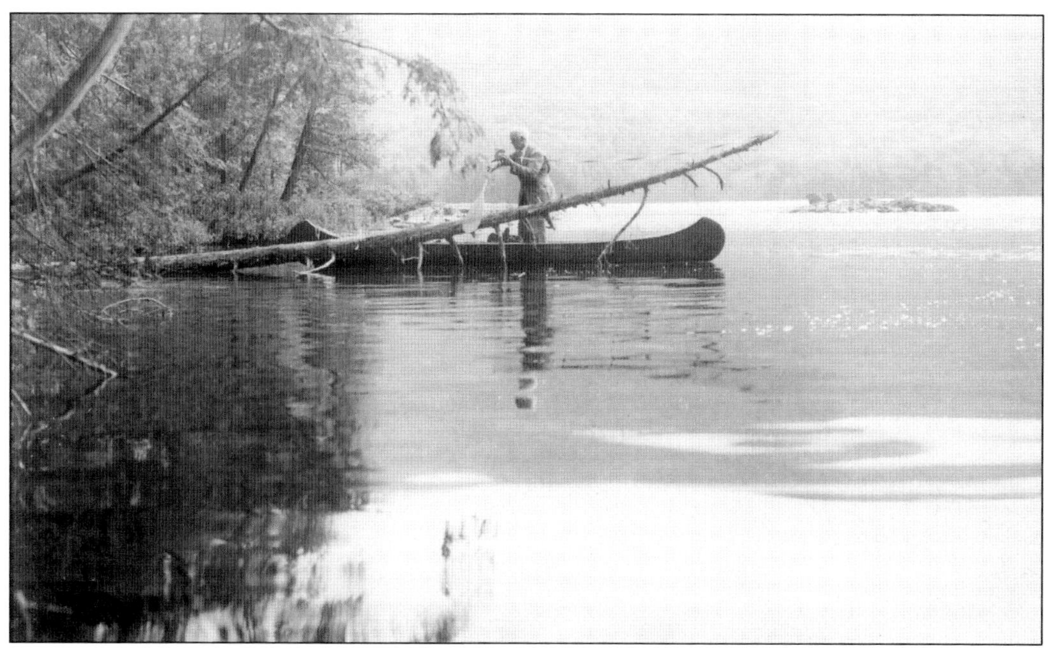

Years after retiring from GE, John Apperson could be seen visiting various trouble spots around the lake, collecting further information to prove that the islands, soils, and trees were still being harmed by high water levels. In the 1950s photograph above, he is out in his canoe, measuring the size of a tree that had fallen into the lake. Seen below is another threat to the forests: the construction of roads. It is easy to imagine Apperson's opinion of the scene captured here at Chapel Pond Road, just a few miles west of Lake George. (Both, courtesy of KARC.)

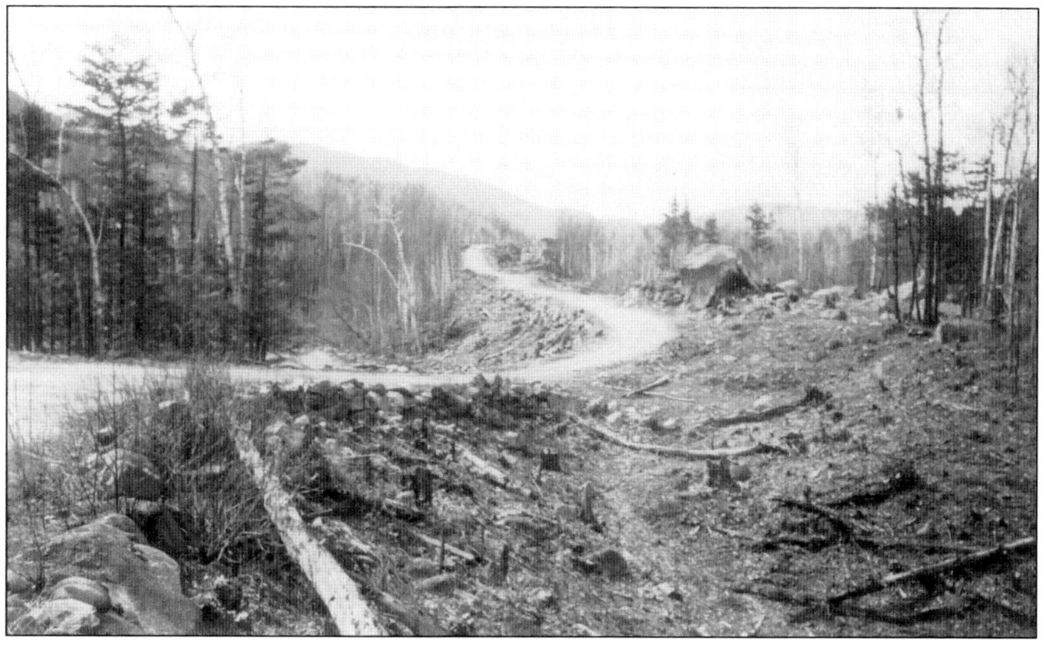

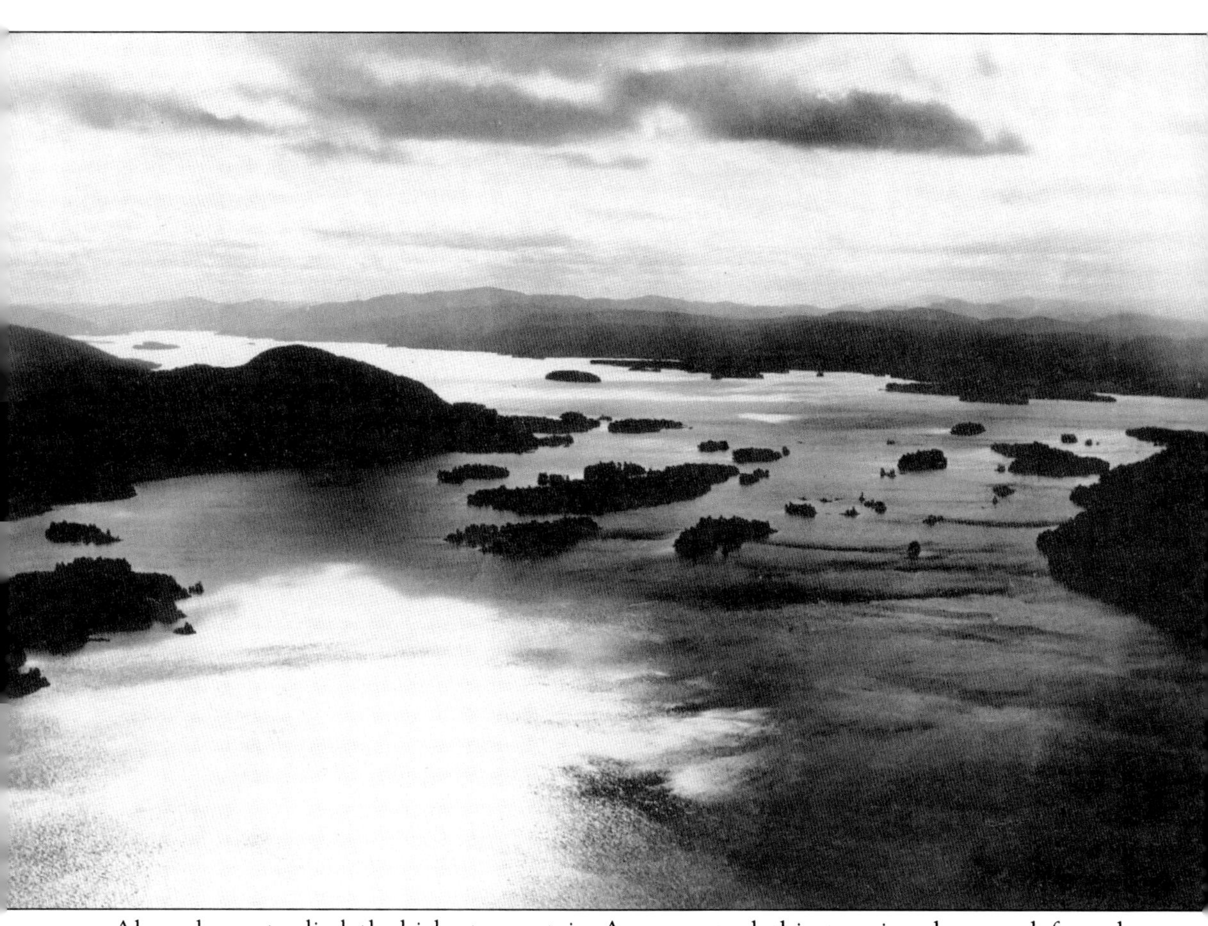

Always happy to climb the highest mountain, Apperson took this stunning photograph from the top of Tongue Mountain looking south toward the Narrows, with Shelving Rock and Paradise Bay on the left and Dome Island just beyond, looking much like the centerpiece of a festive table. (Courtesy of KARC.)

Four

HAULING ROCKS

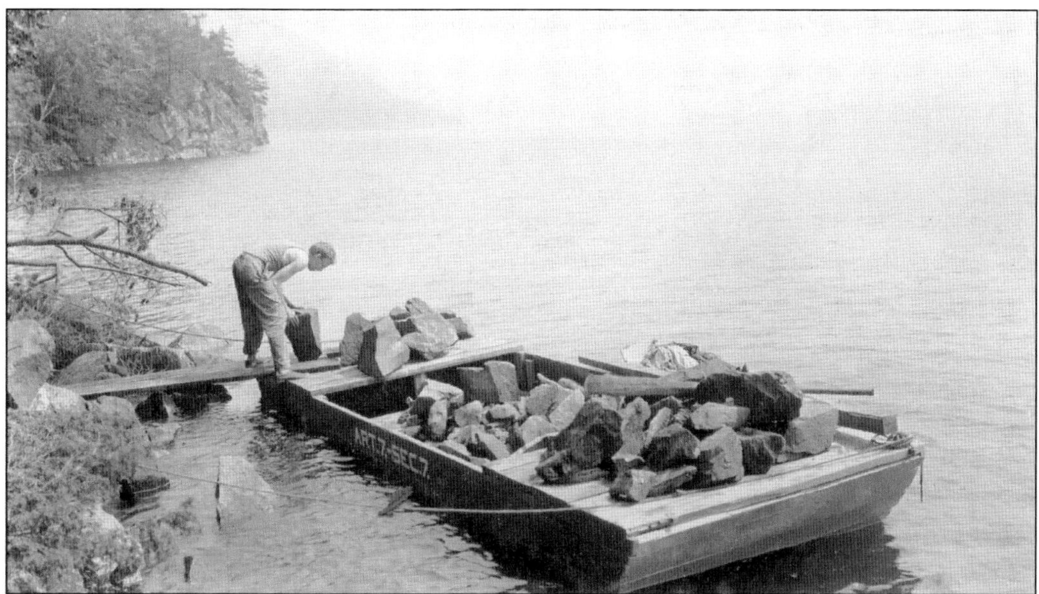

Apperson realized that the islands were threatened by erosion caused by fluctuating water levels, so he came up with a plan to protect them by piling rocks around the shores. This ambitious plan, launched in 1909, required him to recruit friends, asking them to spend a weekend or a summer vacation camping in the islands and contributing many hours of hard physical labor. He built a barge, *ART. 7-SEC. 7*, a reference to the "forever wild" clause of the New York constitution, for use in the summer, and in the winter, he used sleds and even horse-drawn sleighs. By 1917, he had persuaded the legislature to put up $10,000 to expand this project, eventually saving about 50 islands. This photograph, with an accompanying story, was published in the *Conservationist* by the New York State Conservation Commission in 1918. (Courtesy of KARC.)

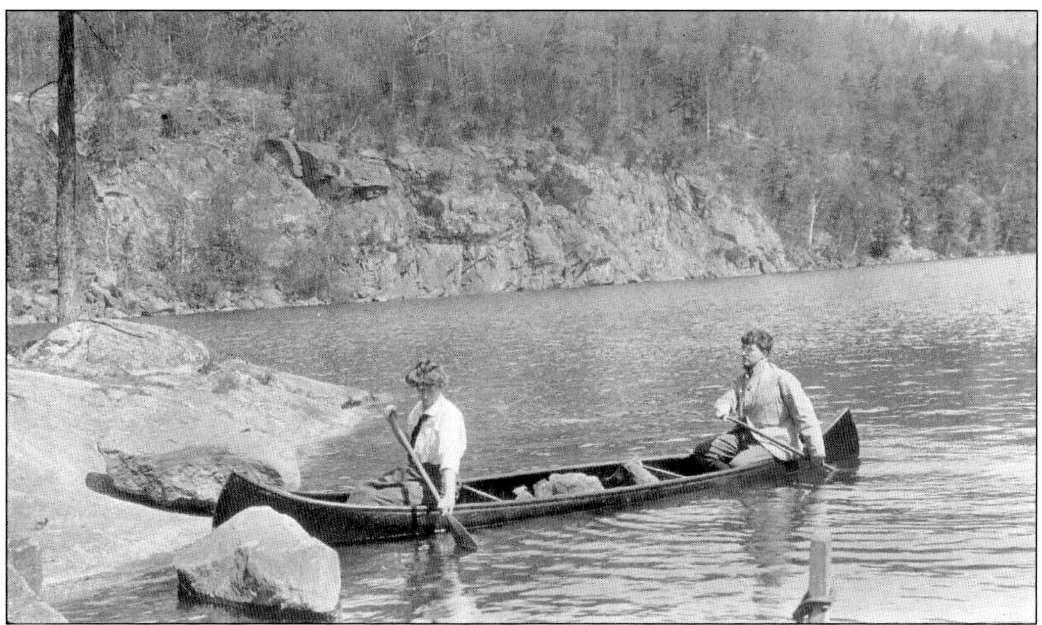

Irving Langmuir and his wife, Marion, were among the early recruits to this project. Irving, who became one of GE's most prominent research scientists, winning a Nobel Prize in chemistry in 1932, was also an avid hiker and skier and helped recruit many others to the cause of preservation at Lake George. Soon after his arrival at GE, he started hiking with Apperson into the high peaks, and it did not take long before he and his wife were recruited for Apperson's riprapping project at Lake George, as seen here, hauling rocks in Apperson's canoe in 1912. Pictured below, Marion Langmuir was well suited for outdoor life and probably did much of the cooking. She is standing at center, with Irving seated second from right. (Above, courtesy of KARC; below, author's collection.)

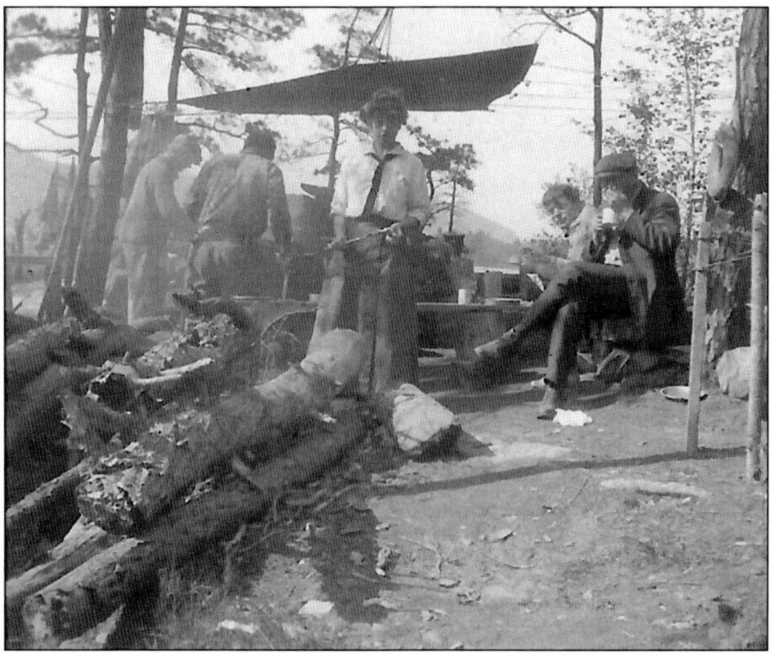

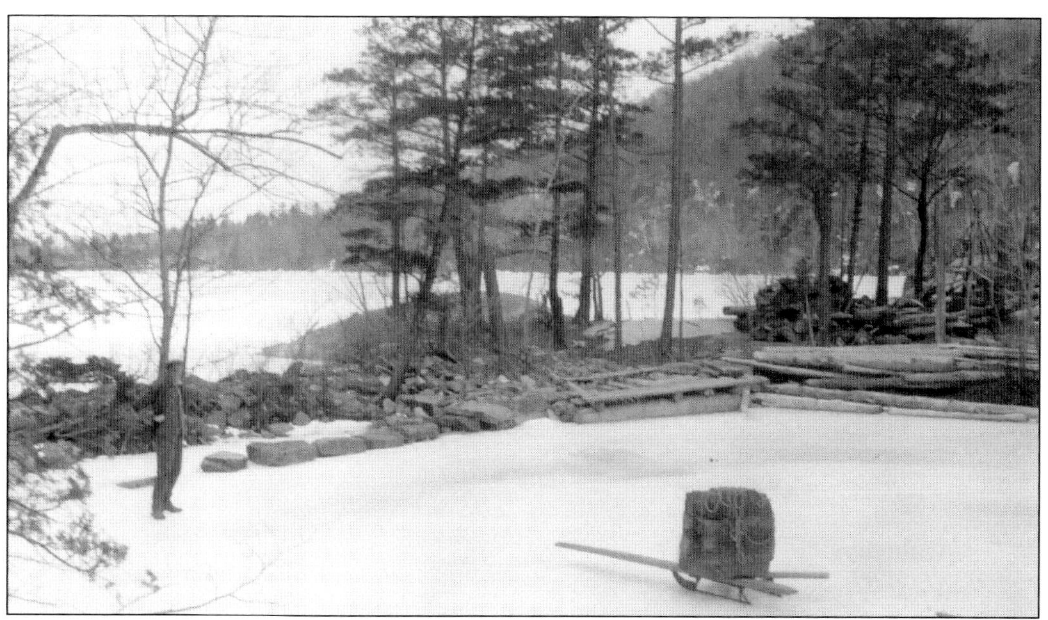

In this winter scene, a man looks over in amazement at a huge boulder he and several friends have just successfully dragged over the ice on a homemade sled. Below, a few minutes later, the rock has been put in place, where it will form the foundation for a protective wall, and the crew has left to find another one. Eventually, Apperson and his friends designed a more substantial sled, but these old-fashioned blades were effective for this job. The engineers used their skills to design a cozy harbor at the Dollar Islands, a design that is still functioning well today. (Both, courtesy of KARC.)

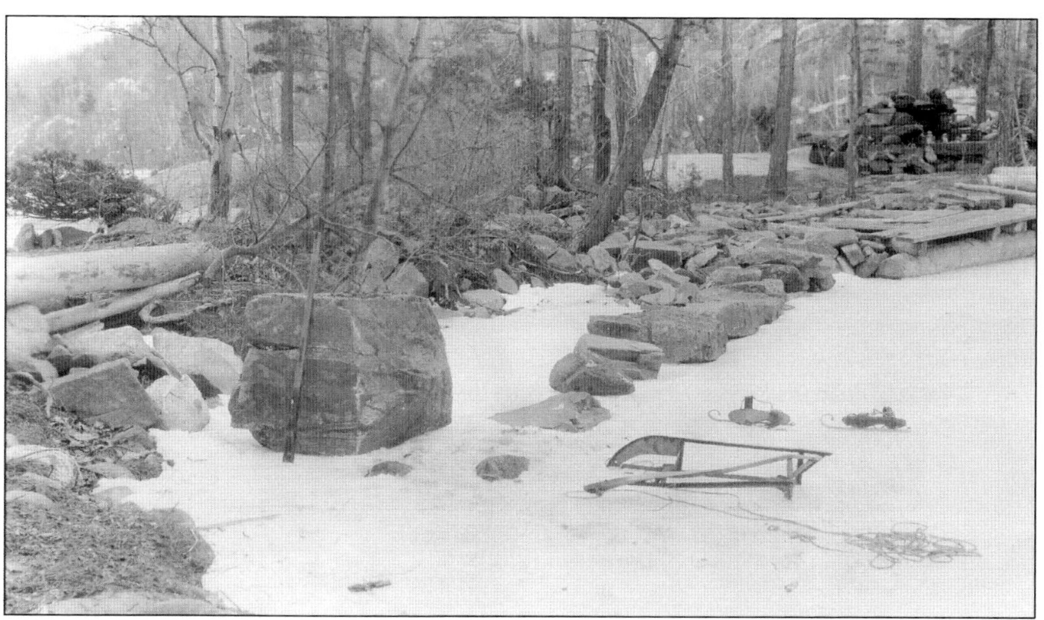

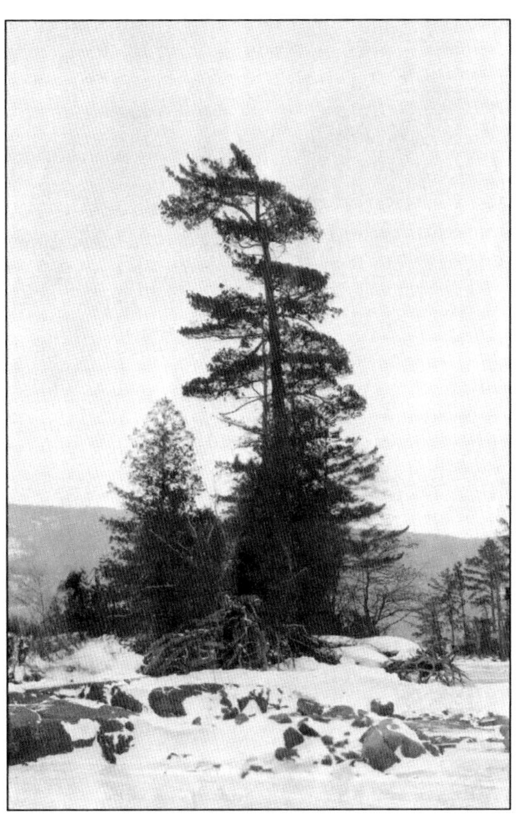

There were many other islands in need of repair, with virtually no soil left to hold the trees in place. The one pictured at left could be protected with a rock wall. Below, Apperson's barge delivers a load of rocks to an island in distress. In 1917, after winning the support of the legislature in the form of $10,000 for island repair, workers from the Delaware and Hudson (D&H) Railway were employed during the off-season, and Apperson directed the operations. (Both, courtesy of KARC.)

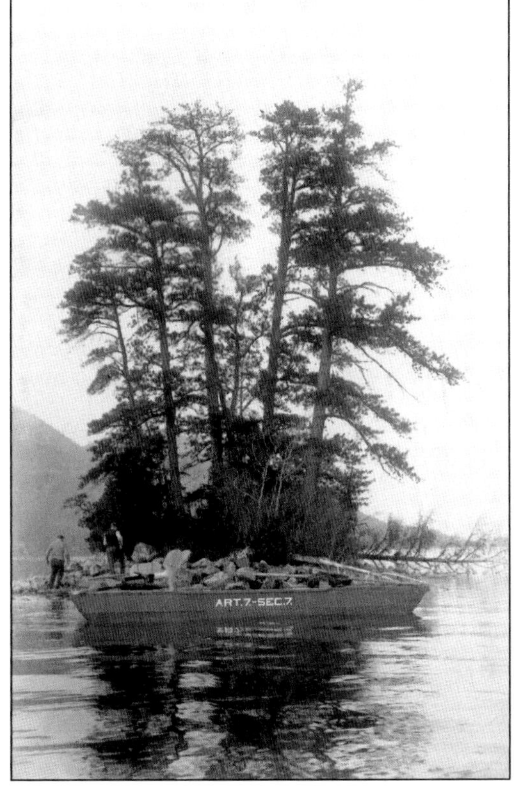

Always interested in teaching the younger generation, Apperson took an active interest in the Camp Fire Girls, helping their leaders find a suitable home base not too far from Lake George and then inviting them to participate in his riprapping project in the Dollar Islands. Here, the girls certainly seem to be having a good time. The Camp Fire Girls had many prominent supporters in those days, including Franklin D. Roosevelt and George D. Pratt. (Both, courtesy of KARC.)

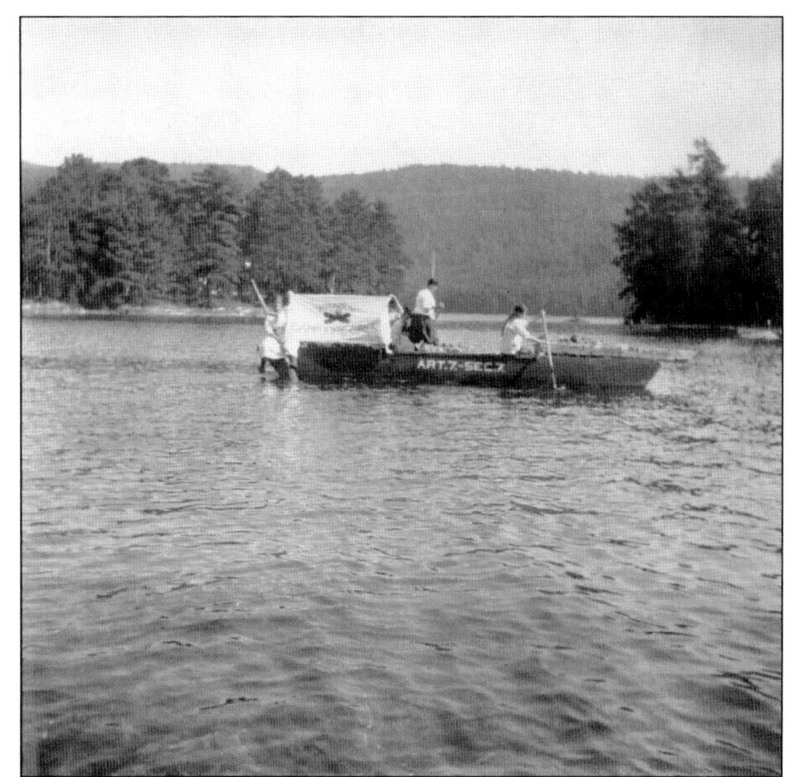

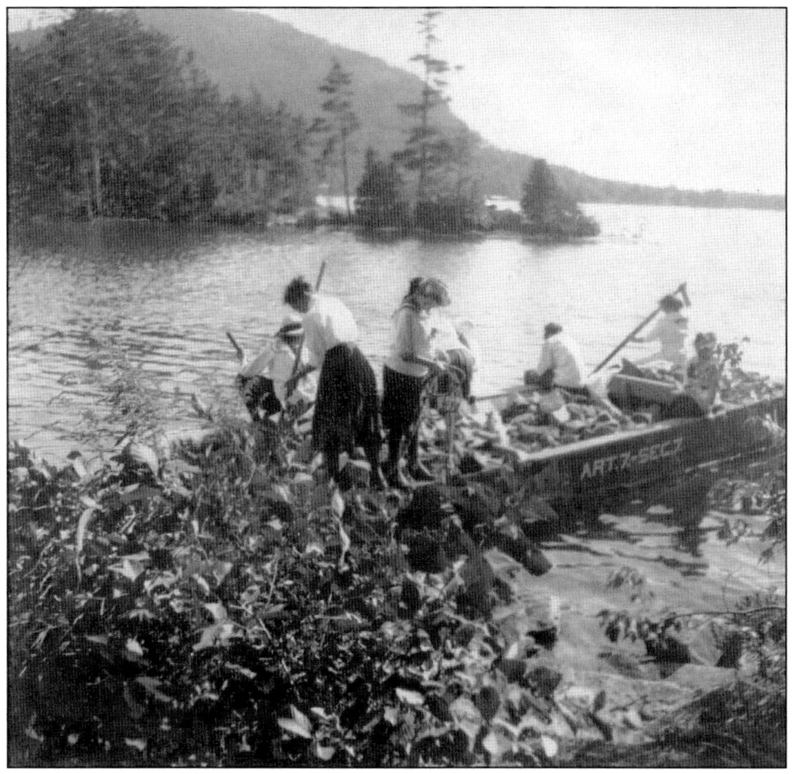

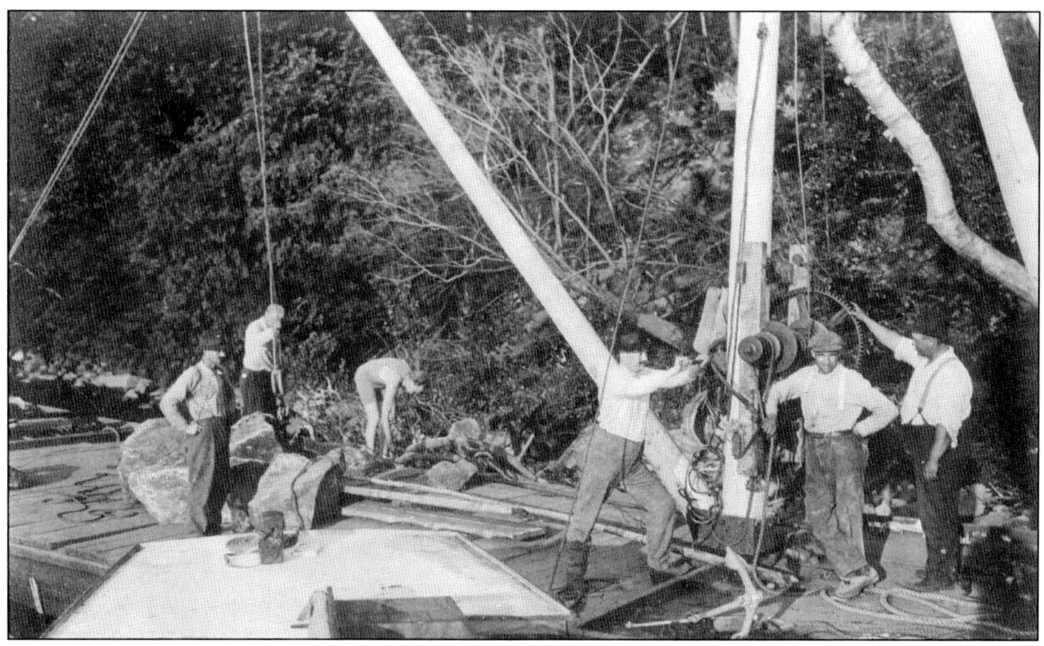

Once the state legislature allocated funds for repairing the shores of Lake George's islands in 1917, Apperson suddenly had an impressive workforce. He could borrow a large barge rigged out with beam and pulleys, capable of lifting and transporting huge boulders. These men are from the D&H Railway, and Apperson is third from the left, wearing a swimsuit. Below is another view of the barge in the harbor of West Dollar Island. According to letters in the Apperson files, the barge was on loan from George O. Knapp, owner of an estate on Shelving Rock east of the Narrows. (Both, courtesy of KARC.)

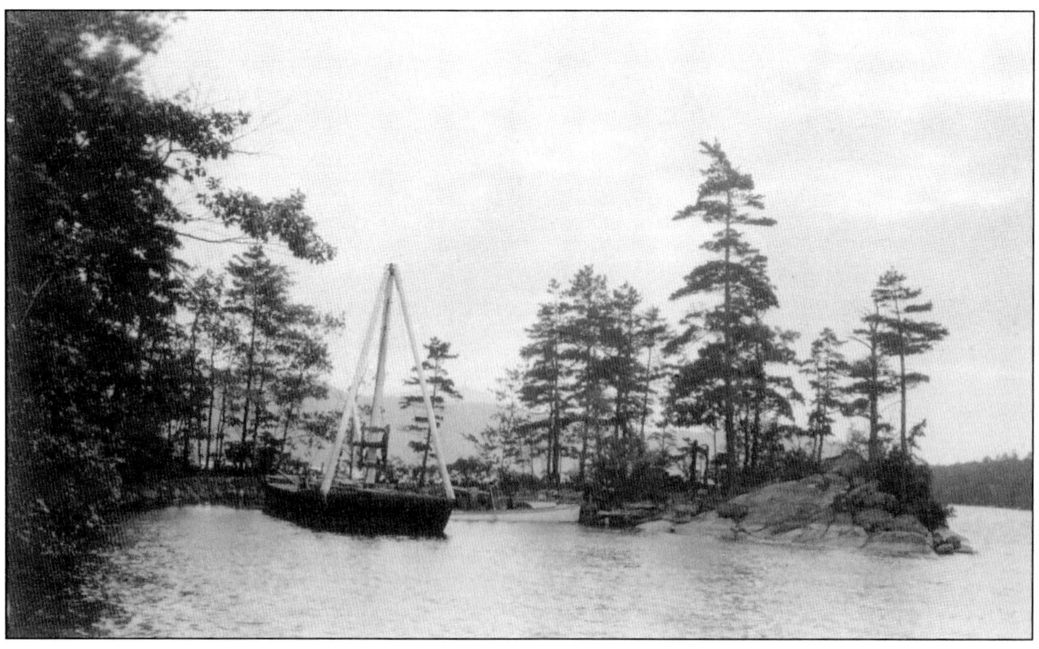

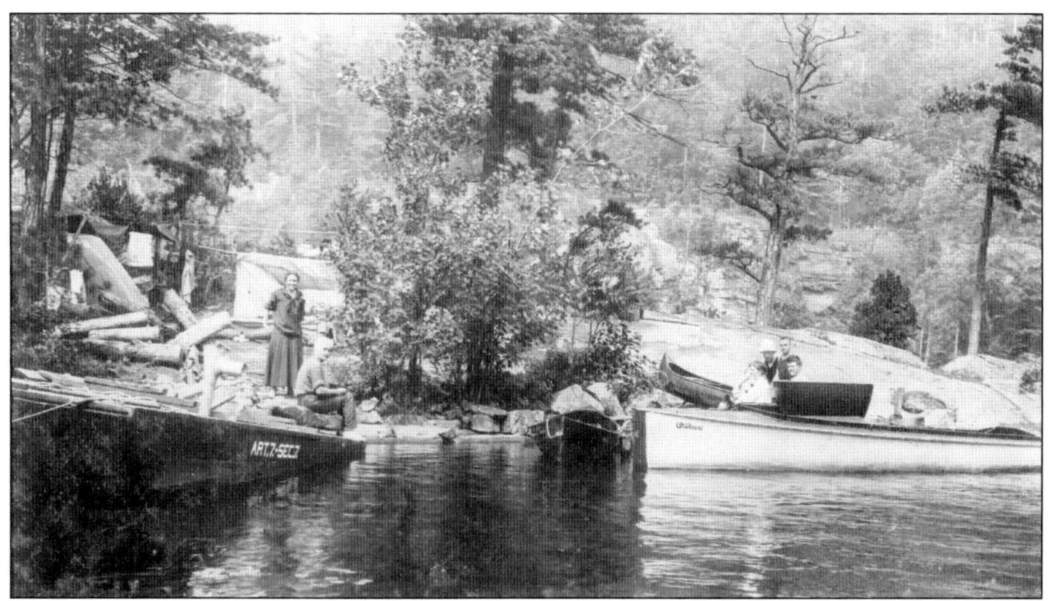

As word spread about the joys of island camping and of the need for volunteers, many GE engineers brought their wives and children to spend a week or two. Above is Apperson's barge and his motorboat *Chilhowie* with a group of friends. Below is a group of unidentified ladies; perhaps they were members of a garden club, but their white dresses certainly seem a bit out of place as they venture into the water to collect rocks around 1914. (Both, author's collection.)

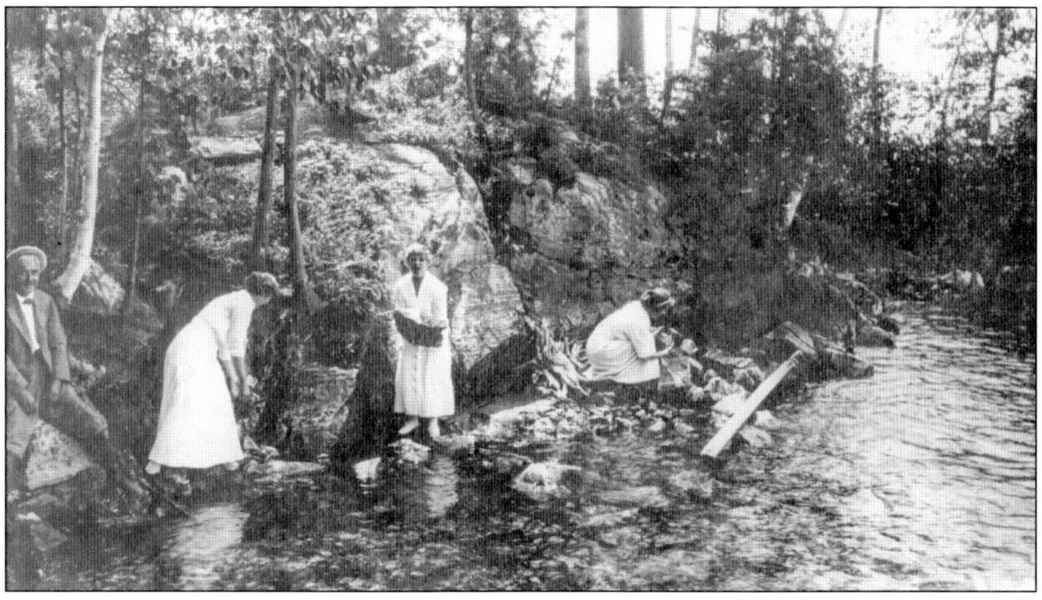

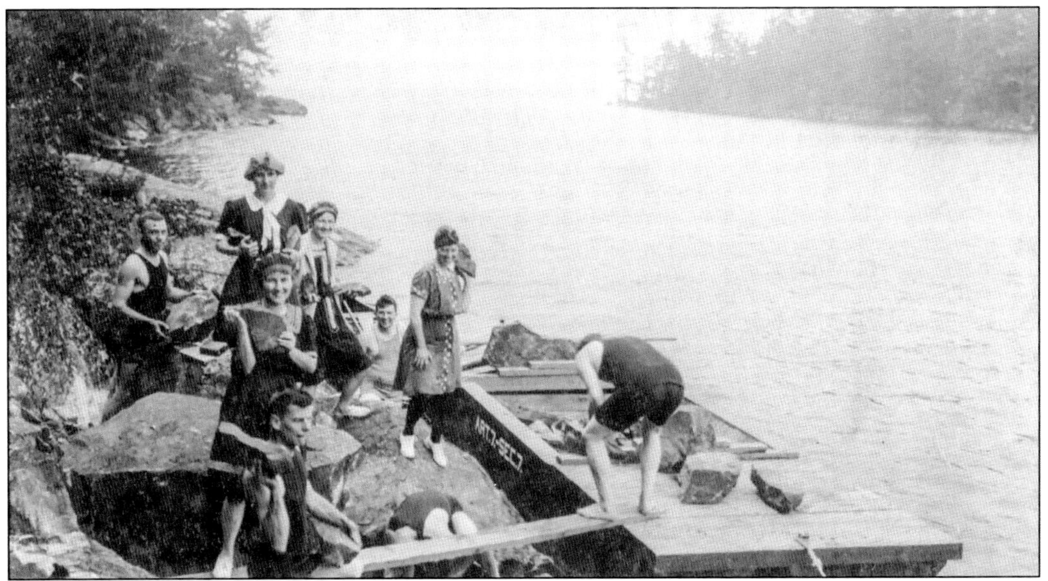

The women in this photograph wear bathing suits instead of dresses. Perhaps this coed group was part of some sort of outing club from Schenectady. They all seem to be happy to flex their muscles and spend the day contributing to a good cause. (Author's collection.)

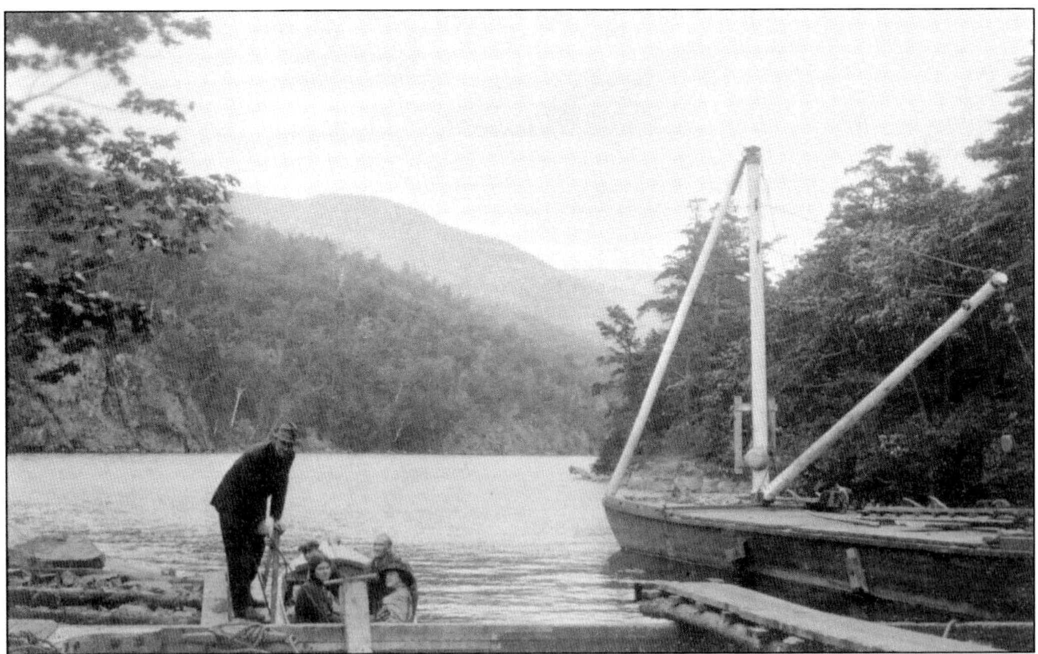

Many local families, or those with summer homes in the area, took notice of the efforts to repair islands and offered to join in the fun. The group in the motorboat may have been taking a tour of the works in progress in the Narrows. The man seated on the right side of the boat may be Ted Dreier, an engineer at GE who married Barbara Loines, granddaughter of Mary Loines, in 1928. (Courtesy of KARC.)

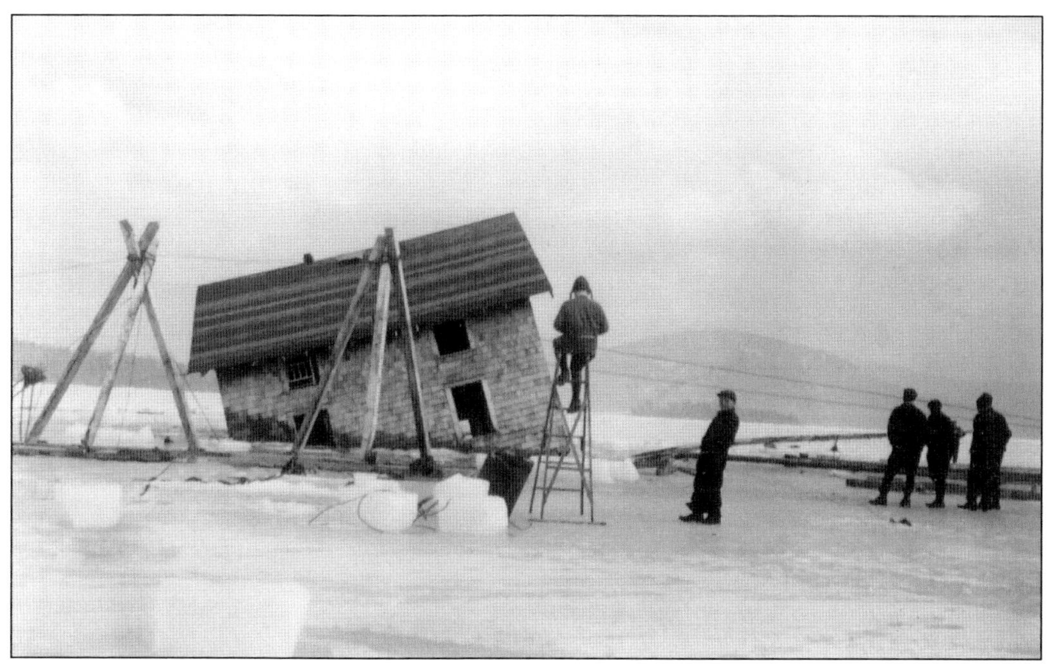

One of Apperson's goals was to put pressure on state officials to force the removal of squatters from state-owned islands. He often took charge of these operations, and not always with great success. Seen above in the 1930s, a work crew tried to haul one such building over the ice, and the heavy structure broke through. They must have had a hard time figuring out what to do. Below is a photograph of the same event taken from a different angle. (Both, courtesy of KARC.)

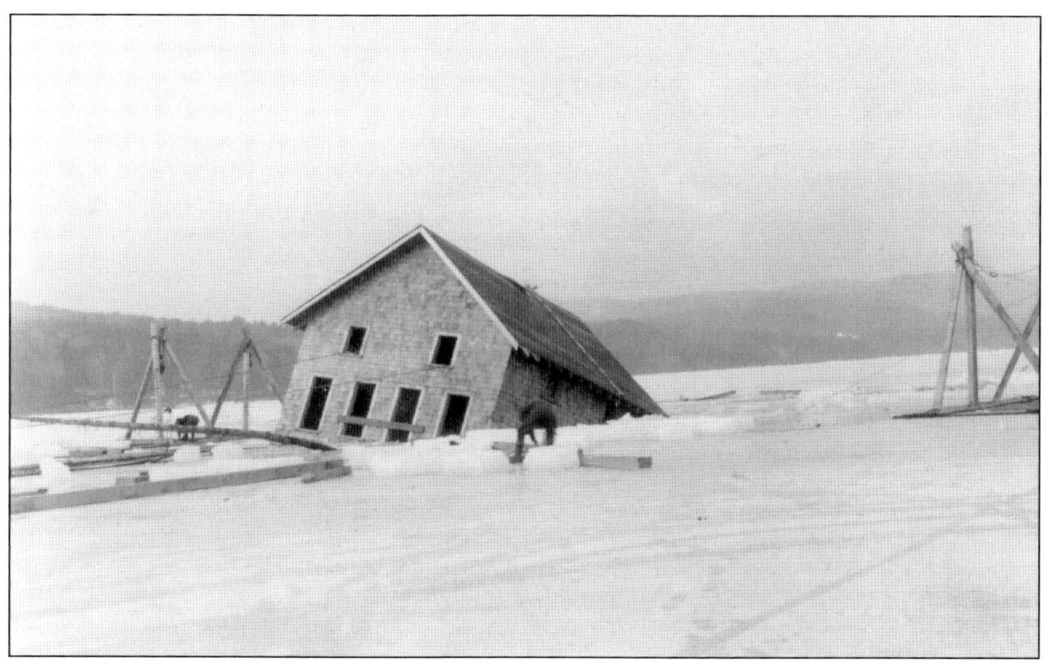

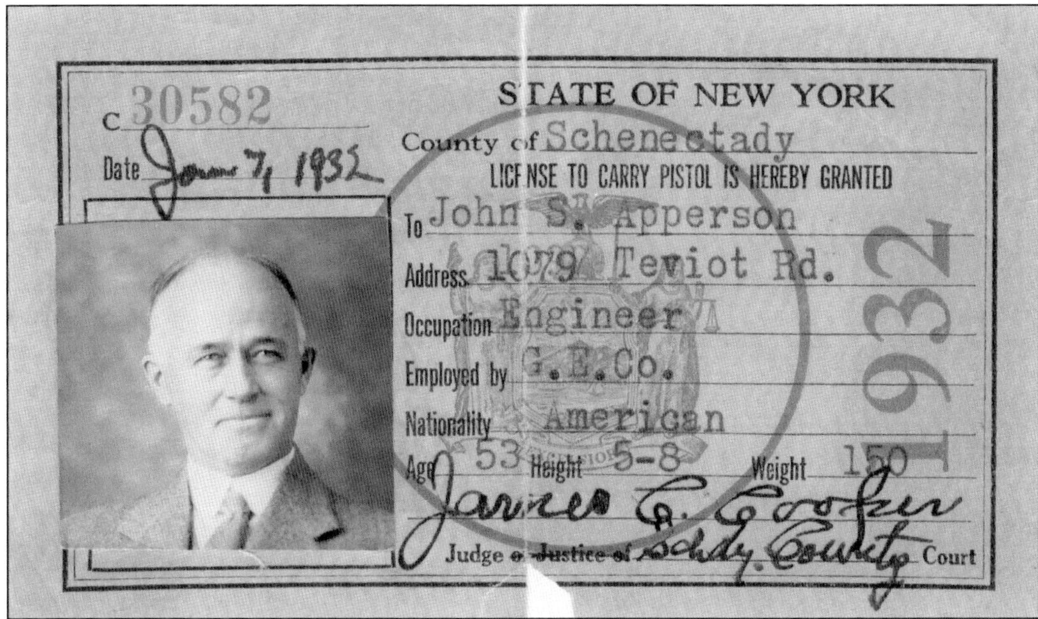
c30582

STATE OF NEW YORK

Date Jan 7, 1932

County of Schenectady

LICENSE TO CARRY PISTOL IS HEREBY GRANTED

To John S. Apperson

Address 1079 Teviot Rd.

Occupation Engineer

Employed by G.E.Co.

Nationality American

Age 53 Height 5-8 Weight 150

Judge or Justice of Schdy. County Court

1932

Local people heard all sorts of rumors and propaganda directed against John Apperson and those "scientists and engineers from Schenectady." Loyal friends warned him of the threats being made against him as early as 1918. He decided to apply for a gun license and purchased a pistol in 1932. (Author's collection.)

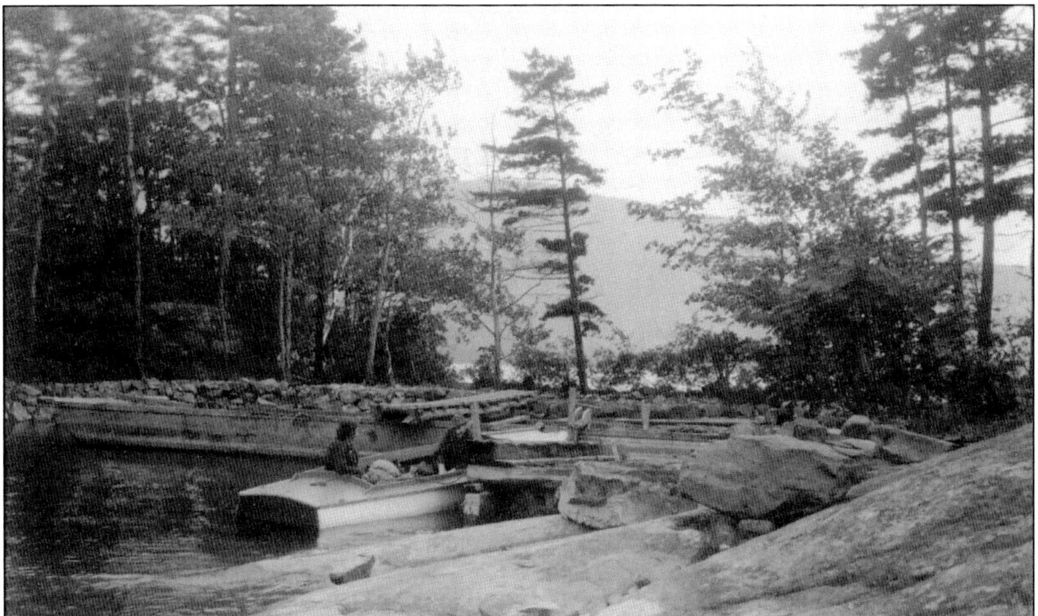

Throughout several decades, Apperson tried to convince wealthy landowners, most of whom were members of the Lake George Association, to pay closer attention to the problems of erosion and acknowledge the damage being done to the islands by high water. He was up against some powerful political foes, however, and had to take comfort in the tangible progress he was making, especially at the Dollar Islands. Here is a view of the dock and harbor Apperson and his friends constructed. (Courtesy of KARC.)

Five

HUDDLE BAY

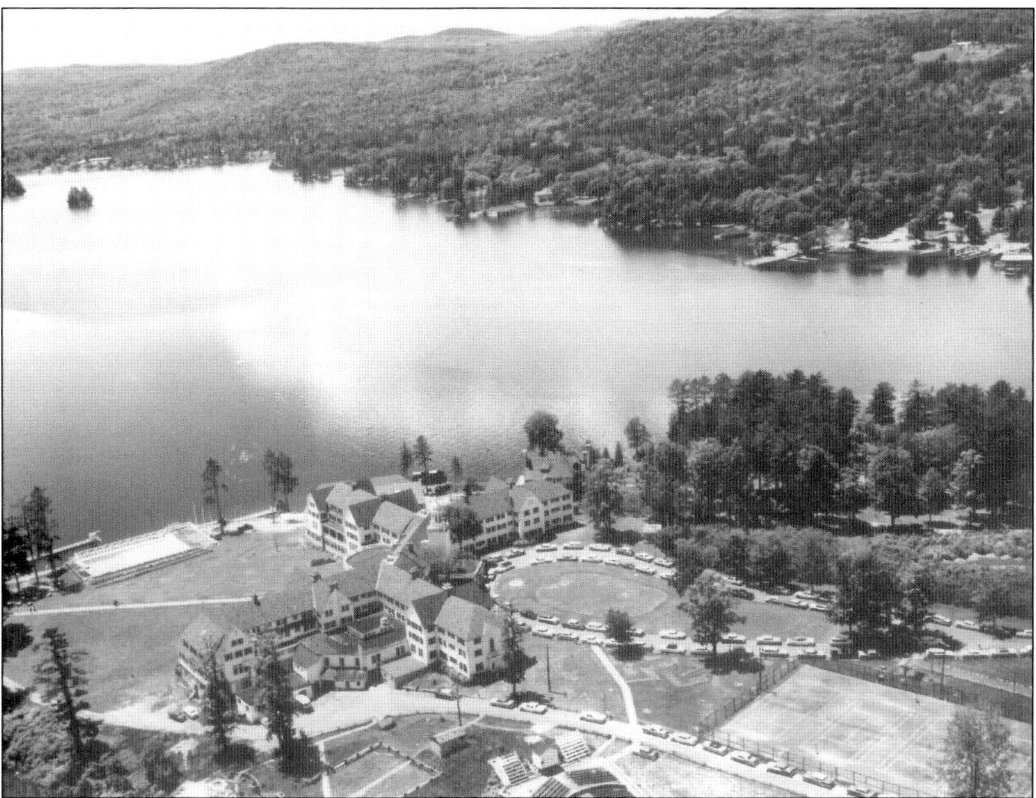

By 1920, John Apperson started looking for property in Bolton as a place to store his boats and camping gear. This photograph shows Bolton in the 1940s, with the Sagamore Hotel at the bottom and Mohican Point, home of William K. Bixby, at the top. Just to the south, or left, along the shore is Huddle Bay, where Apperson and two others purchased an old hotel in 1920. Apperson was delighted with the possibilities and began transforming an old icehouse into his version of an Adirondack camp, naming it Chilhowie, after his hometown in Virginia. (Author's collection.)

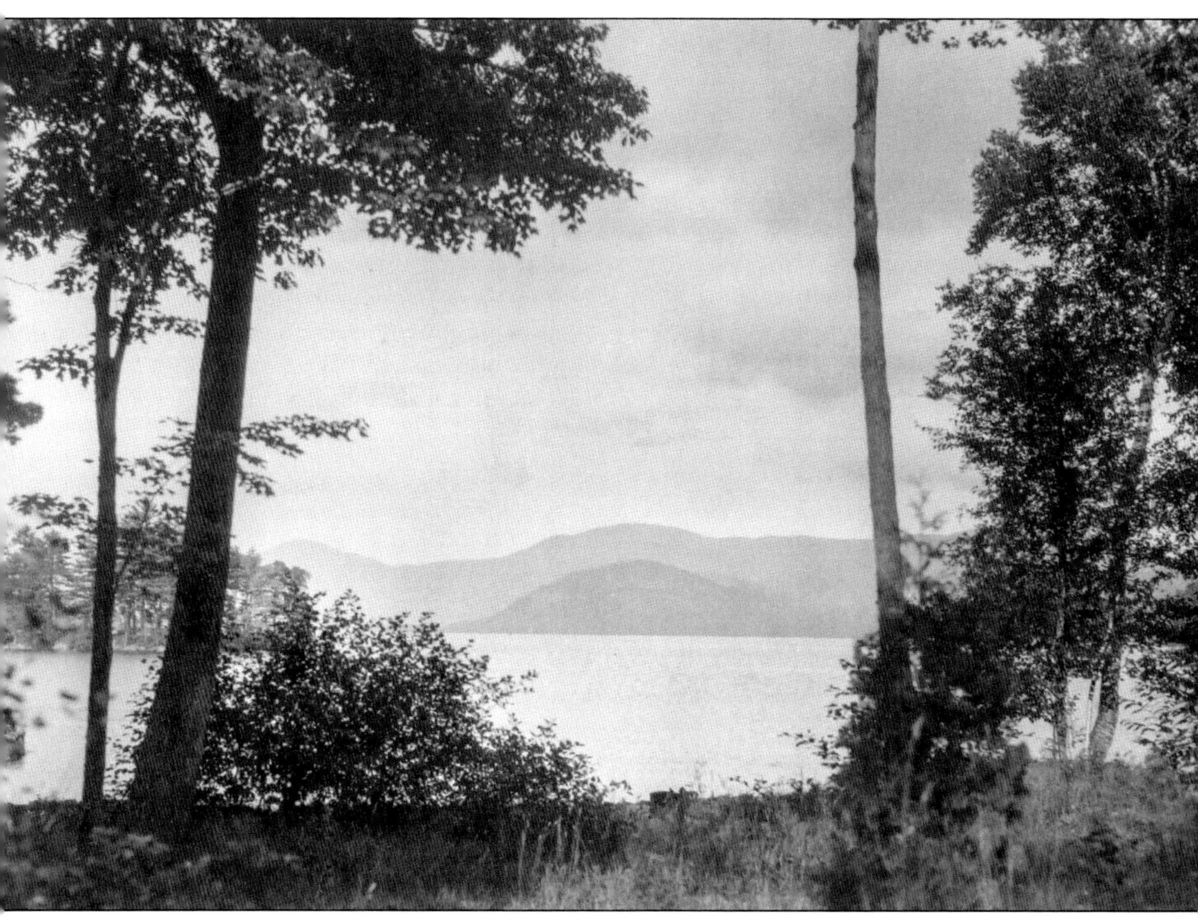

Although Apperson always preferred the islands to the busy town of Bolton, the old Lake View Hotel property was relatively peaceful and undeveloped. One of Apperson's early photographs shows the view from Lake View House on Parodi Point, looking out toward Shelving Rock with Black Mountain in the distance. (Author's collection.)

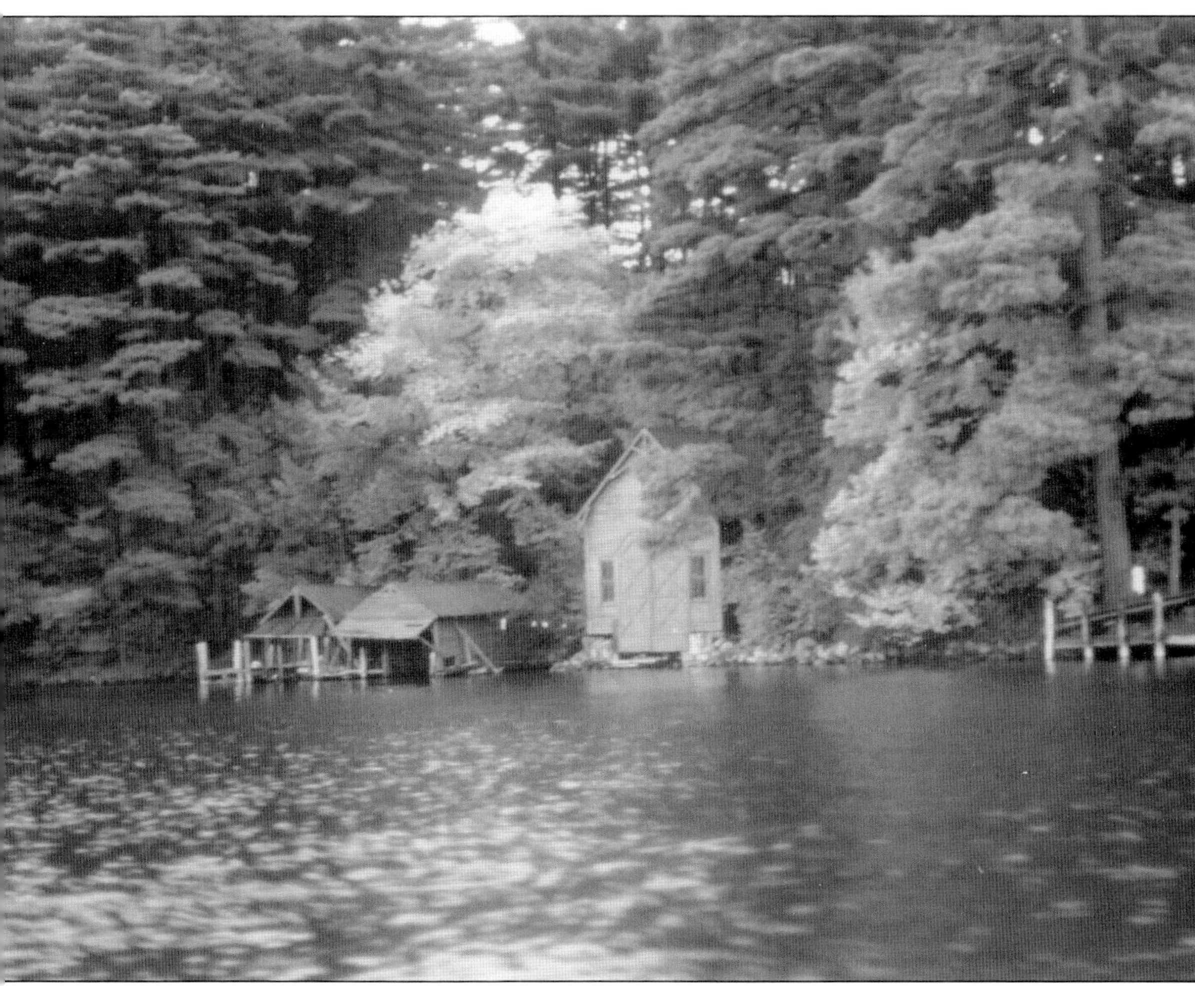

After dividing up the hotel property into three parcels, John Apperson took over the southern piece with several boat slips, a large boathouse (full of old rowboats that had been used by the hotel), a little camp near a dock (that was probably used as a bar for some of the hotel's patrons), and a huge icehouse, which he promptly renovated. This photograph, taken in the 1940s, shows the old boathouse looking much the same as it did in the early 1900s, still painted a shade of forest green to blend in with the trees. (Author's collection.)

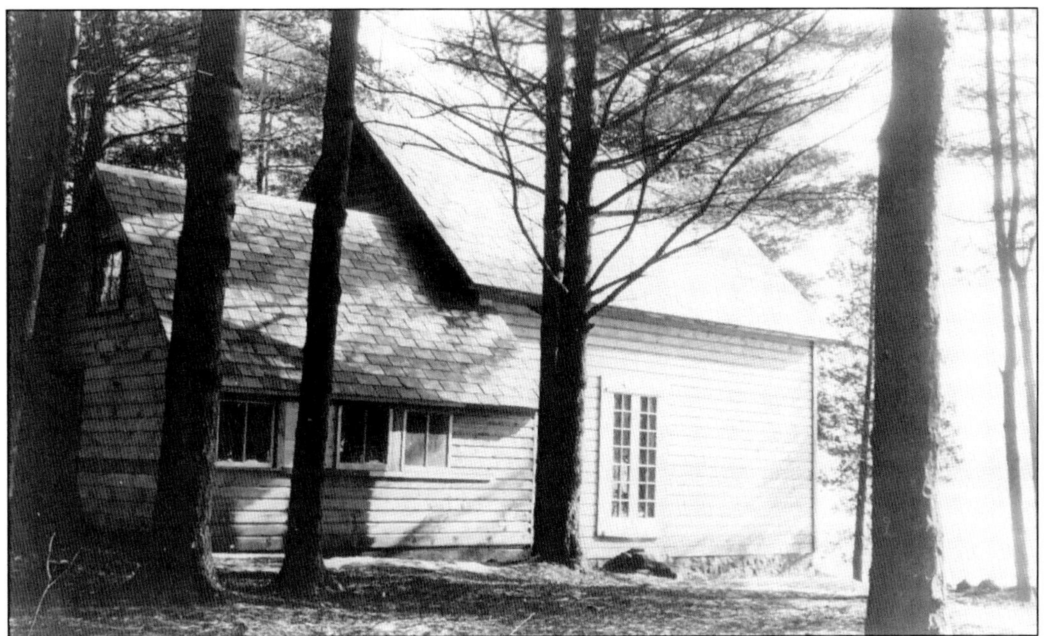

Apperson recruited local builder William Hill to help him transform the old icehouse into a two-story camp with a fireplace, wood stove, bathroom, additional storage space, and a large dormitory-style sleeping space upstairs. Apperson delighted in putting on all the final touches and thinking about every detail. He loved being able to offer hospitality to friends and family and invite them to spend their vacations at the beautiful lake. Below is a view of his camp from the back in about 1925. He deliberately chose to leave trees growing all around, hoping to screen it from view. He wanted the shoreline to be as natural as possible and objected to the construction of elaborate houses with lawns and formal gardens, preferring to repurpose existing structures like this old icehouse. (Both, courtesy of KARC.)

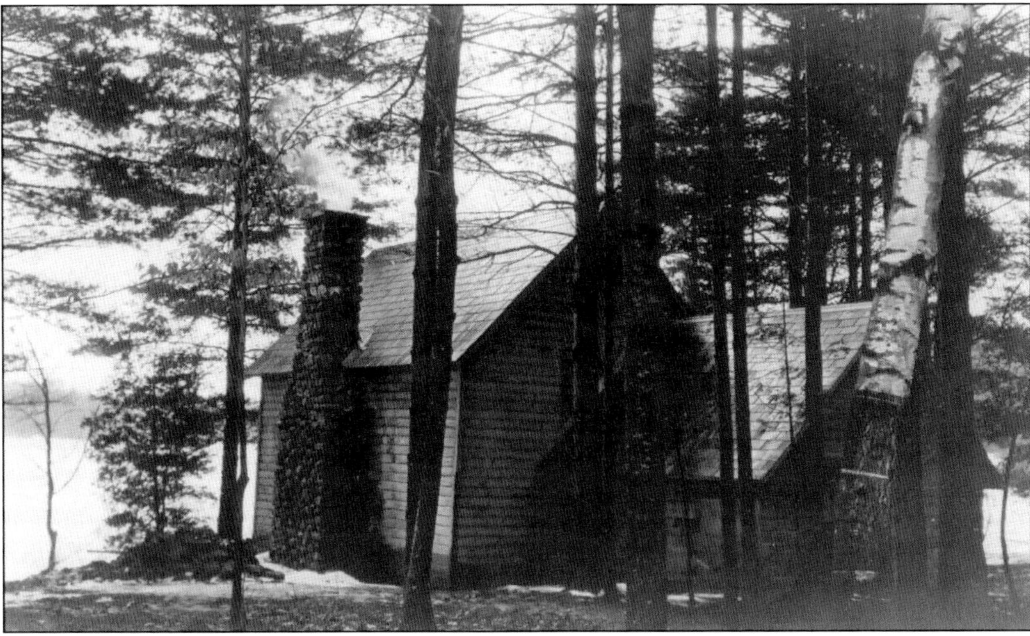

In the winter of 1926, when good friends came for a visit, they were eager to try out their new sports equipment. Jim Cawley (left), vice commodore of the American Canoe Association, was working closely with Apperson to plan a regatta on Turtle Island for the following summer. Apperson was happy to help, knowing that some of the club's members might become allies in his efforts to create a Lake George Park. Below, Jim and Margaret Cawley must have been enthusiastic about winter sports, having already purchased a pair of skis for their young daughter Margaret. She grew up to become a college professor and fondly remembered her childhood visits to Lake George. Jim worked in the publishing business for McGraw Hill. (Both, courtesy of KARC.)

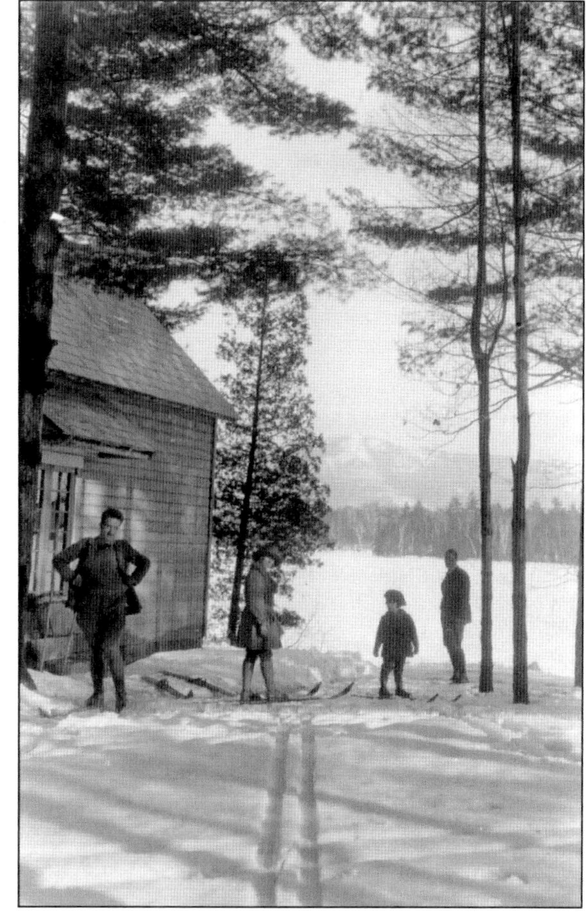

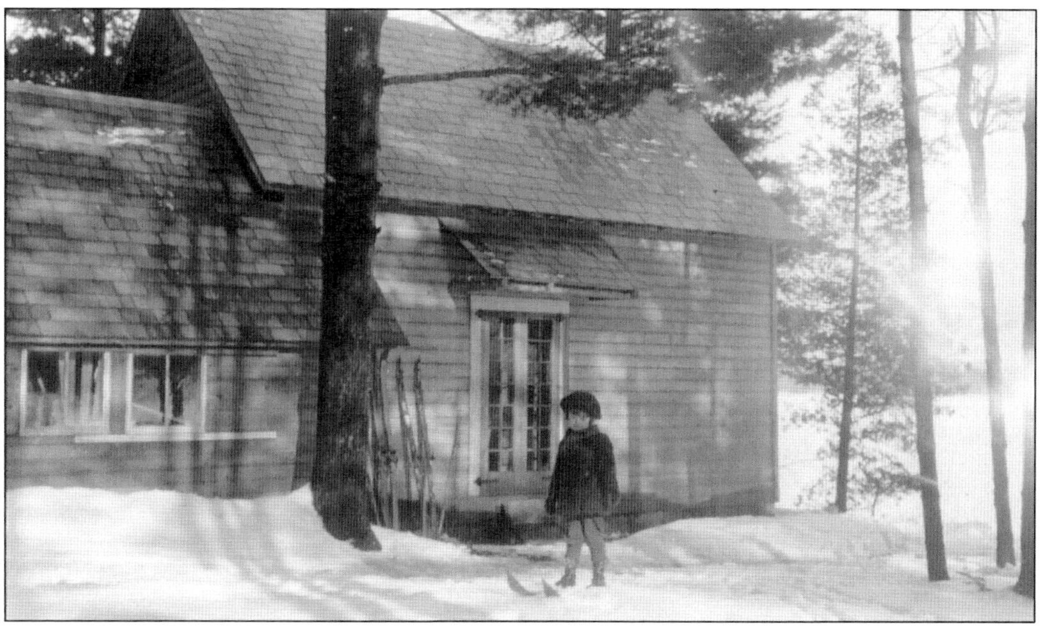

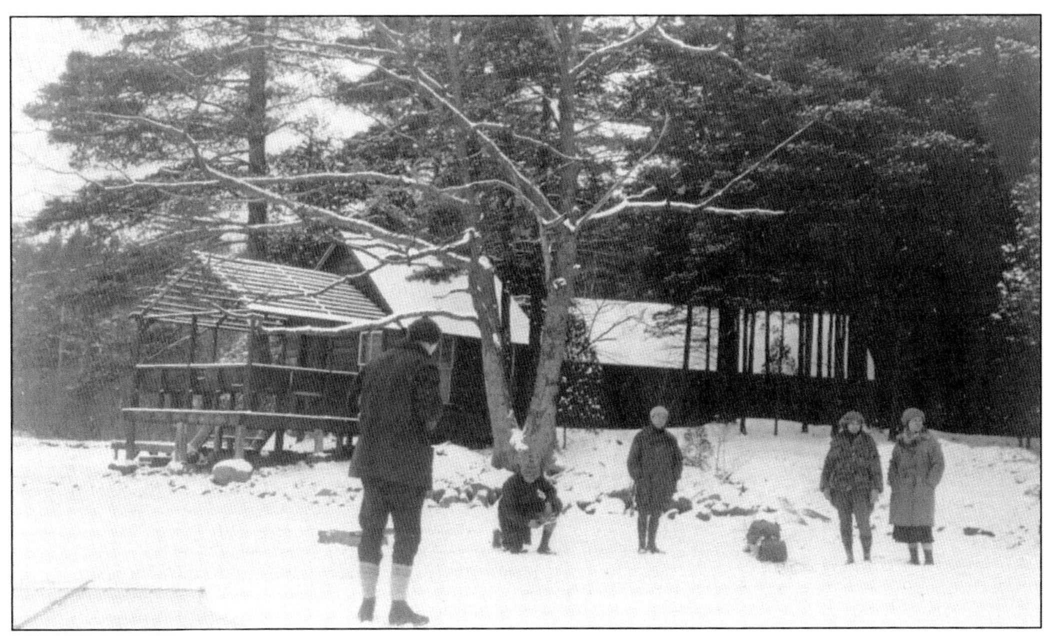

The photograph above shows a porch under construction, an extension of the little shack by the water. This building became known as the Little Camp. The tradition was for the men to sleep outside on the porch, while the women slept upstairs in the Main Camp, also known as Chilhowie, or "Chill House." The long roof in the background was the boathouse, and the Main Camp was off to the right, out of view. Below, three friends try out their skis in front of the camp. There were huge doors, like shutters, at the front of the building, and stone steps leading down to the lake. It was designed so that huge chunks of ice could be cut from the lake in early spring and dragged inside to be packed in straw and preserved for use by summer guests at the old hotel. (Both, courtesy of KARC.)

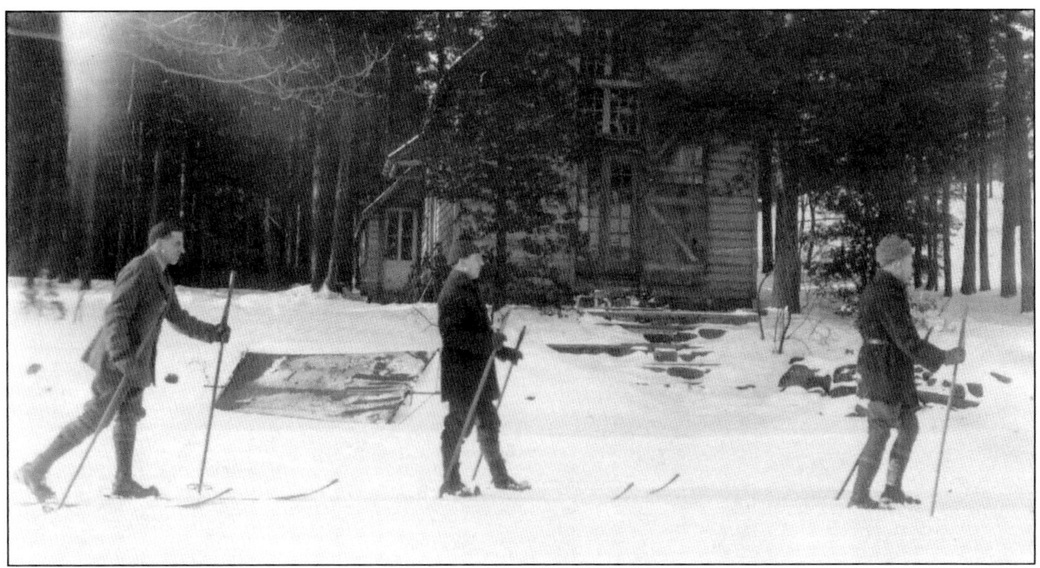

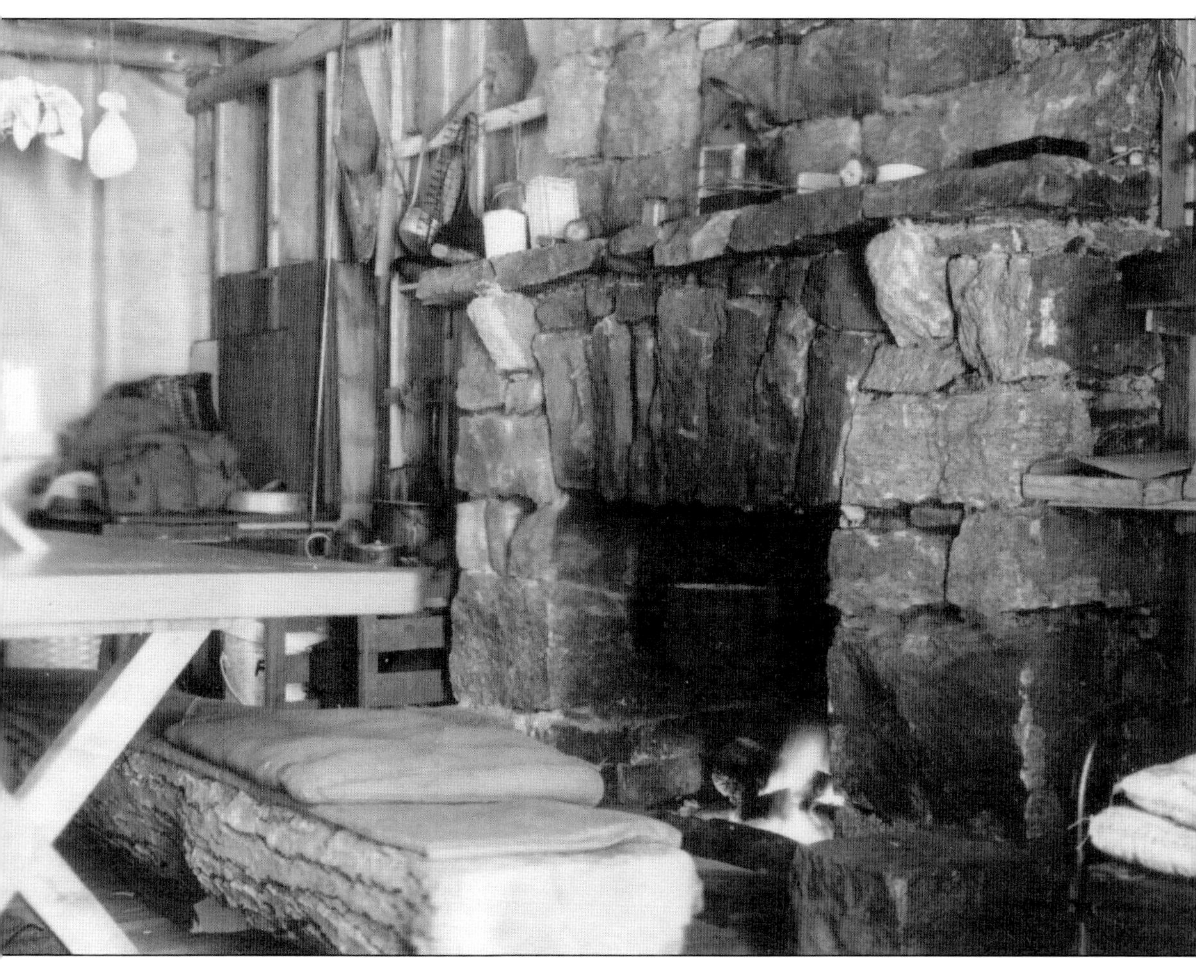

Here is look at the interior of the building, with a fire burning brightly in the fireplace. On the opposite wall was a wood stove. Apperson had two identical eight-foot-long tables made of ash wood in the shop at GE. He brought one to his camp in Huddle Bay, and the other was delivered to his camp in Turtle Bay. (Author's collection.)

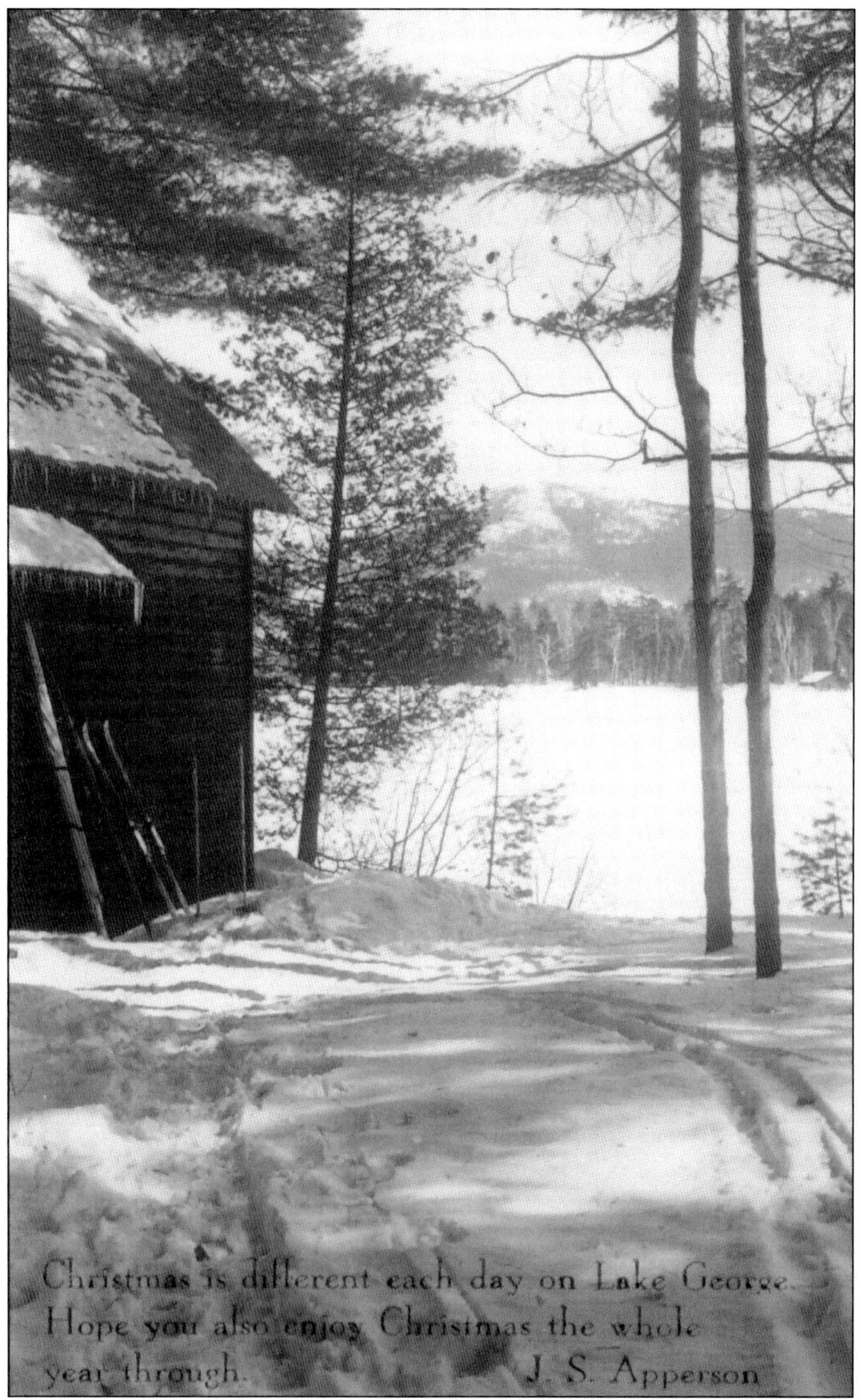

To express his delight over his new camp, Apperson designed Christmas cards featuring this lovely view of Huddle Bay, reading, "Christmas is different each day on Lake George." He sent them to a long list of friends, including Gov. Al Smith, state officials, and members of important organizations such as the Association for the Protection of the Adirondacks and the American Canoe Association. (Courtesy of KARC.)

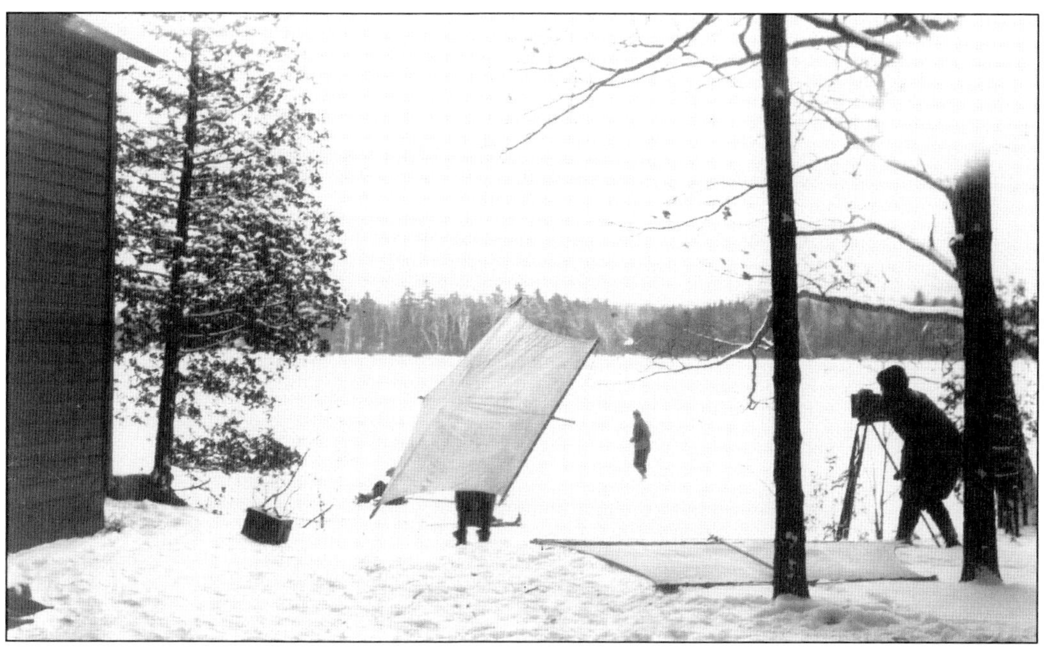

Apperson's camp became a hub of winter activities. Above, good friend Irving Langmuir tries out one of his latest hobbies, using a movie camera to record skate sailing and other winter sports. According to the caption on the back, this took place in 1923—a very early example of filmmaking in the Adirondacks. Below, perhaps on that same day, Langmuir parked his elegant automobile at Apperson's camp. Later that year, the Roosevelts moved away, and Apperson and William Dalton struggled to figure out how to divide up the property. In 1928, the Daltons gave up and sold their land to Apperson. (Both, courtesy of KARC.)

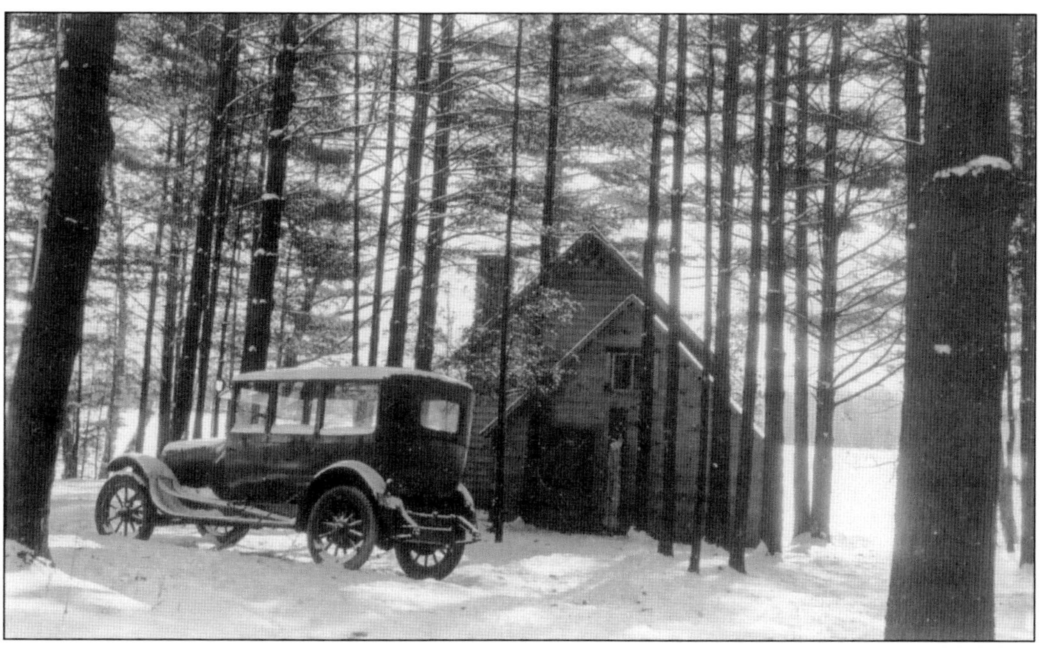

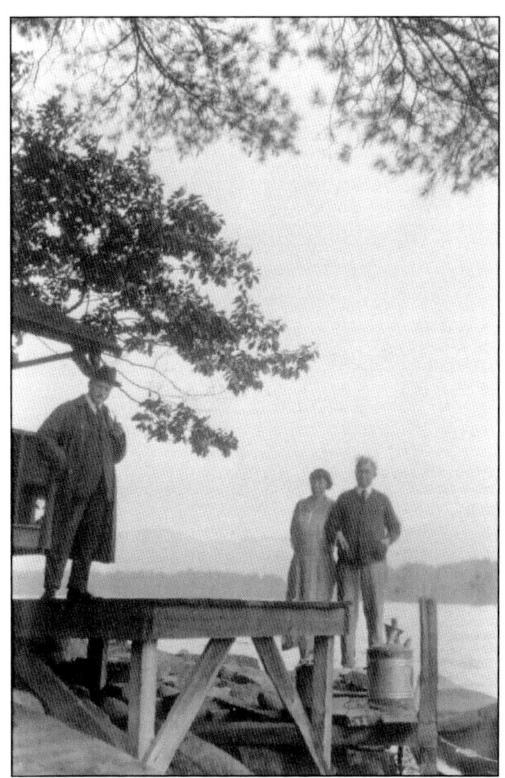

By a stroke of good fortune, Apperson found a childless couple from Schenectady to purchase the annex. Florence and Kilgore Christie, seen at left standing on the dock near Apperson's Little Camp, became the ideal neighbors. They were not wealthy, so Apperson offered them the deed to the property for just $1, and they only had to pay the yearly taxes. Irving Langmuir helped find others to purchase lots nearby, thus creating a very friendly and compatible community of like-minded people. Below are the Christies, with Florence on the left and Kilgore on the right, sitting at the front steps of Camp Chilhowie in 1928. The man in the doorway is unidentified. (Both, courtesy of KARC.)

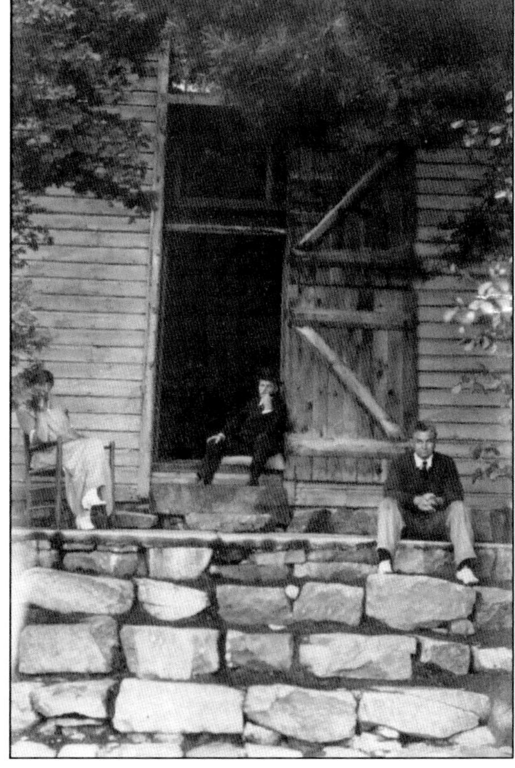

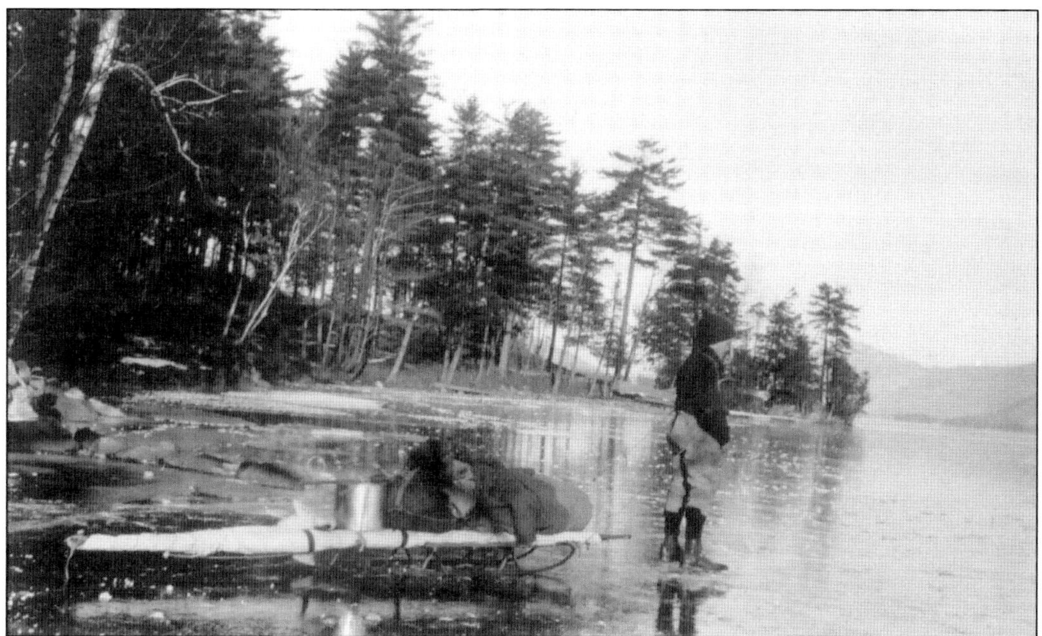

John Apperson's nieces and nephews from Virginia began coming to Huddle Bay, where their Uncle John could offer them a wonderful adventure in the outdoors. Hull Apperson, John's older brother, lived in Richmond, Virginia, with his wife and five children. Above is their youngest, John Apperson III, who spent a week or so in the winter of 1925 and learned all about winter sports. Wearing knickers, a warm sweater, a knit hat, and a pair of skates, he had just finished loading up the sled for a day of skate sailing. He is also pictured below on another morning later in the same week. There was snow covering the ice, making it a perfect day for ice fishing. (Above, KARC; below, Author's collection.)

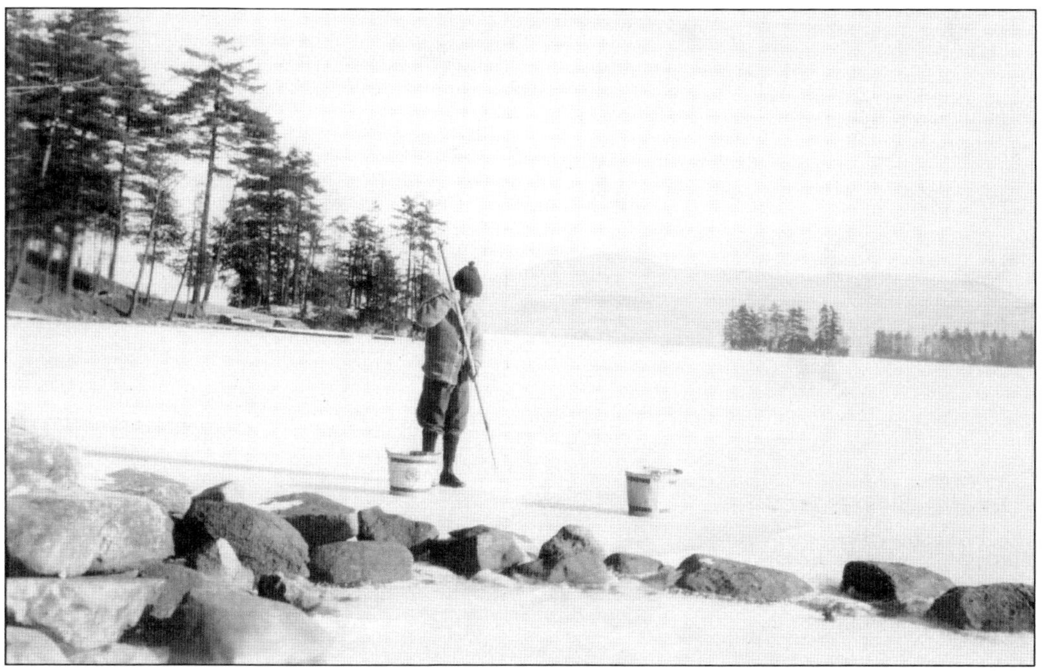

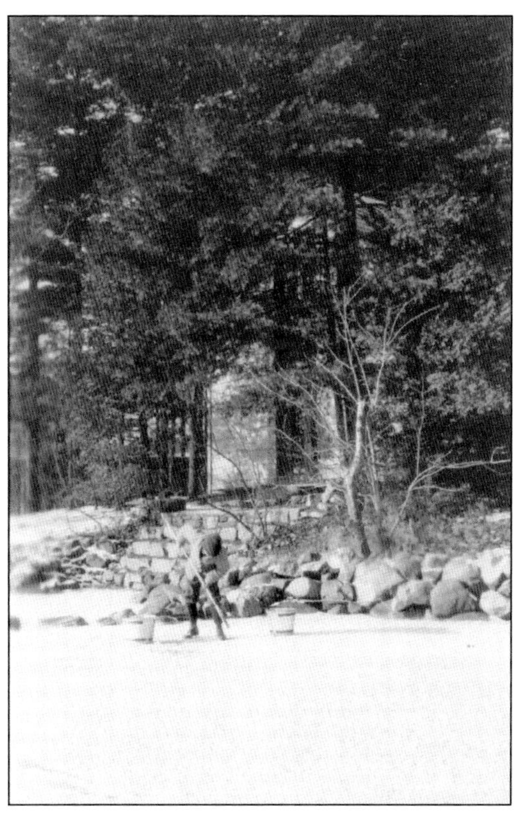

As a bachelor uncle, Apperson must have enjoyed introducing his nephew to this exotic world of snow and winter sports. At left, notice how hard it is to see the building Chilhowie through all the trees. Below, a few years later, another member of Hull Apperson's family, Jim, helped his uncle John entertain a crowd of cousins from Virginia who were eager to take a tour of the lake. Jim is seated near the stern, close to his attractive first cousins. His aunt, Nancy Apperson Dickinson, is seated in the middle row. She is the same woman who came on a trip to the Fulton Chain in 1906. Notice the second wooden boat, a Sponson canoe, resting on the other dock near Parodi Point in Huddle Bay. (Both, courtesy of KARC.)

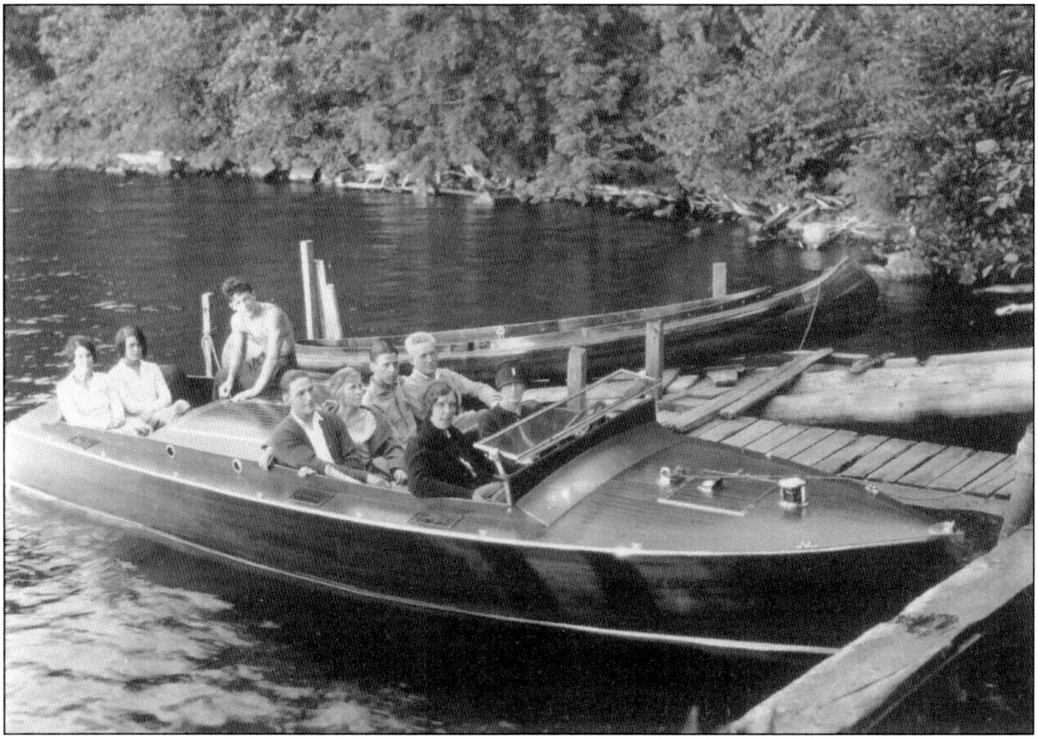

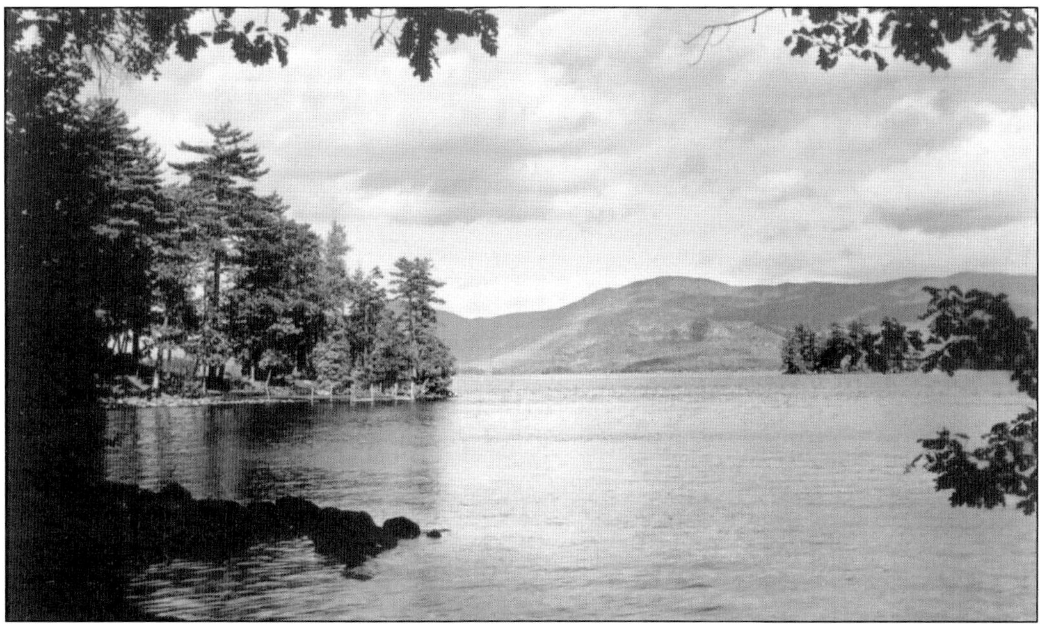

The photograph above captures the beauty of Huddle Bay, showing the docks near Parodi Point and the tiny feature called Tadpole Bay, outlined by a semicircle of rocks, where youngsters could swim. By the time this was taken in the 1940s, a new generation of Appersons were regular visitors at Lake George. John Apperson III came to Schenectady to work at GE in 1940 and married a girl from Virginia; they soon had three children, John, Tom, and Ellen. Below, by the late 1940s, the buildings in Huddle Bay were well hidden by trees, making it hard to even catch a glimpse of the old icehouse. John Apperson III understood that trees helped to hold the soil and hated to see estates with large lawns using chemical fertilizers. He was working to protect the water quality at Lake George long before other environmental organizations took up the cause. (Both, courtesy of KARC.)

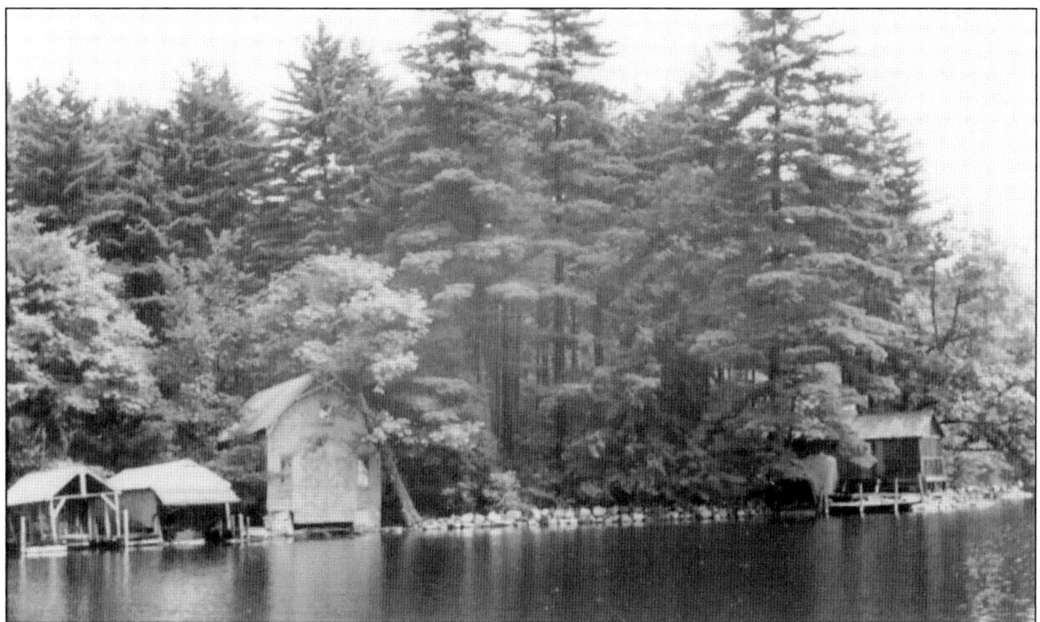

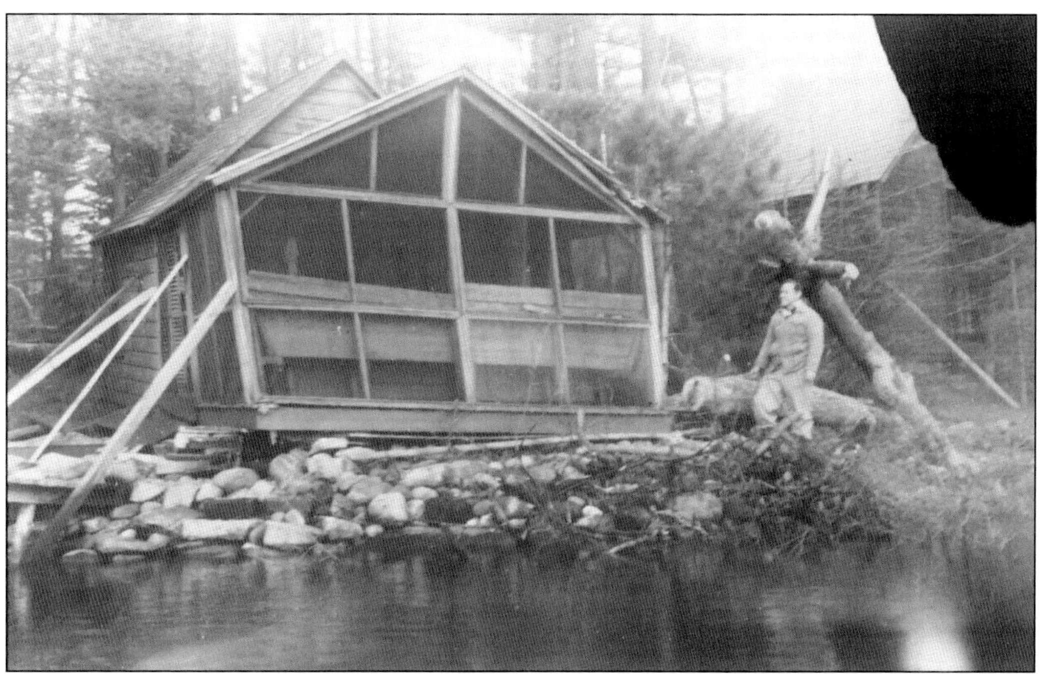

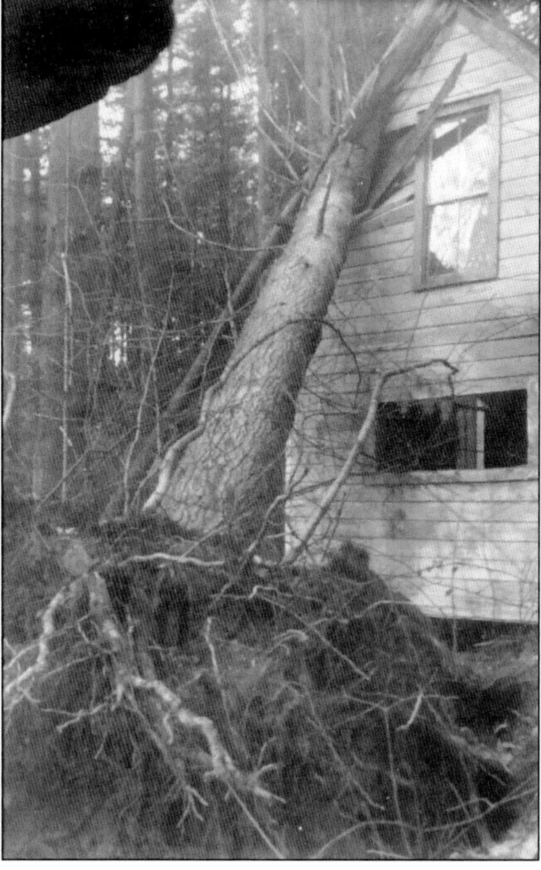

A terrible storm, a nor'easter, came through the region in the fall of 1950, causing many of the majestic trees to come crashing down around the buildings. The Little Camp, seen above, took a direct hit and had to be shored up with poles. At left, this uprooted tree came awfully close to destroying the main building. Apperson and his friends and family worked frantically to make repairs. (Both, courtesy of KARC.)

Apperson loved to entertain people at his camp. Alvin Whitney from the New York State Museum spent a week's vacation at Apperson's camp while recuperating from an illness. These two men had many common interests, and together, they hatched a scheme to protect Dome Island. Whitney was a founding director of the Nature Conservancy, and when they got through the plan, Dome Island at Lake George became the first acquisition of the new organization in 1956. Pictured below in the 1950s, Florence Christie, now a widow, and her brother Bert Keys came to Apperson's camp for a visit and to enjoy slices of fruitcake. Seated clockwise from the left are John Apperson, Bert Keys, Florence Christie, three unidentified guests, and Alvin Whitney. (Both, courtesy of KARC.)

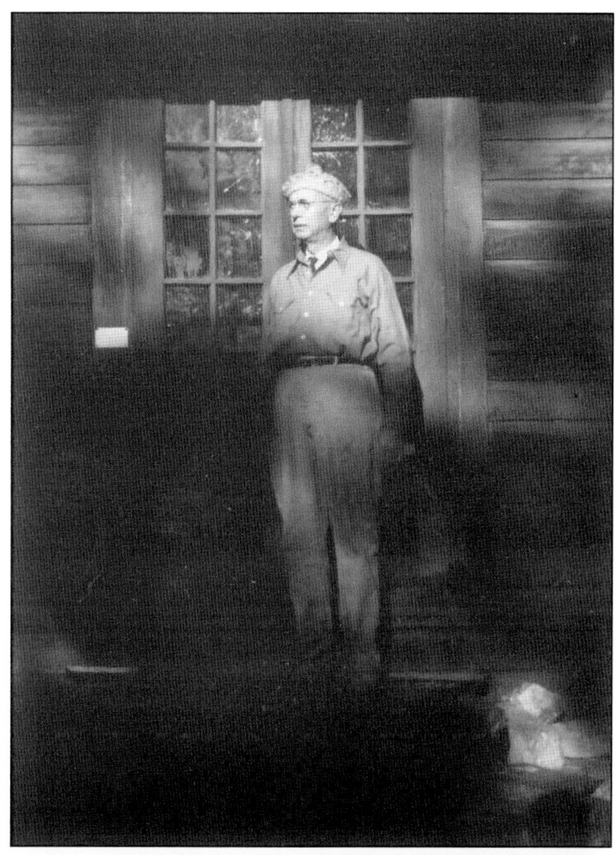

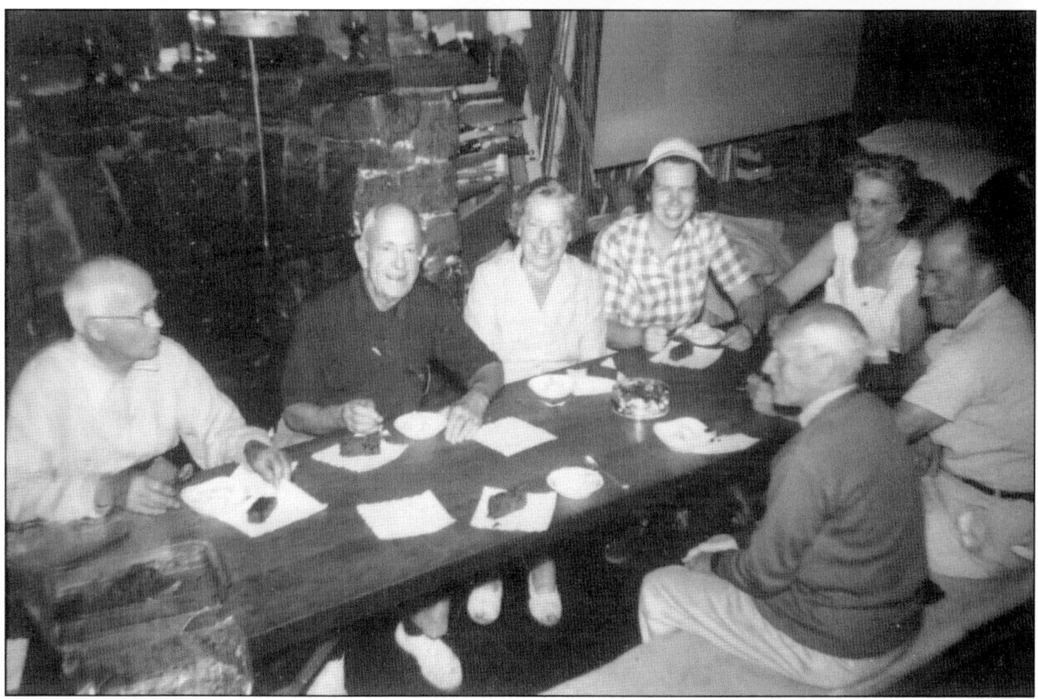

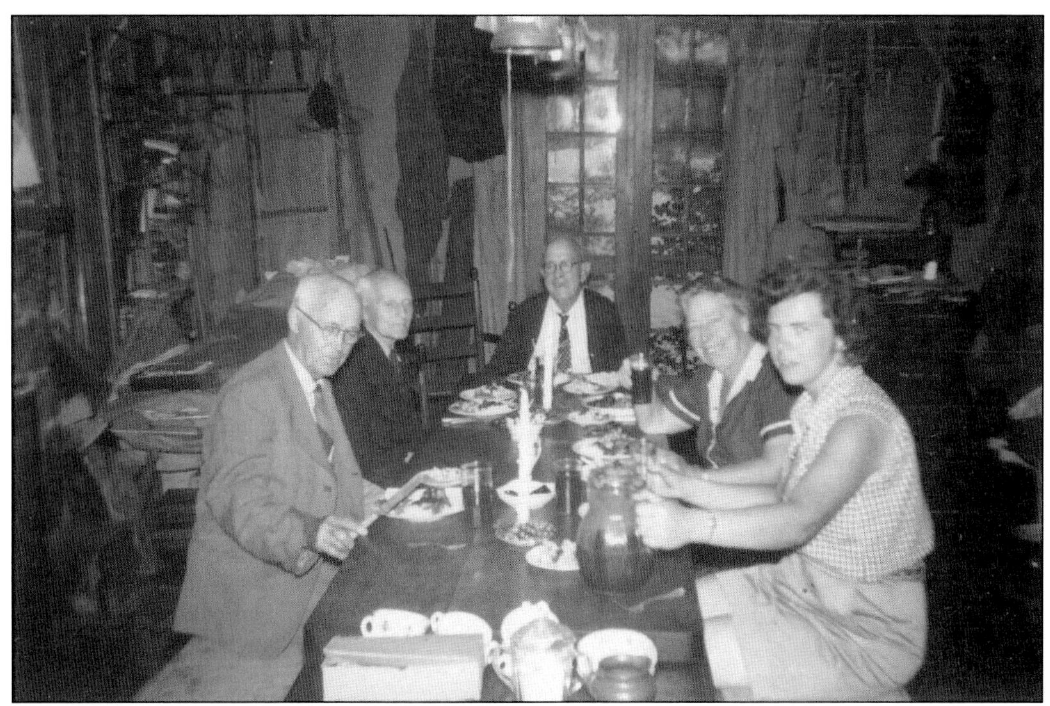

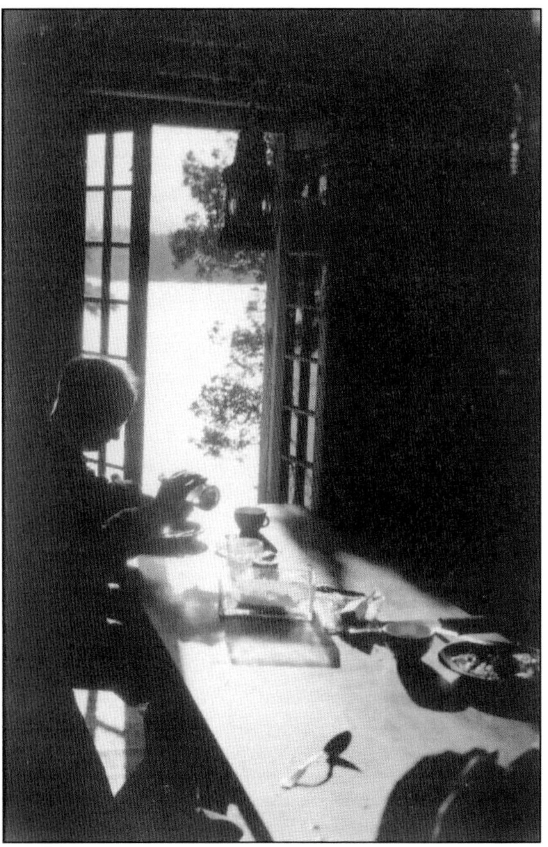

Apperson and his guests shared another meal together that week, this time with candles and china dishes. Above, seated around the table are, clockwise from left, John Apperson, Alvin Whitney, Bert Keys, Florence Christie, and an unidentified woman. A fireplace is behind Apperson, and a wood stove is behind Christie; French doors lead to the lake. At left, another good friend, Earl Paxton, who owned a camp on Tongue Mountain, came by to share a cup of coffee and a meal around 1960. (Both, courtesy of KARC.)

Six

Getting Organized

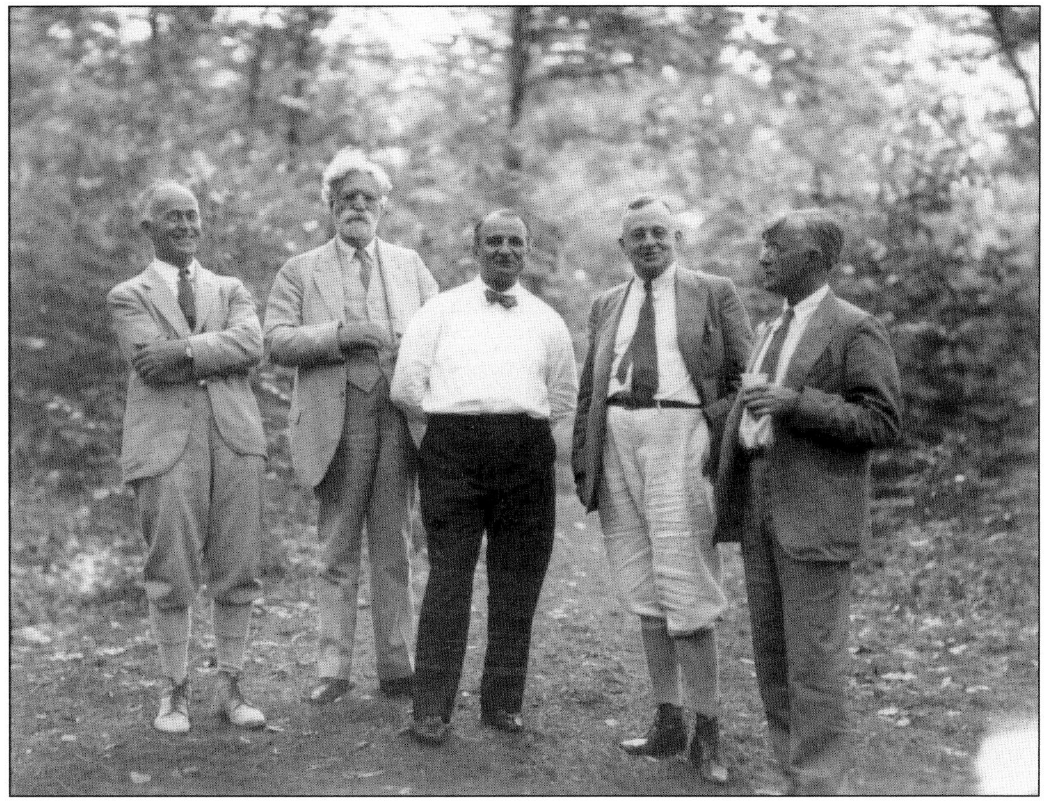

Many people at Lake George thought of Apperson as a loner, or perhaps even a troublemaker, but others knew differently. The New York Forest Preserve Association (FPA) was formed in 1934 to provide an organizational structure to raise money and use it to support important preservation causes. John Apperson (far left) served as the CEO but without a salary, and the others pictured (from left to right, George Foster Peabody, Ellwood Rabenold, E. McDonald Stanton, and Irving Langmuir) provided funding, legal expertise, and political connections. At age 56, working full time as an engineer at GE, Apperson had achieved a remarkable feat, persuading men of such caliber and influence to become directors of his organization. (Courtesy of KARC.)

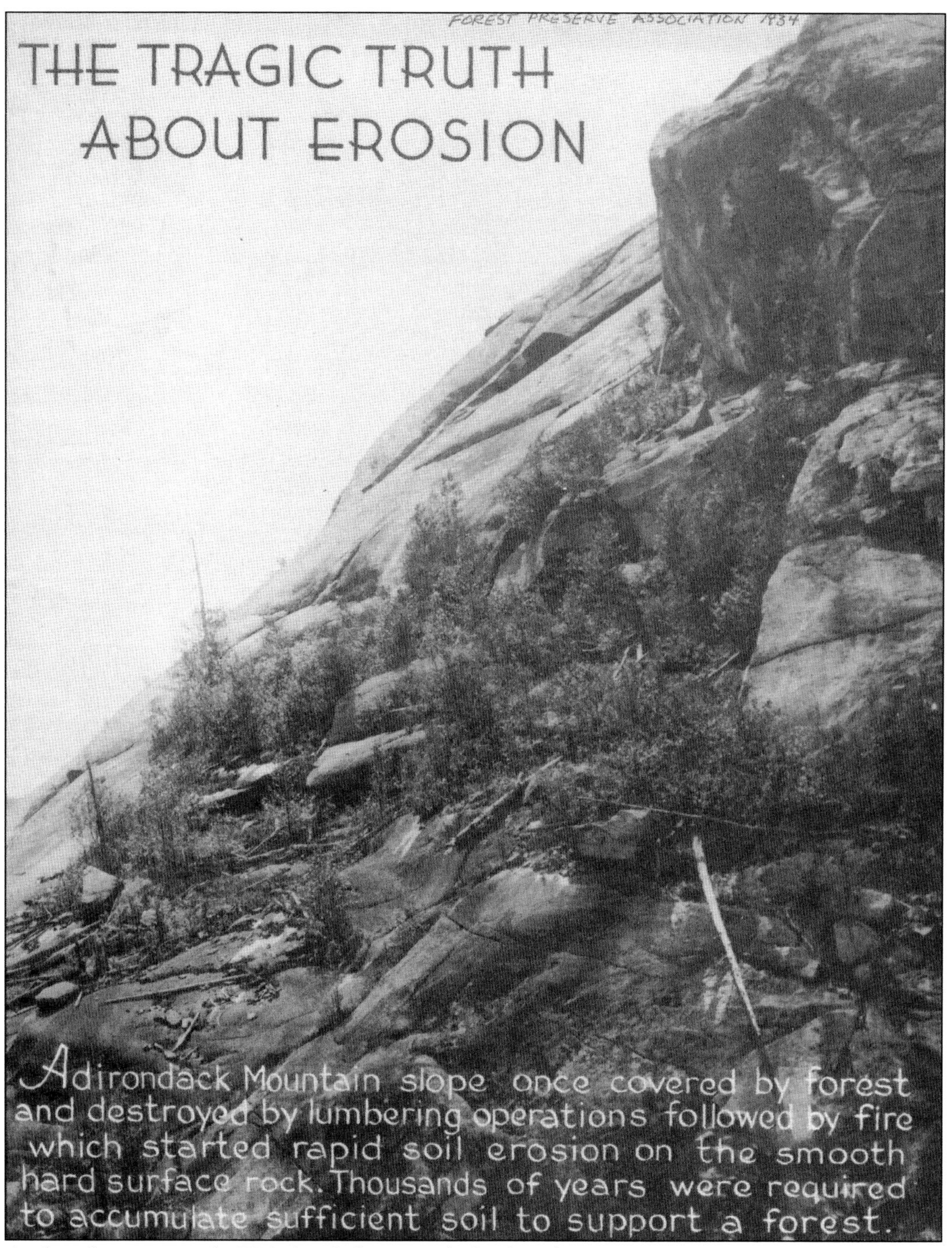

As their first project, the FPA decided to provide funding for an important educational publication on behalf of the US Soil Conservation Service, entitled *The Tragic Truth About Erosion*. Forty-thousand copies were distributed to extension offices around the United States at the height of the dust bowl. The photograph on the cover was taken near Lake George. (Courtesy of KARC.)

Always fascinated by gadgets and the latest technology, Apperson took up photography as a hobby early on but soon began to think of how to document problems at Lake George and use the images to tell a story. As early as 1917, he began offering his photographs for use in magazines and journals. (Author's collection.)

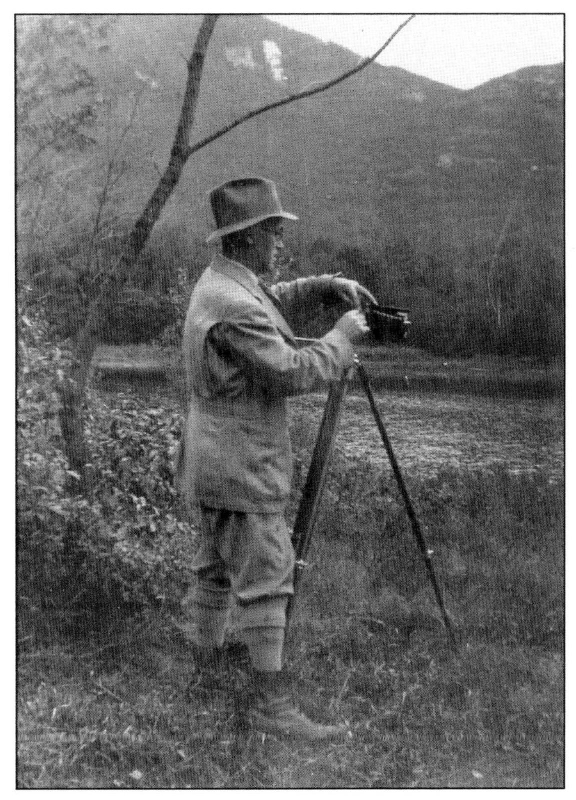

Apperson's efforts to riprap the islands of Lake George caught the attention of Warwick Carpenter, the secretary of the Conservation Commission. In 1917, Carpenter visited Lake George, became friends with the energetic activist Apperson, and invited him to submit his photographs for use in the first editions of the *Conservationist*. Here is a page from a later publication from 1922, *Mountain Slope Protection*, as an example of their ongoing collaboration. (Author's collection.)

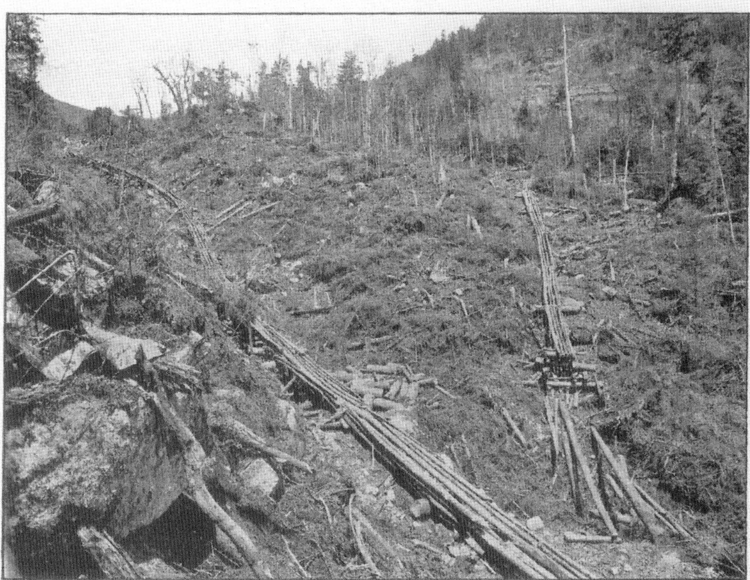

14 MOUNTAIN SLOPE PROTECTION

SLASH AND "SLIPS" IN HUNTER PASS

The steep sides of the high mountains make "slips" more feasible than horses for getting out logs. On such slopes loss of the soil after fire is quick and certain.

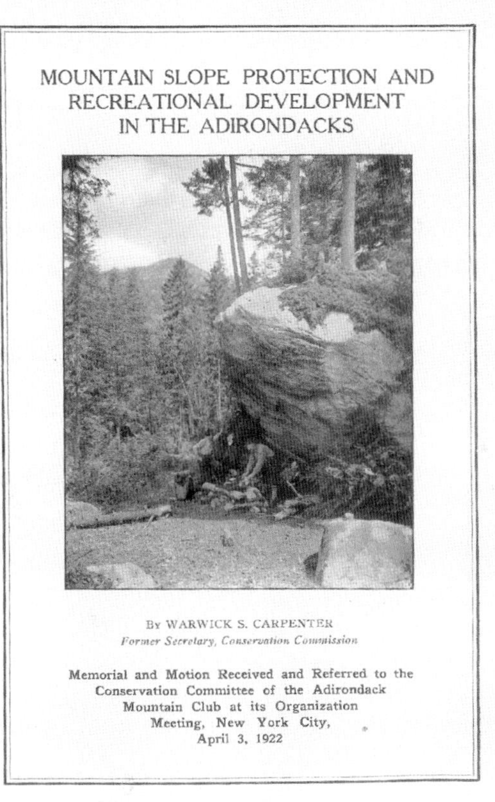

MOUNTAIN SLOPE PROTECTION AND RECREATIONAL DEVELOPMENT IN THE ADIRONDACKS

BY WARWICK S. CARPENTER
Former Secretary, Conservation Commission

Memorial and Motion Received and Referred to the Conservation Committee of the Adirondack Mountain Club at its Organization Meeting, New York City, April 3, 1922

As it turned out, Carpenter had a brief career as secretary of the Conservation Commission. He rocked the boat, speaking out against illegal practices, and was fired from his job in 1922. Apperson had to continue the fight alone. Soon after Carpenter lost his job, he found backers to publish this memorial. He delivered an impassioned plea to the newly formed Adirondack Mountain Club, asking them to take a stand against logging in the high peaks. (Author's collection.)

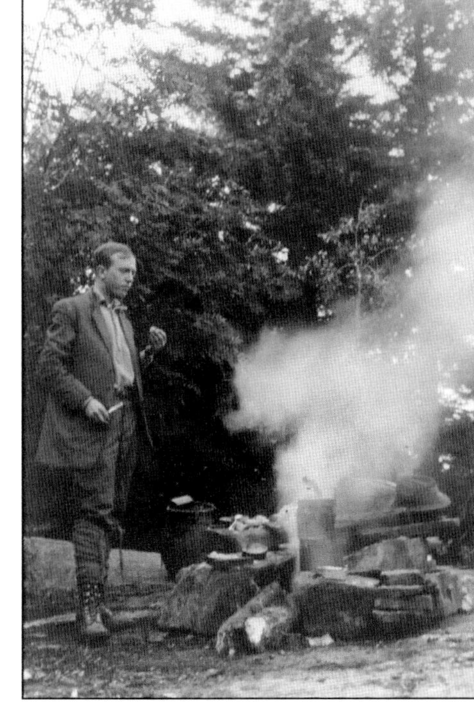

Carpenter never did find another job in New York State, and moved to California. This photograph of him was taken by John Apperson at Lake George in about 1919. They kept in touch with each other, and in 1962, Carpenter sent a huge file of his papers to the New York State Museum to the attention of Warder Cadbury, hoping that some historian would eventually read through all the papers and tell his story. (Courtesy of KARC.)

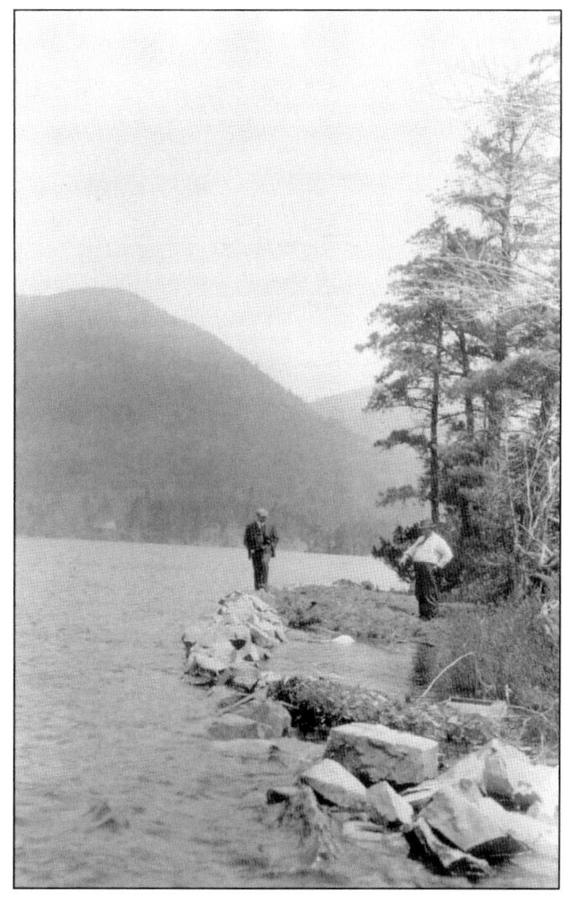

For a brief time, however, Apperson enjoyed having the support and encouragement of a highly placed government official. In 1918, Warwick Carpenter visited Lake George, inspected the rock walls around one of the islands, and had a conversation with Jay Taylor, the forest ranger. After Carpenter left for California, Taylor reported to others in the commissioner's office, and Apperson was cut off from any trusted source of information. Below, in another scene from 1918, Taylor (left) and Carpenter are inspecting a rock wall on one of the islands. Unfortunately, many individuals and organizations were spreading propaganda against Apperson and the preservationists, especially lumber companies and those affiliated with the International Paper Company. (Both, courtesy of KARC.)

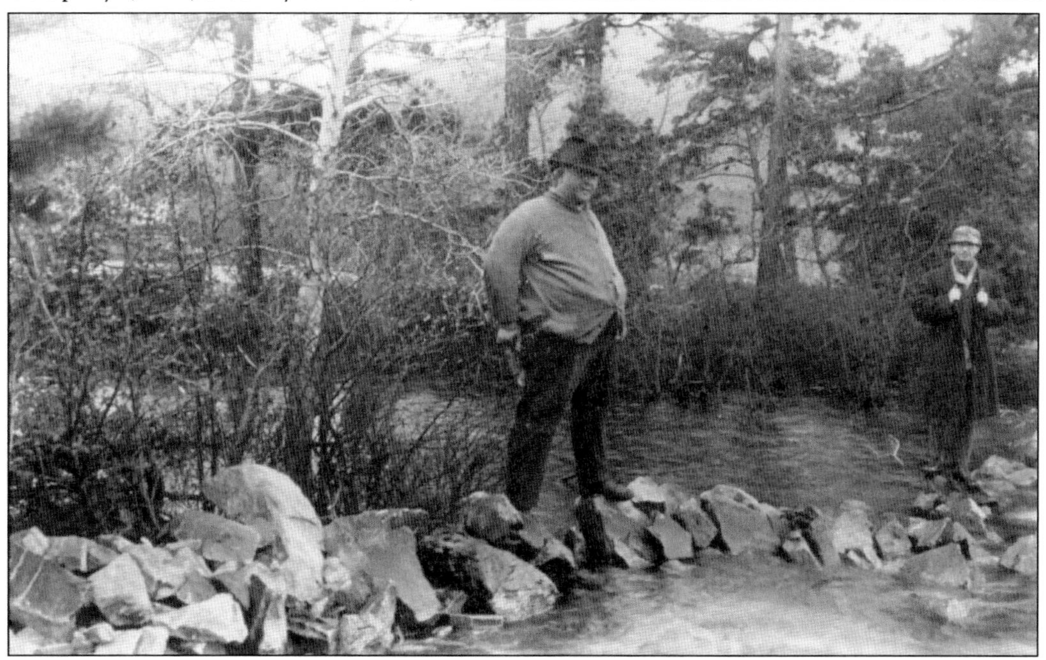

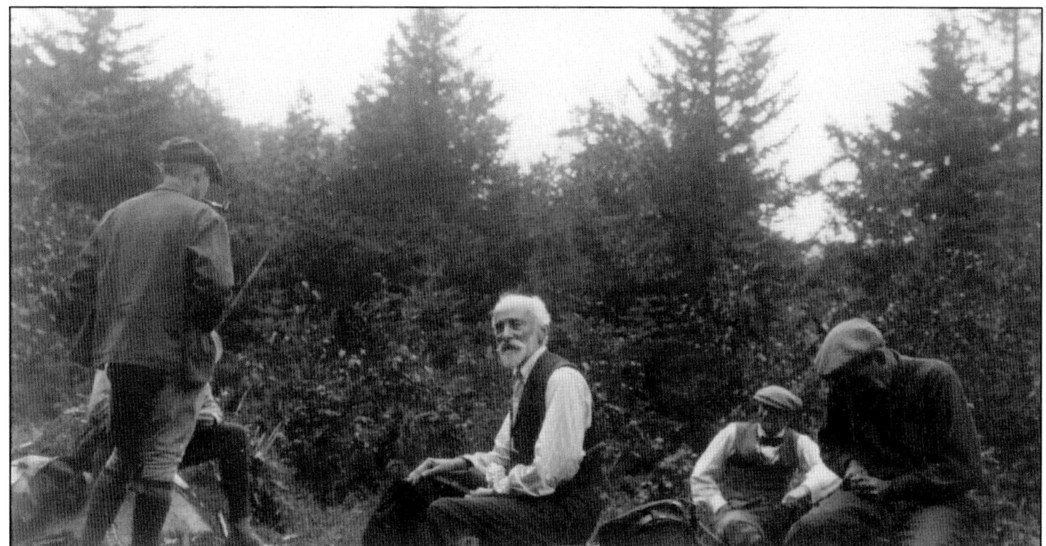

According to a note on the back of this picture, several of the top people in the New York State Conservation Commission took a hike into the high peaks area in 1920. They were getting ready to launch the Adirondack Mountain Club. It is possible that George D. Pratt, conservation commissioner, was in this group, but the bearded man at center has not been positively identified. Among the others are Clifford R. Pettis, William G. Howard, and Arthur S. Hopkins. Apparently, Apperson organized this excursion and took this photograph. (Courtesy of KARC.)

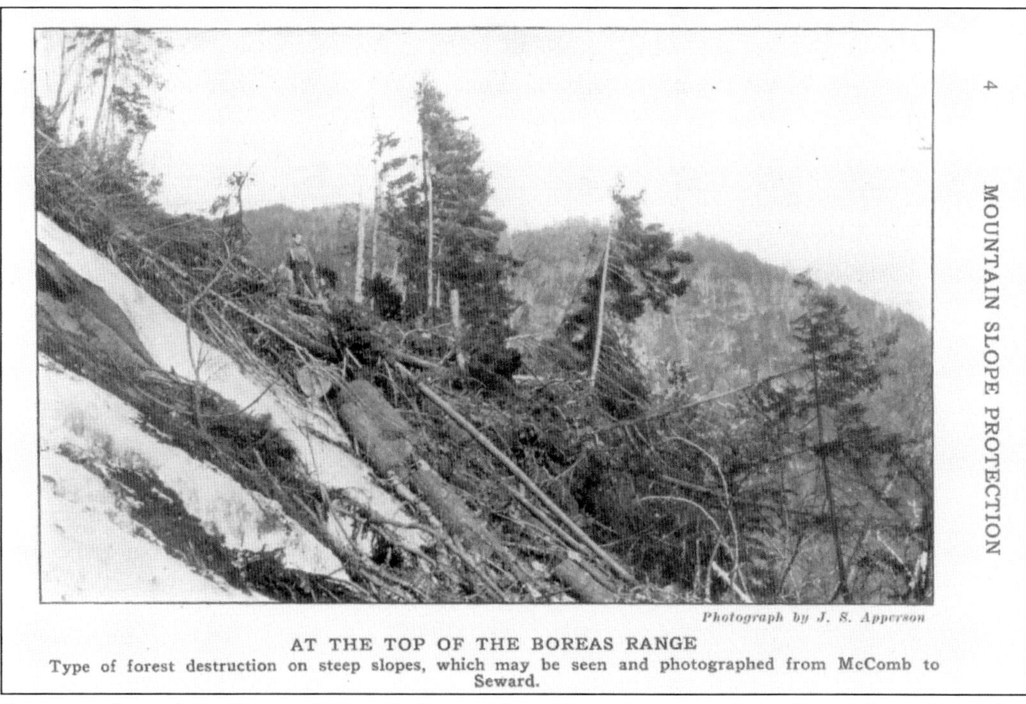

4 MOUNTAIN SLOPE PROTECTION

Photograph by J. S. Apperson

AT THE TOP OF THE BOREAS RANGE

Type of forest destruction on steep slopes, which may be seen and photographed from McComb to Seward.

Apperson hoped the State of New York would purchase forest lands in the high peaks and at Lake George. Here is one more page from the important document he helped Warwick Carpenter present to the newly formed Adirondack Mountain Club in 1922 to try to convince them to take a stand on this important issue. (Author's collection.)

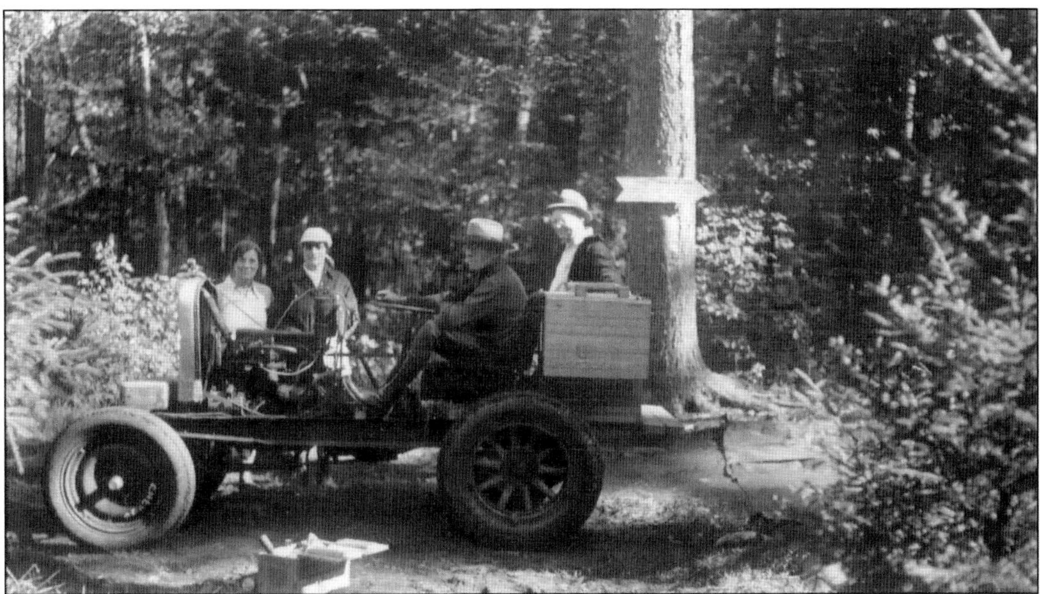

Many of the photographs in the archives are unmarked, and this one is particularly intriguing. One educated guess, however, is that this might be Franklin D. Roosevelt in 1926, driving an early version of a Jeep, possibly on the trail to the fire tower near Mount Adams. This would have been after he had caught polio and before he became governor. (Courtesy of KARC.)

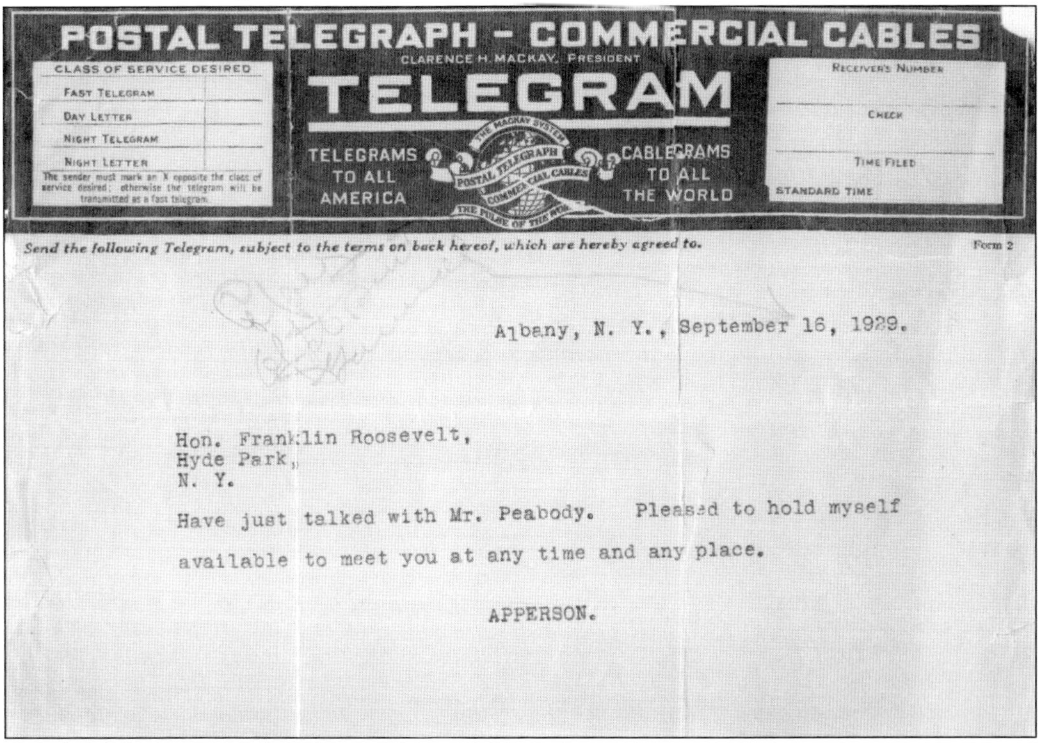

POSTAL TELEGRAPH - COMMERCIAL CABLES

CLARENCE H. MACKAY, PRESIDENT

TELEGRAM

TELEGRAMS TO ALL AMERICA — CABLEGRAMS TO ALL THE WORLD

THE MACKAY SYSTEM — POSTAL TELEGRAPH — COMMERCIAL CABLES — THE PULSE OF THE WORLD

CLASS OF SERVICE DESIRED	
FAST TELEGRAM	
DAY LETTER	
NIGHT TELEGRAM	
NIGHT LETTER	

The sender must mark an X opposite the class of service desired; otherwise the telegram will be transmitted as a fast telegram.

RECEIVER'S NUMBER
CHECK
TIME FILED
STANDARD TIME

Send the following Telegram, subject to the terms on back hereof, which are hereby agreed to. Form 2

Albany, N. Y., September 16, 1929.

Hon. Franklin Roosevelt,
Hyde Park,
N. Y.

Have just talked with Mr. Peabody. Pleased to hold myself available to meet you at any time and any place.

APPERSON.

This telegram from Apperson to Roosevelt indicates the two men were working together on a scheme, possibly to try to persuade W.J. Knapp to sell his land (Paradise Bay) to the State of New York and thus complete their dream of a Lake George Park. (Author's collection.)

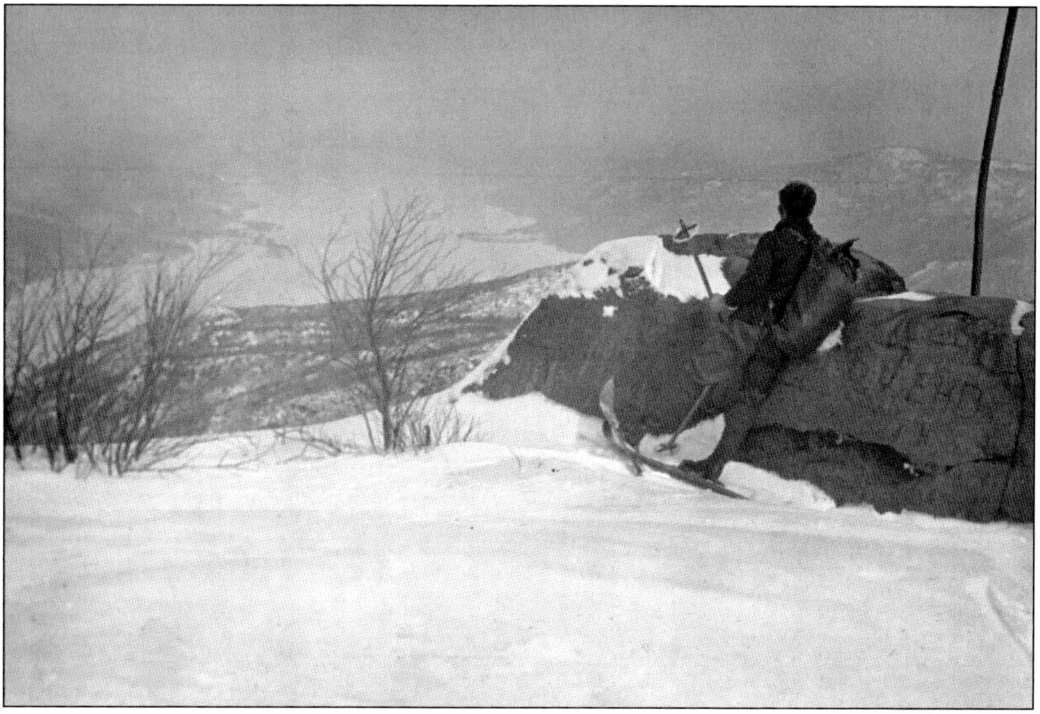

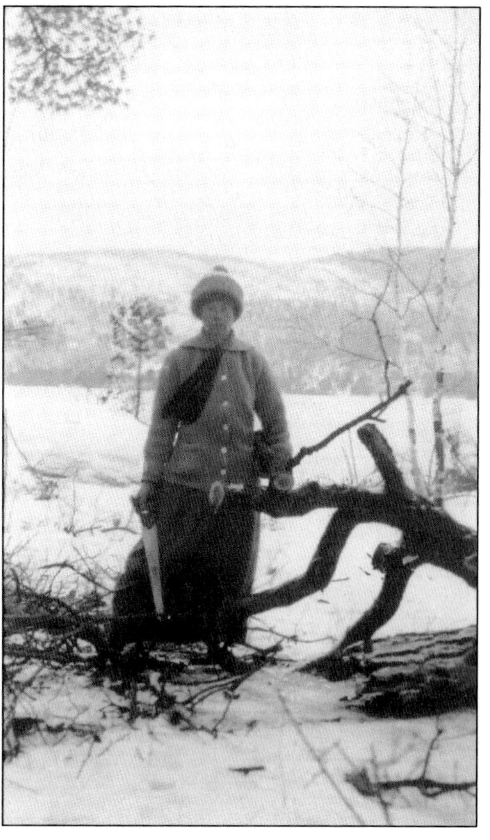

Irving Langmuir, shown here resting on skis and looking down on a snow-covered lake, shared Apperson's enthusiasm for winter sports, island repair, and advocacy on behalf of the Forest Preserve. As the top scientist in the GE Research Department and winner of the Nobel Prize in chemistry in 1932, Langmuir had considerable political and financial resources, helping Apperson find good neighbors in Huddle Bay and providing him a loan to purchase Dome Island in 1939. At left, Marion Mersereau, who married Irving Langmuir in 1912, shared his enthusiasm for the outdoors and did not mind the cold or hard work, as seen in this photograph, where she is helping collect firewood. (Both, courtesy of KARC.)

Irving and Marion Langmuir began looking for property at Lake George in the early 1920s, eventually purchasing a lot in Huddle Bay. Years earlier, however, they made use of one of the cottages in Northwest Bay belonging to the Loines family. Marion and Irving are standing, preparing a meal, and the others are unidentified in this c. 1915 photograph. (Courtesy of KARC.)

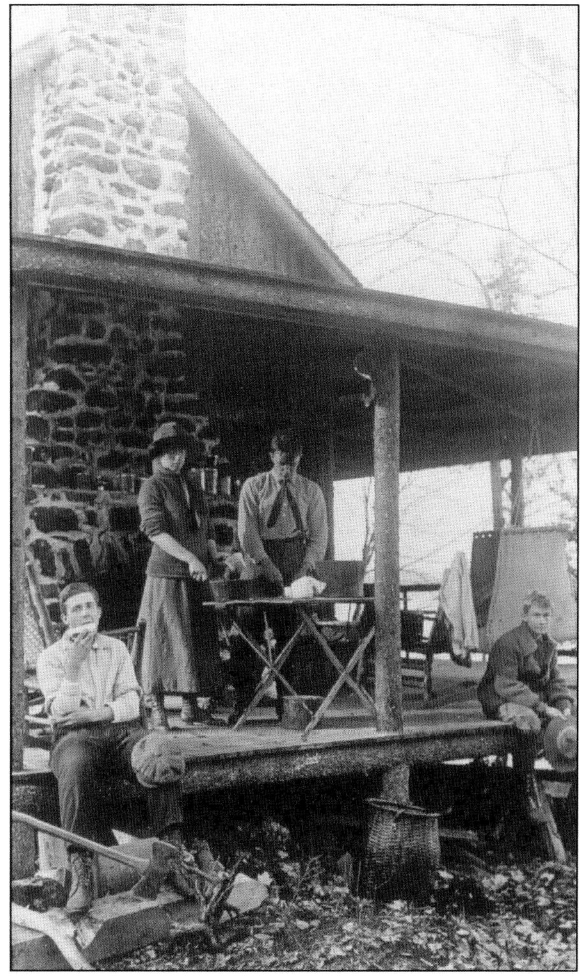

The Langmuirs eventually purchased several properties at Lake George in Huddle Bay and Turtle Bay and on Crown Island, thus affording them a nice variety of retreats. Always the scientist, Langmuir was constantly making scientific observations, as he is here, watching steam rising from the frozen lake. (Courtesy of KARC.)

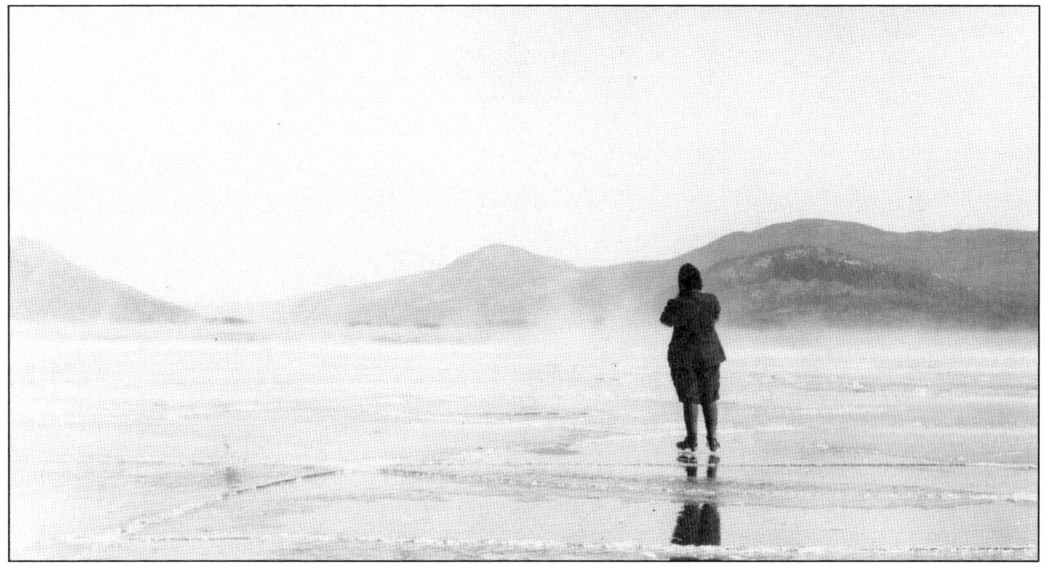

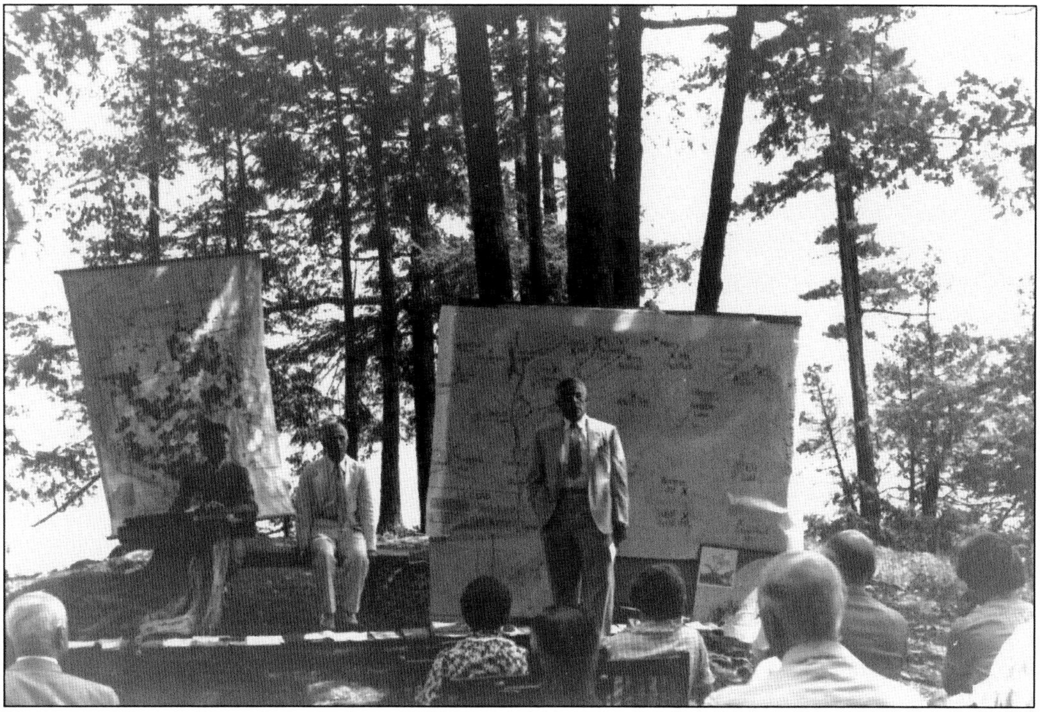

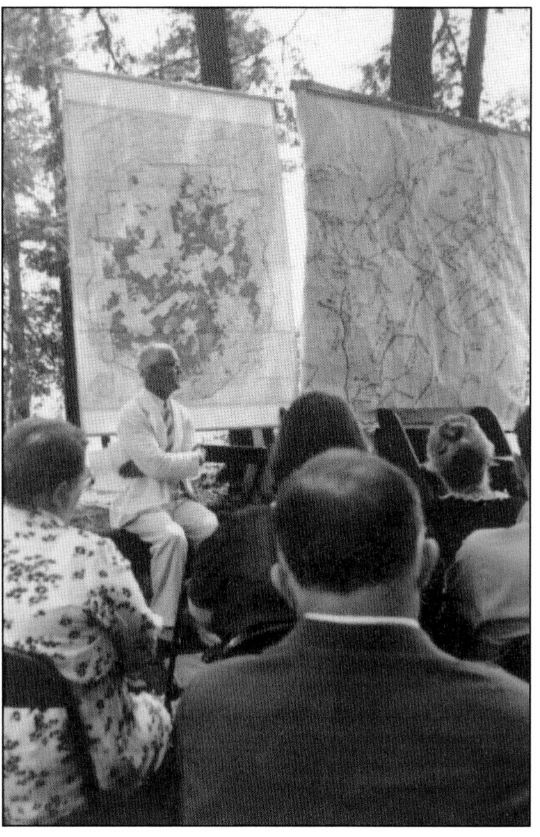

Apperson and Langmuir were concerned about sloppy record keeping and the lack of accurate information concerning land ownership throughout the Adirondack Park. One way to address the problem was to create maps. Above, Irving Langmuir (standing) with Apperson (seated directly to his right) are at a meeting of the Forest Preserve Association, showing off their large and well researched maps, in 1938. At left, 50 or more people were seated on the lawn that day and heard from John Apperson about all the trouble spots where illegal logging continued and roads and dams were threatening the land, and about the continued problems of regulating the dam at Ticonderoga. Many of these guests came a good distance, and were put up in rooms at Florence Christie's annex just a few yards away. (Both, courtesy of KARC.)

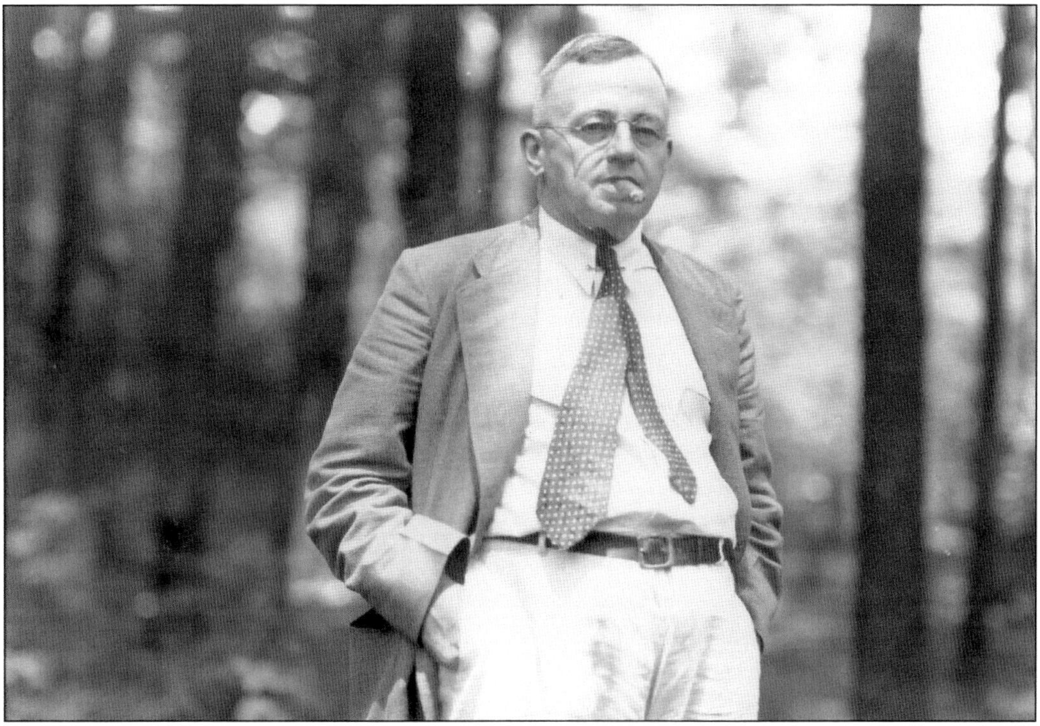

One member of the FPA, Dr. E. McDonald Stanton, a physician from Schenectady, offered to investigate the fluctuating water levels at the dam near Ticonderoga. He tried to persuade other property owners at Lake George, especially members of the Lake George Association, to understand the need for regulation. (Courtesy of KARC.)

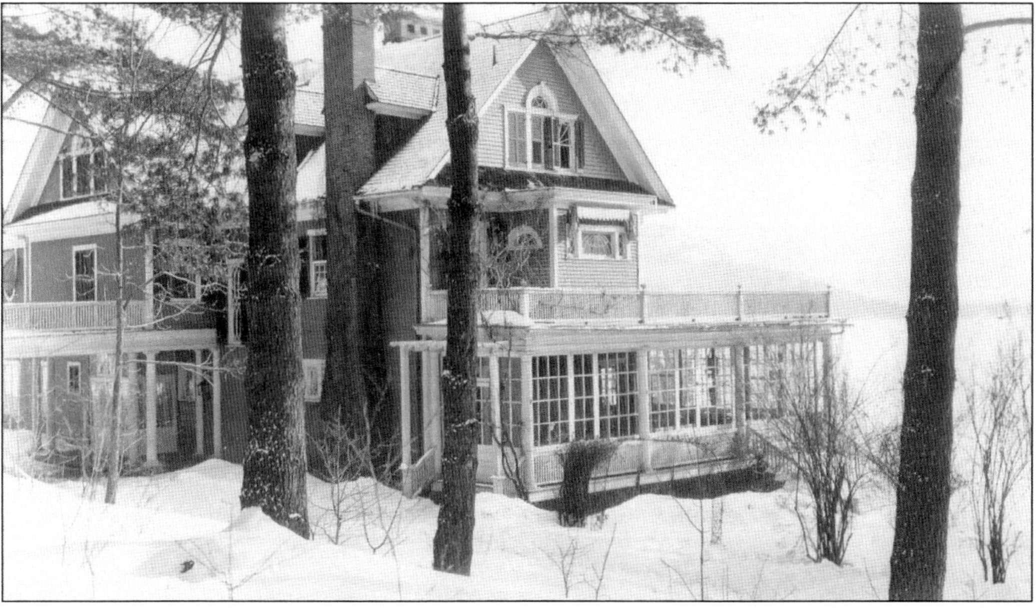

This beautiful home belonged to Rev. Ernest Stires, an Episcopal clergyman who was sympathetic to the concerns of Apperson and his organization, the FPA. He was known for being a progressive and for taking bold stands on controversial issues. (Courtesy of KARC.)

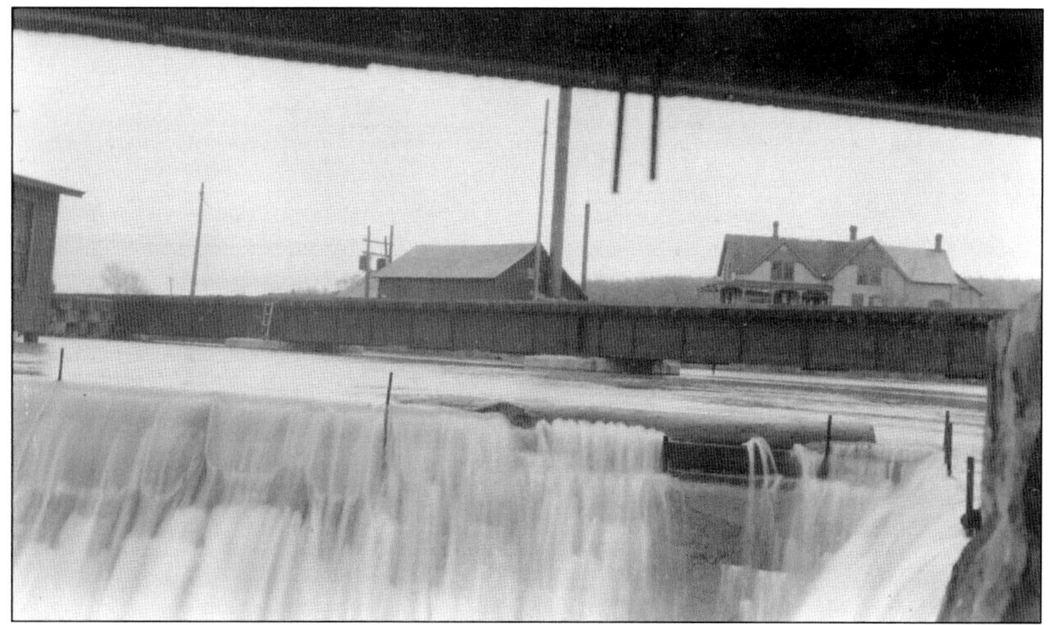

Over several decades, as Apperson and his associates watched and worried, the water levels at Lake George continued to fluctuate, as much as 15 to 30 inches a year. Unwilling to accept the official reports, Apperson sent friends to take pictures and make accurate readings. This picture was taken in Ticonderoga and shows the flashboards that caused Lake George water levels to back up. (Courtesy of KARC.)

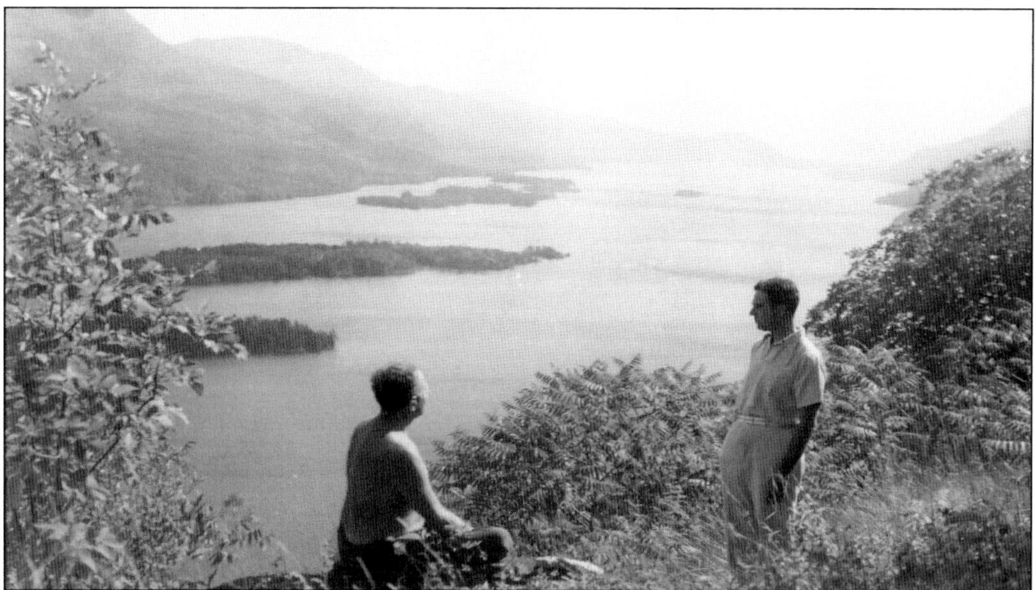

During World War II, many of Apperson's young recruits to the cause of conservation were called up for military service instead. Apperson persisted, however, and persuaded the state's solicitor general Orrin Judd to support him in a legal fight against the International Paper Company to protest the operations there. Judd and another attorney came to see the famous scenery first hand. Apperson took them to Deer Leap, a great place from which to get a look at the islands. (Courtesy of KARC.)

LAKE GEORGE A MILL POND

PREVIOUSLY UNLAWFUL BUT NOW AUTHORIZED BY THE LEGISLATURE

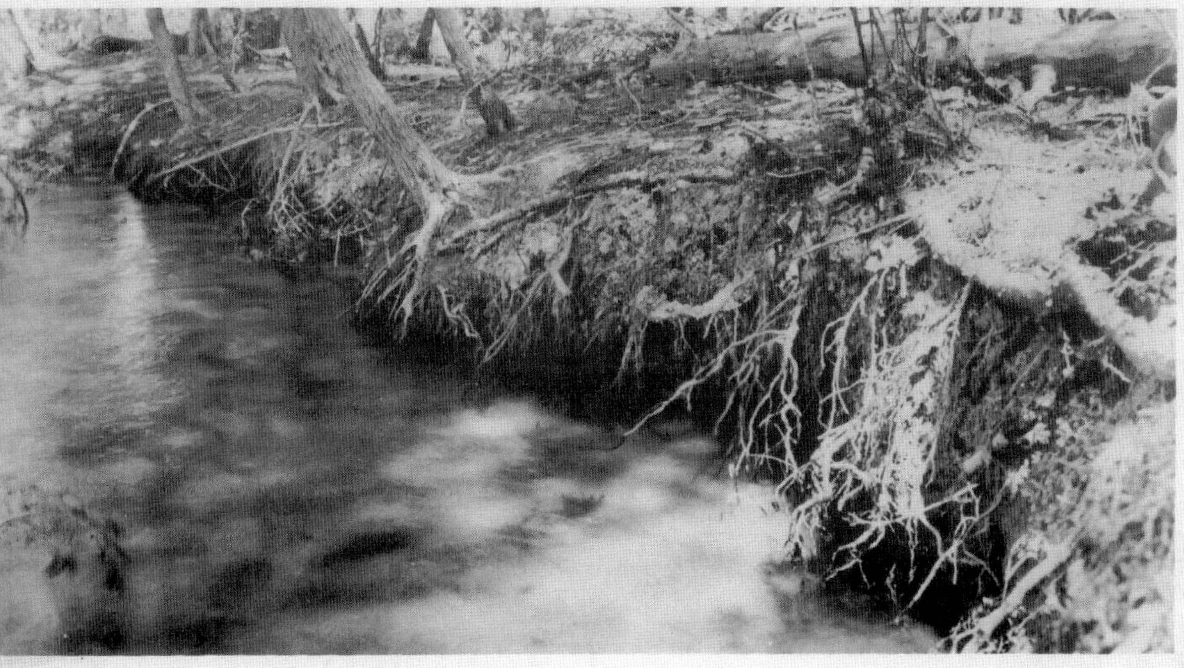

Exhibit 193: Phenita Island; Apr. 29, 1944. Lake elevation 4.21 USGS. Graphic view of under-cut bank and exposed tree roots.

Despite all these hearings and court battles, high water levels continued to threaten the islands, and Apperson continued to take dramatic photographs. Here is a pamphlet published by the Lake George Protective Association in 1956, stating, "for fourteen years (1942–1957) the state was in the courts to establish its sole right to control lake levels to prevent this kind of damage from high water which had eroded eighty-seven islands and washed away several others." (Author's collection.)

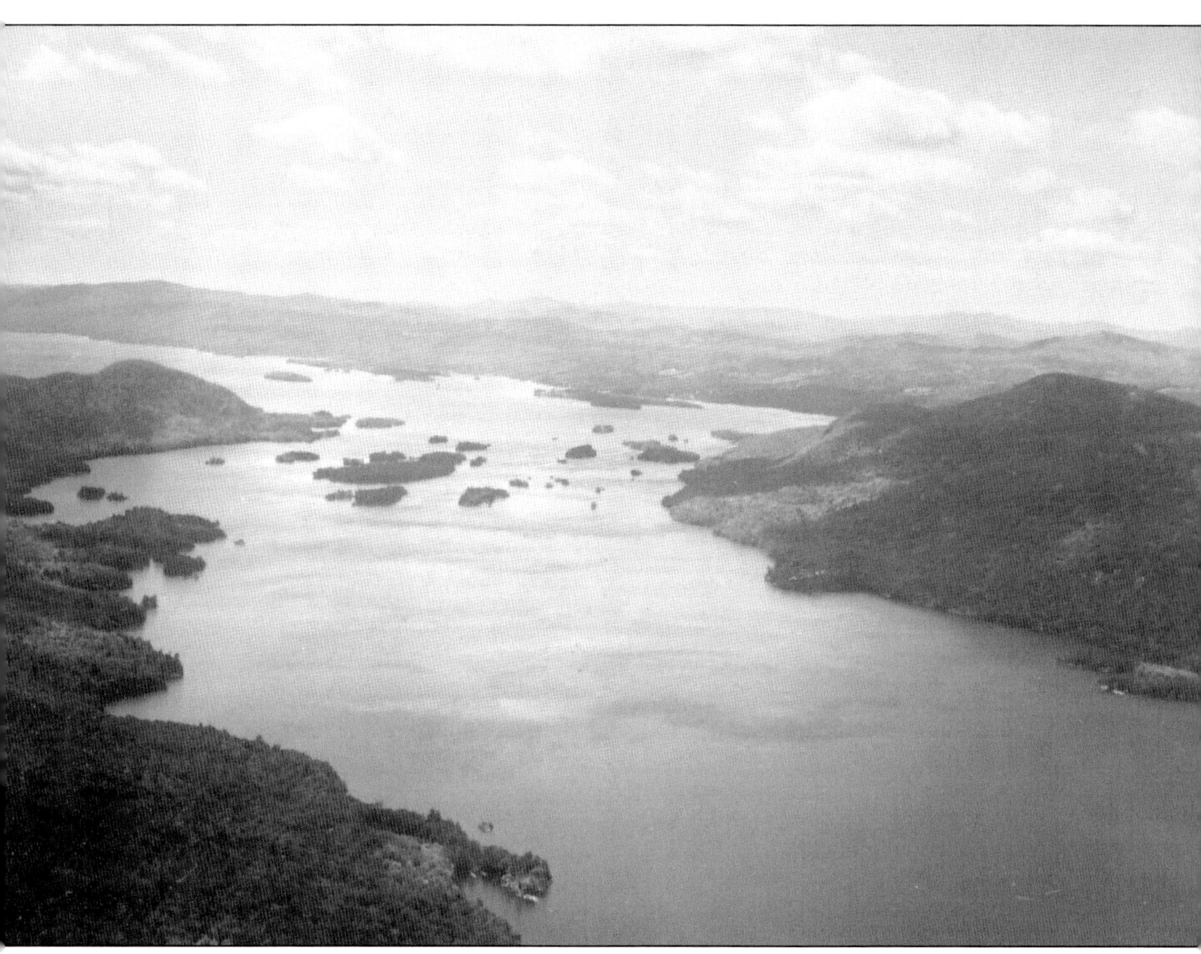

In this spectacular view, most likely taken from the fire tower on Black Mountain in 1920, the islands and shores Apperson was working so hard to protect can be seen. The entire shoreline on the left, or eastern side, of the lake was finally sold to the State of New York in 1941 by W.J. Knapp for just under $200,000, though it was probably worth about $4 million. (Courtesy of KARC.)

Seven

BATTLEGROUNDS

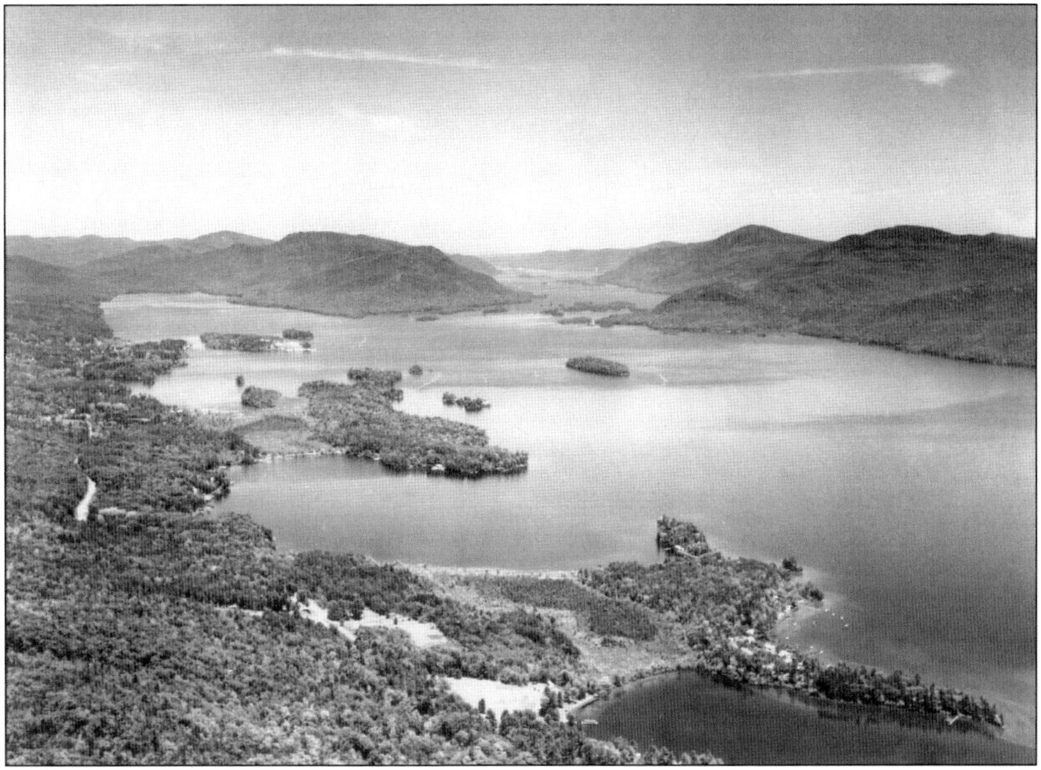

In this panoramic view, almost all the places Apperson fought so hard to protect can be seen. At top left is Northwest Bay, where the Loines family had a large farm. The next landmark is Tongue Mountain, aptly named since it juts out into the lake like a huge tongue. French Point and Turtle Bay are perched along the eastern shores of Tongue Mountain. Across the lake from Tongue Mountain is Black Mountain, with Shelving Rock just to the south. Apperson and his friends took a photograph of a sign posted there, with the name W.J. Knapp, that read, "Hunting and Fishing Forbidden on this Property, W.J. Knapp, Owner, Shelving Rock, Lake George, N.Y." (Author's collection.)

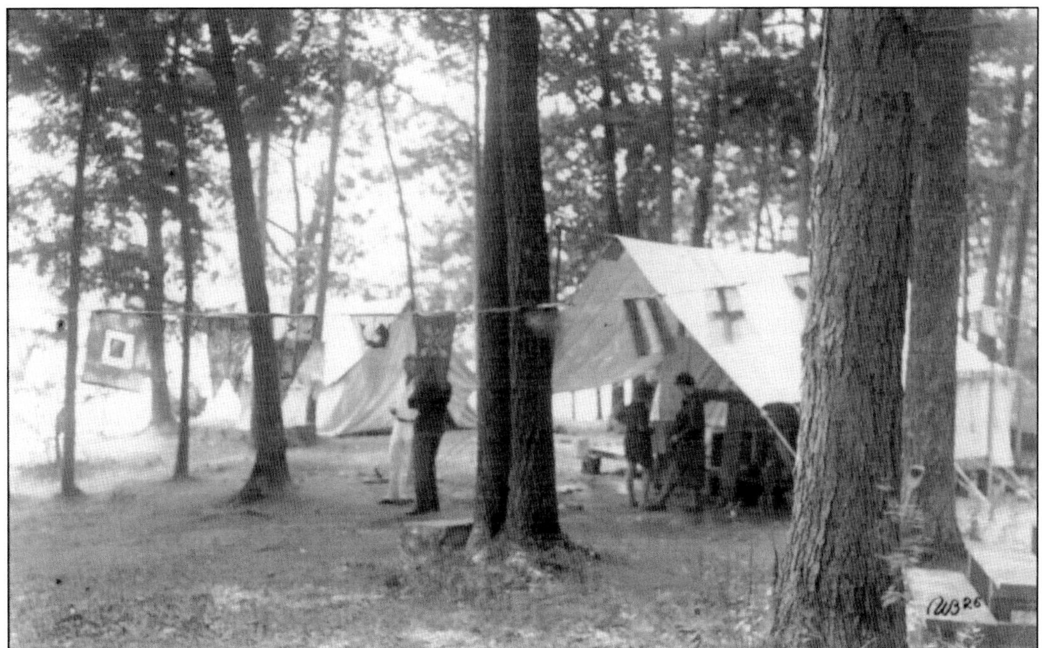

In 1921, the American Canoe Association held a regatta in Huddle Bay, putting up members in the annex, the icehouse, and several tents. In 1926, Apperson helped arrange for the club to hold another regatta at Lake George, but this time, it took place in the Narrows on Turtle Island. Apperson and his old friend Jim Cawley arranged to provide tents and sanitary facilities. Pictured are some of those tents as well as the festive banners they had on display. (Courtesy of KARC.)

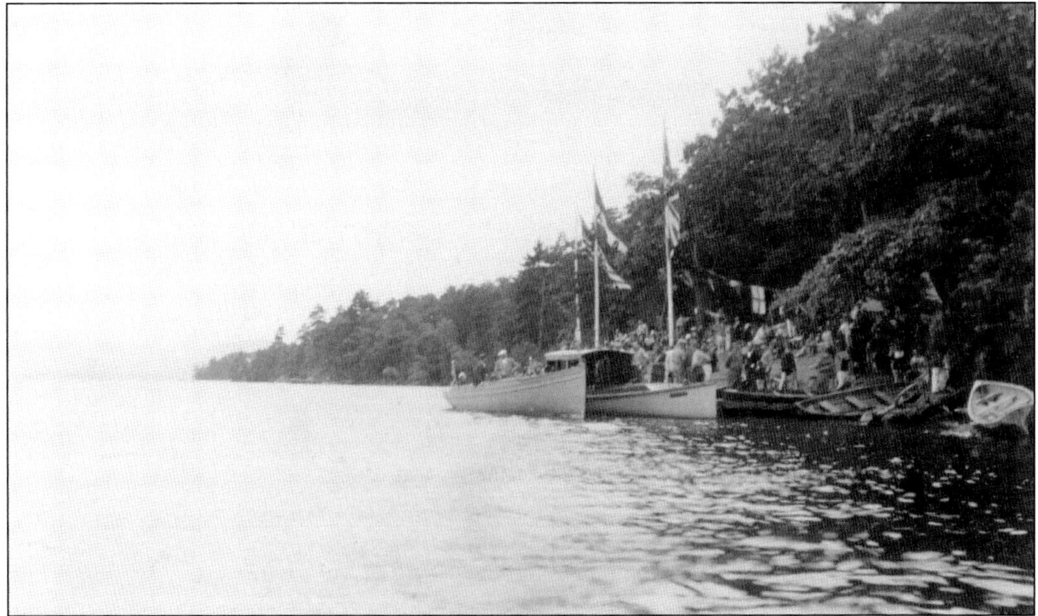

Here are some of the boats assembled for the big event. Several engineers at GE were members of the American Canoe Association, so they shouldered many of the responsibilities. Apperson was pleased to have an opportunity to impress on these influential sportsmen his dream of preserving the islands for the enjoyment of future generations. (Courtesy of KARC.)

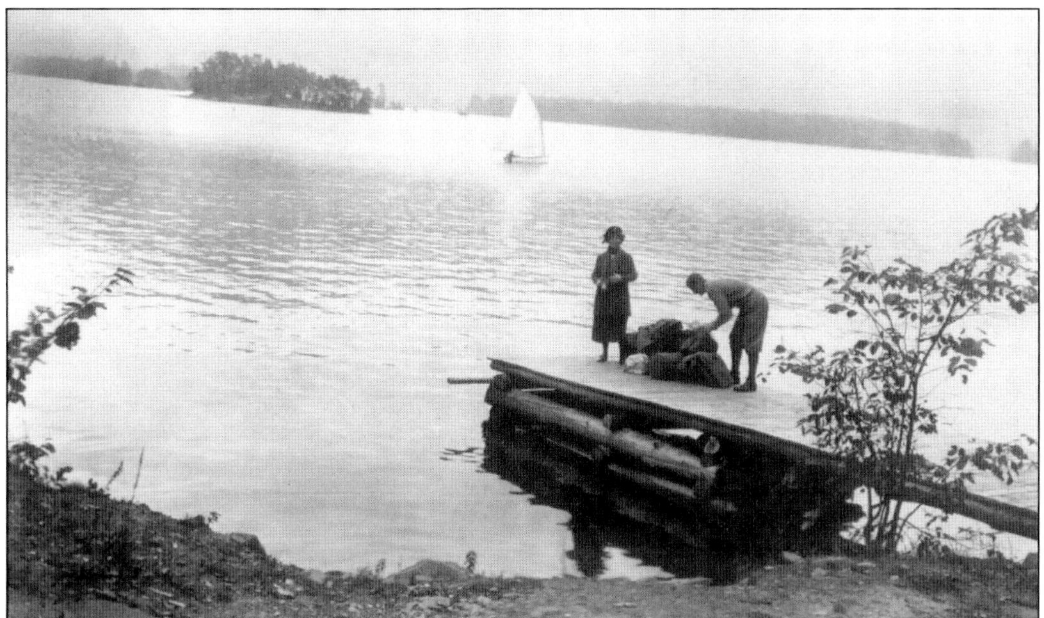

Two unidentified figures stand on a dock with baggage during the summer of 1926. They are probably waiting for a ride to Turtle Island. (Courtesy of KARC.)

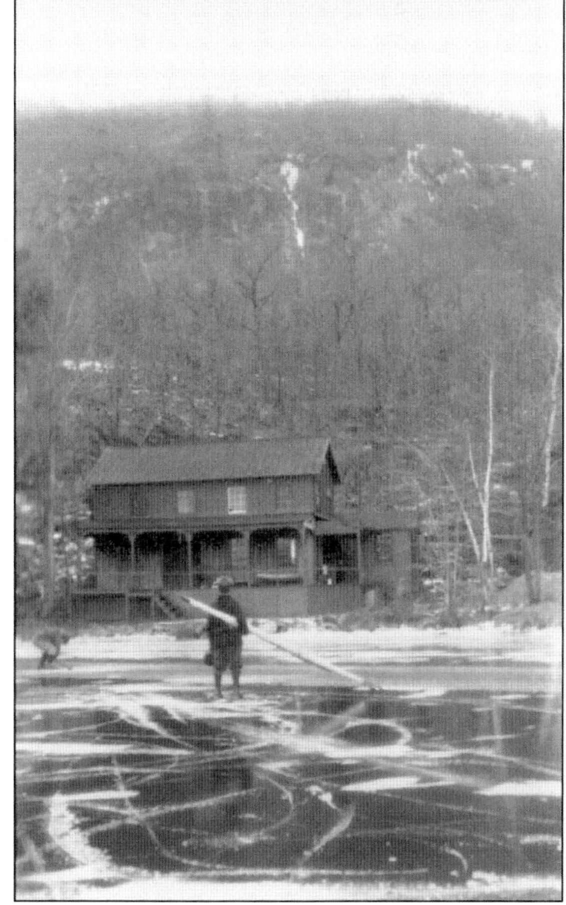

Apperson became friends with widow Mary Loines in Northwest Bay and introduced her daughters Sylvia and Hilda to various forms of recreation. In this c. 1925 photograph, Apperson's nephews John (left) and Jim Apperson have skated over to Northwest Bay to the Quarterdeck to see if anyone can come out to play. (Author's collection.)

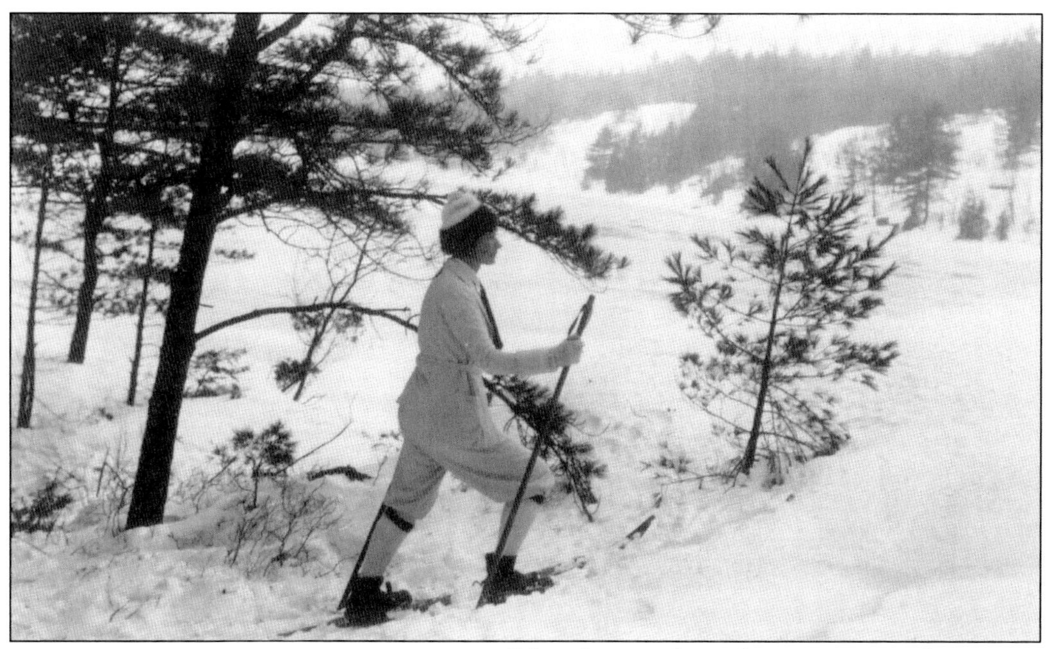

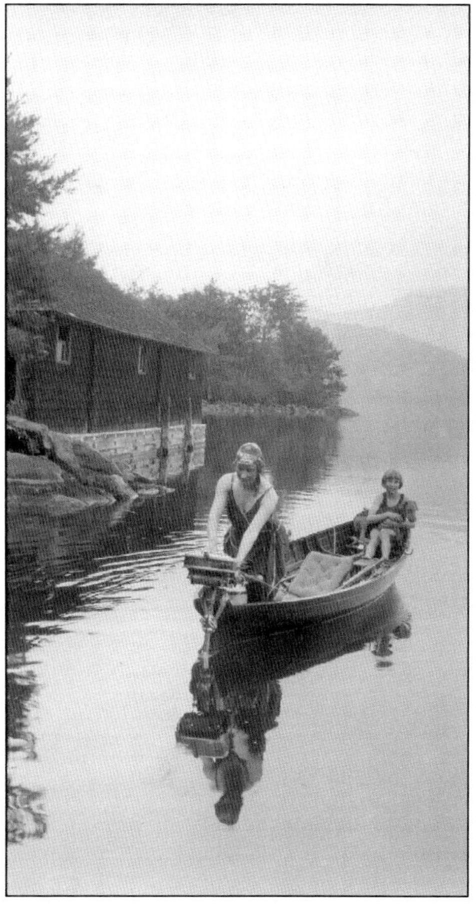

Sylvia Loines, shown here wearing a white snowsuit, loved winter sports and had a very adventurous spirit; Apperson probably considered proposing marriage to her. When her family made a generous donation of land on Tongue Mountain to the State of New York, it set off a firestorm of angry comments from others in the community, and Loines may have had second thoughts about a life spent fighting for conservation causes. As it turned out, she married William Dalton, whose wife had died soon after selling their lot in Huddle Bay, and the Dalton family began enjoying the use of the Loines property in Northwest Bay. (Courtesy of KARC.)

Hilda Loines, the oldest sister in the family, developed a close friendship with Apperson and supported his efforts to establish a Lake George Park. She was active in garden clubs on a national level, and helped Apperson get introduced to influential women. One such woman was Ethel Dreier, mother of Ted Dreier, an engineer at GE. For many years, Ethel was the president of the New York City Women's Club and with advice from Apperson, established a conservation committee, made speeches at hearings, and helped get out the vote in key elections. In this photograph, Loines is getting ready to start the engine, while her niece Barbara holds her pet dog. (Courtesy of KARC)

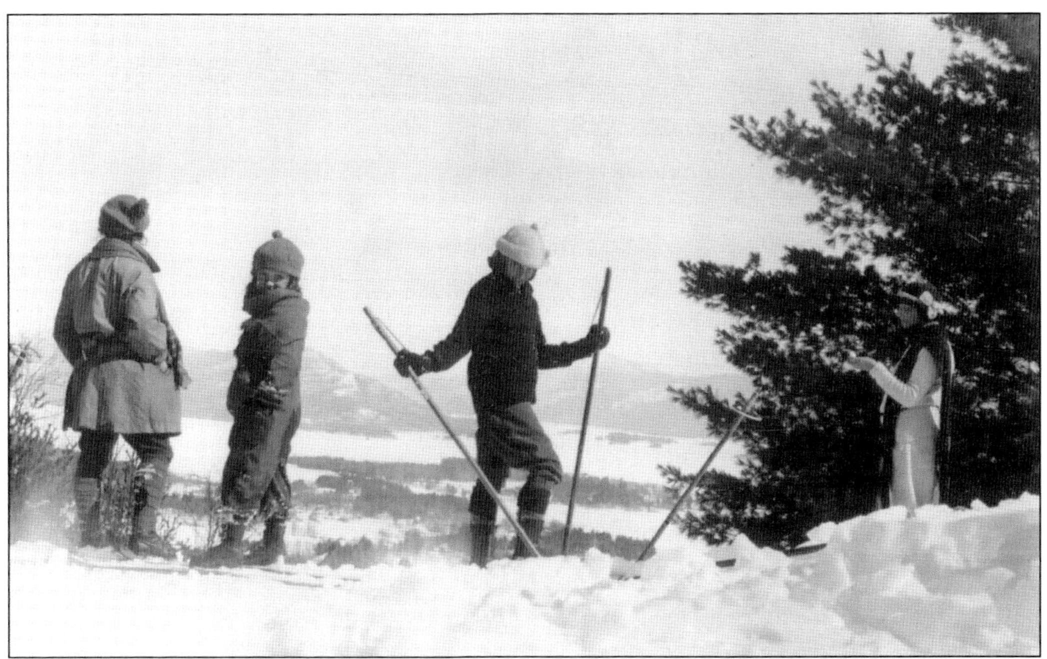

After the death of Russell Loines in 1922, his sisters, especially Sylvia and Hilda, made a special effort to look out for his two daughters Barbara and Margot. In this c. 1923 photograph, Apperson has invited them on a little ski expedition to climb "Appie Top," also known as Barber Mountain, behind Apperson's camp in Huddle Bay. From left to right, the skiers are Katherine Conger Loines, Margot Loines, Barbara Loines, and Sylvia Loines. (Courtesy of KARC.)

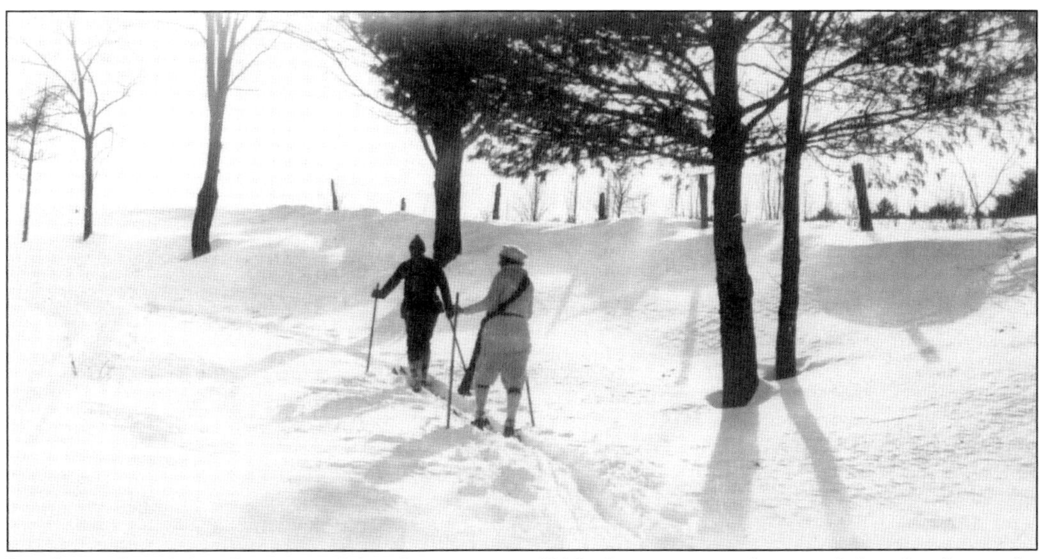

In a letter from Mary Loines to John Aspersion in 1923, she mentions the possibility that he might become her son-in-law. He and Sylvia did have a romantic relationship, but it became complicated when she and her family were harshly criticized in an editorial in the *Lake George Mirror* for their efforts to turn over their land in Northwest Bay to the state. (Courtesy of KARC.)

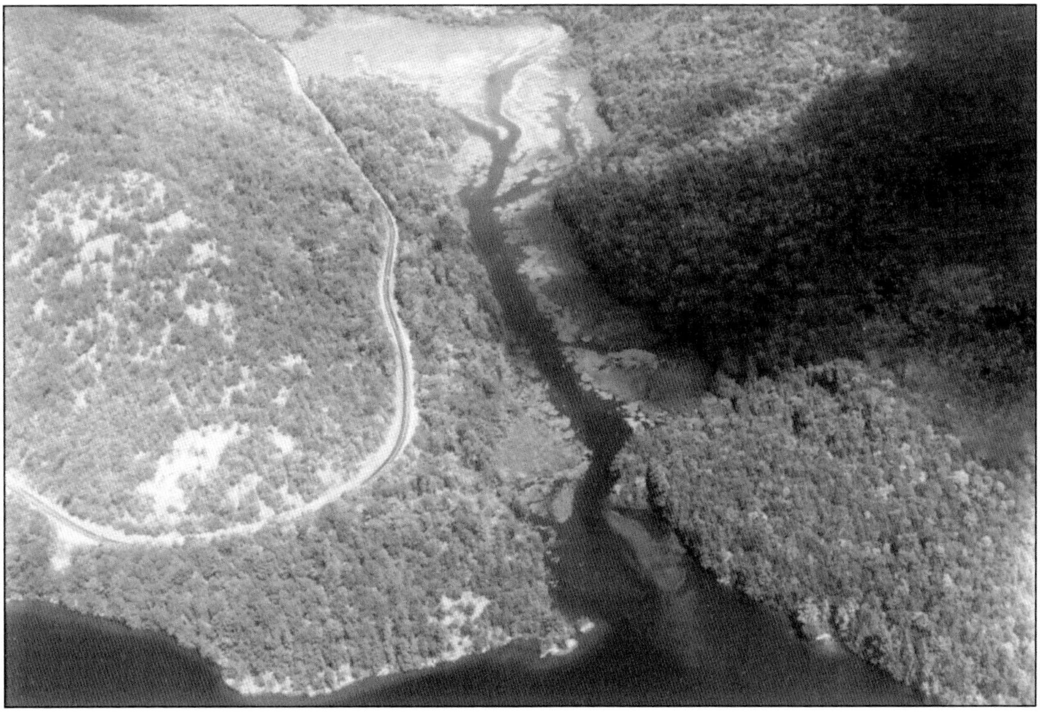

Many commercial interests were trying to open Northwest Bay to development. Apperson fought and won a particularly interesting battle in 1923 against Robert Moses, who was grabbing control of the state park system and tried to put through a proposal to build a highway around the rim of Tongue Mountain. This photograph, taken by Art Newkirk in the 1950s, shows the land that once belonged to the Loines family. Below, in this view of Northwest Bay, it is easy to imagine how alarming it must have been to think of a highway being constructed along the edge of Tongue Mountain. Apperson fought hard for many years to find a way to get the state to control all the land on Tongue Mountain and Northwest Bay Brook to prevent anyone from building unsightly structures or gas stations in the middle of this pristine wilderness. (Both, courtesy of KARC.)

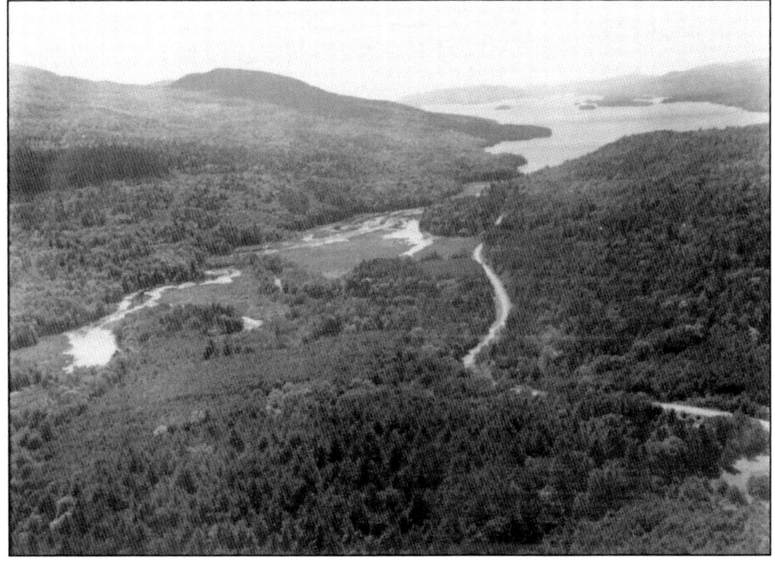

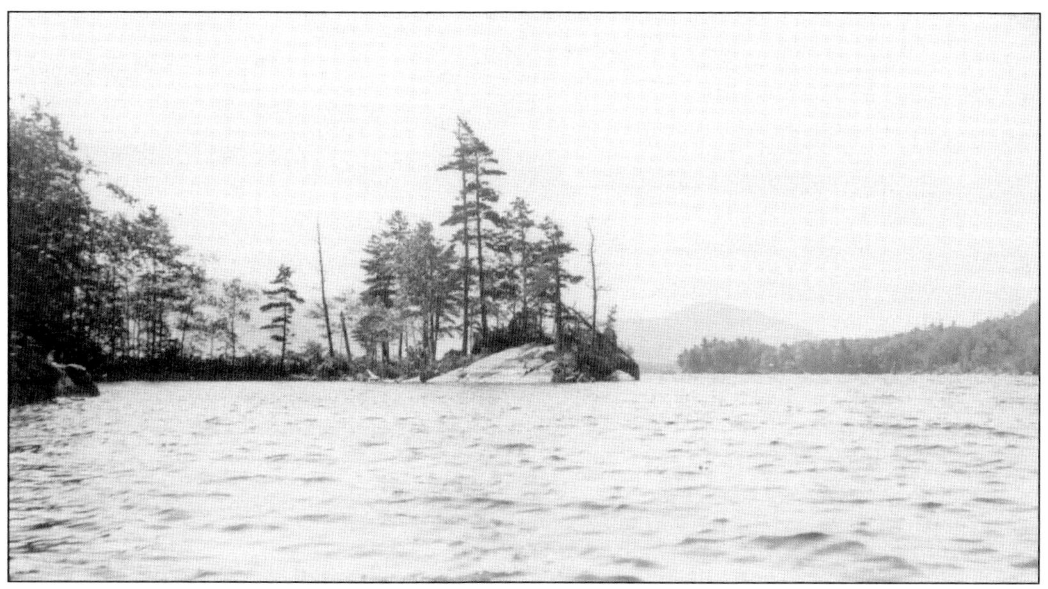

While camping on the Dollar Islands, Apperson and his friends must have had frequent contact with people on the shores nearby. This picture clearly shows how very close they were to French Point, the site of the old Sherman House Hotel. Apperson apparently used his influence at GE and persuaded them to purchase the property to prevent it being sold to a developer or logging firm. He then persuaded GE to establish a summer camp on French Point for female employees, using the old house (below) and cabins still on the site. The camp started operations in 1921 and provided scores of women a chance to enjoy a summer vacation on a beautiful lake at a very low cost. (Both, courtesy of KARC.)

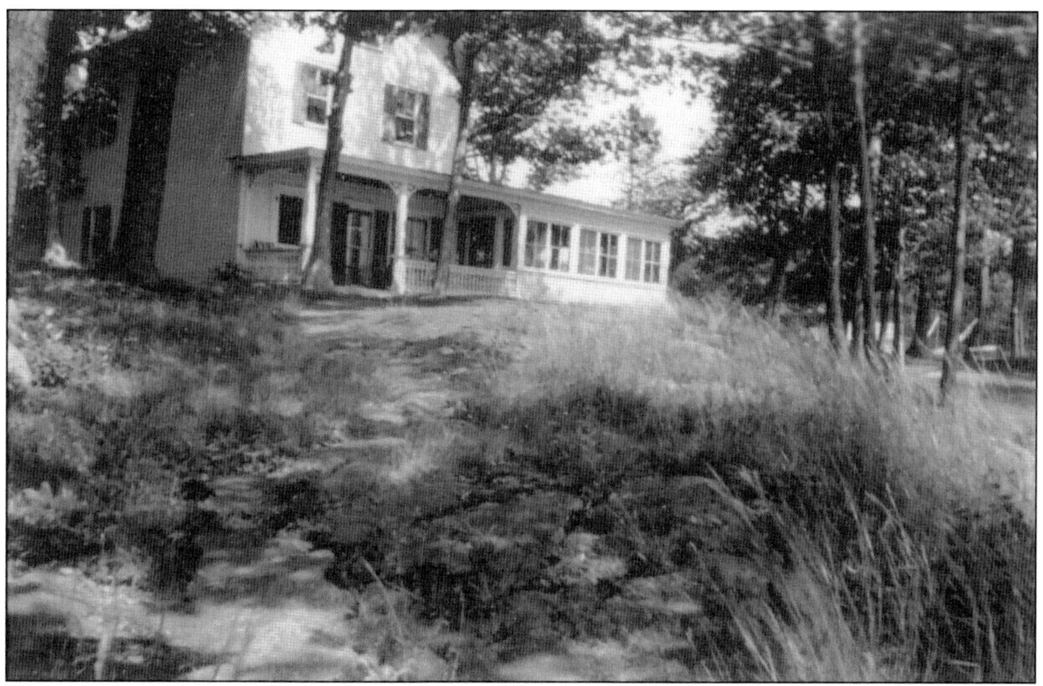

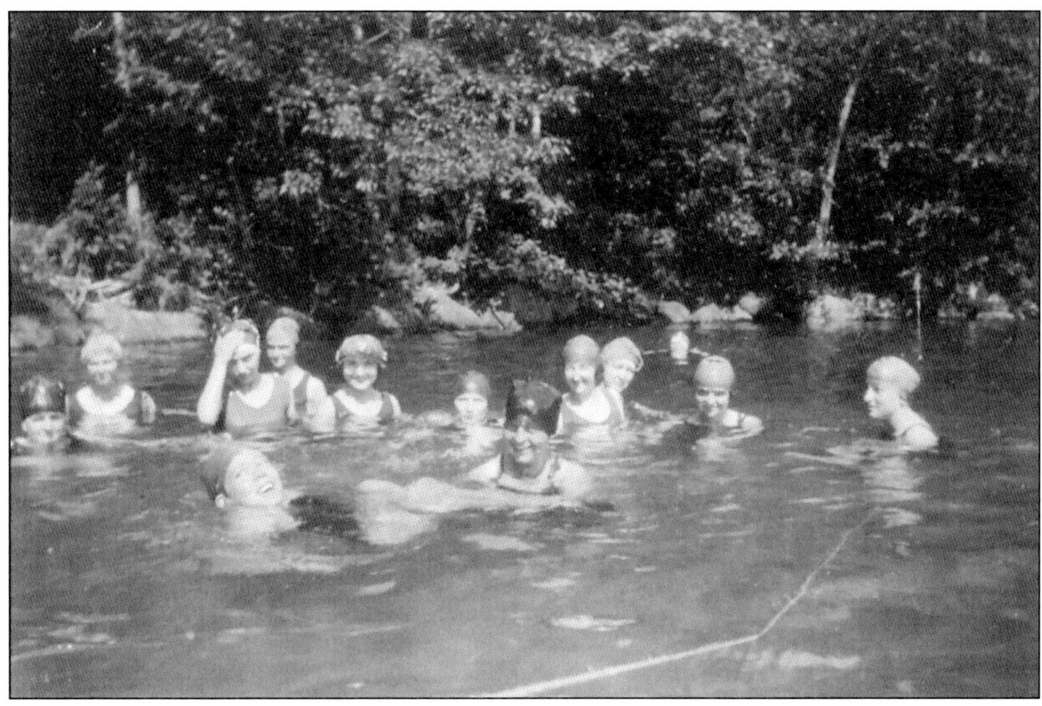

Pictured in the remarkable c. 1922 photograph above are about a dozen women enjoying a swim near French Point. GE eventually lost interest in running this camp and considered putting it back on the market, but Apperson intervened, getting his wealthy friends to raise enough money to buy it from GE and then donate the property to the State of New York. It became a memorial to George Foster Peabody. Below, in another glimpse of French Point from the Apperson archives, men are unloading a barge full of rocks to repair the shores of the Dollar Islands, with Sherman House in the background, around 1918. (Above, courtesy of KARC; below, author's collection.)

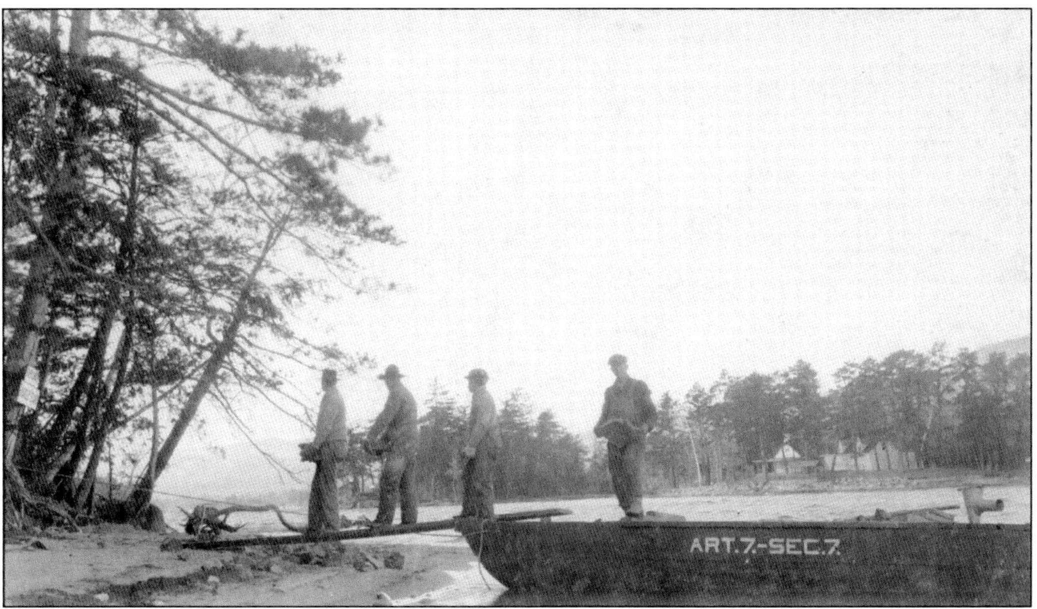

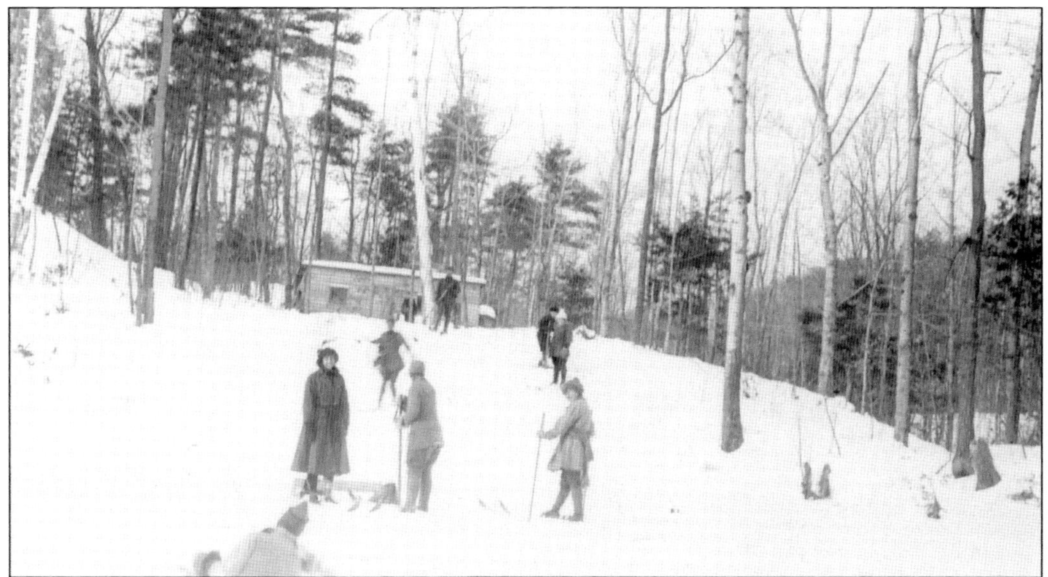

Apperson purchased a lot on the shores of Tongue Mountain in Turtle Bay, and his friends flocked there to enjoy winter sports. The building served as a nice shelter, and Bolton residents often came over to join in on the fun. Below, the last large parcel of land on Tongue Mountain to come under state control was French Point. In the 1930s, when GE lost interest in running the camp, Apperson raised money to purchase the land from GE at a reduced price and give it to the state. He used some of the donations to establish a memorial to George Foster Peabody in 1938. (Both, courtesy of KARC.)

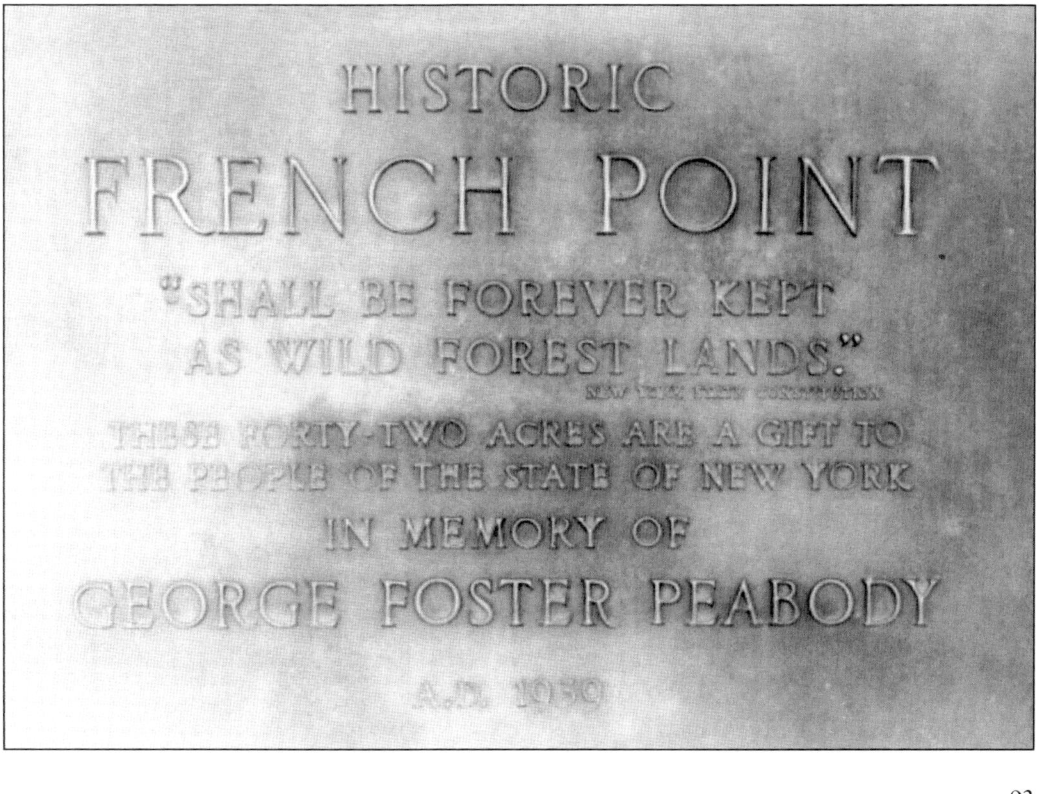

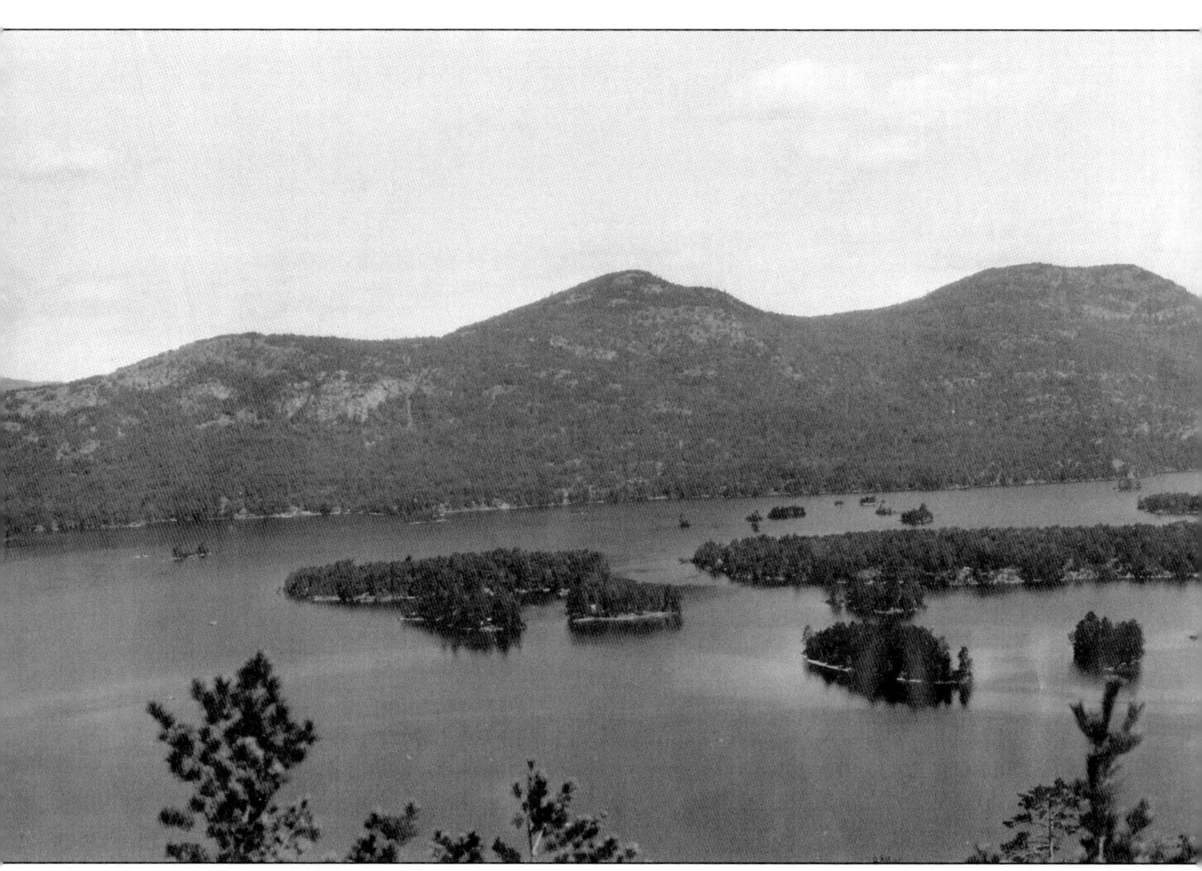

This view from Shelving Rock, looking across at Tongue Mountain, seems almost to have been taken from an airplane, but it was taken while hiking. Most of these islands were saved by the process of riprapping, thanks to John Apperson. (Courtesy of KARC.)

Shelving Rock had wonderful hiking trails and was a popular destination for hikers and skiers, as seen in these two photographs from 1915. The owner of this property, W.O. Knapp, also owned Paradise Bay, one of the most popular tourist destinations, and about 10 miles of shore property extending as far as Black Mountain Point. Apperson kept up his efforts for many years, determined to bring most of this land under state protection and ensure that the public had access. (Both, courtesy of KARC)

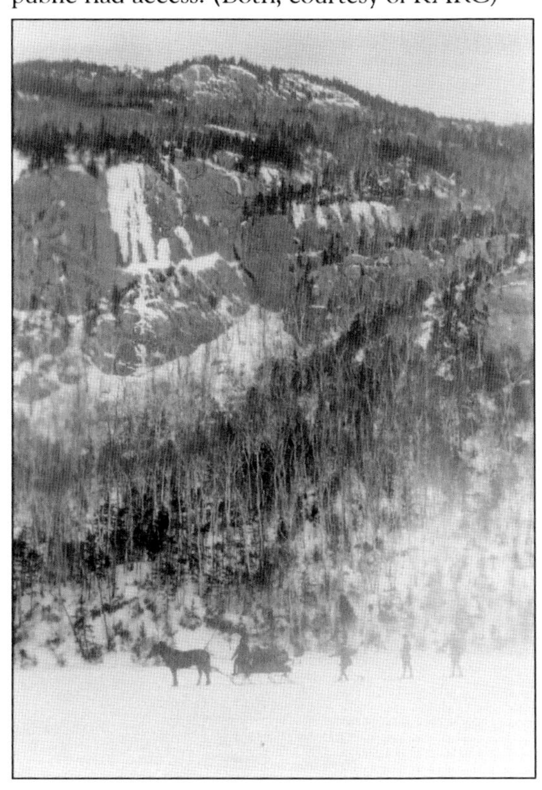

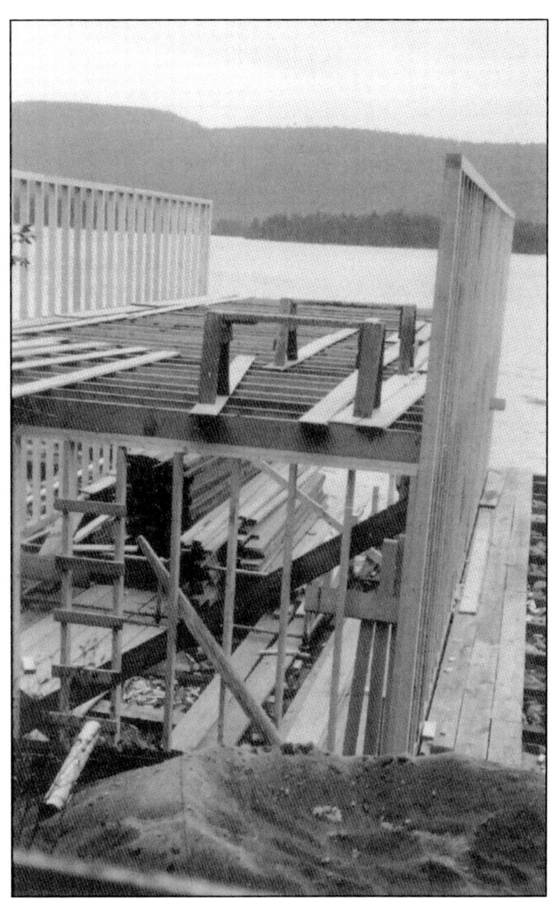

By 1928, after most of the Tongue Mountain Peninsula had come under state control, a group of like-minded people formed the Turtle Bay Association, agreeing to put a limit on the construction of new buildings. They were all very upset when another neighbor, who did not sign their agreement, started building a huge two-story boathouse. Below, someone alerted Apperson and even sent him pictures, so he immediately complained to state officials. It was a dangerous precedent, he argued, if owners of shoreline property could erect a boathouse far out into the lake on state land. After asking around, Apperson learned that Jay Taylor's son had been employed as the contractor for the job. (Both, courtesy of KARC.)

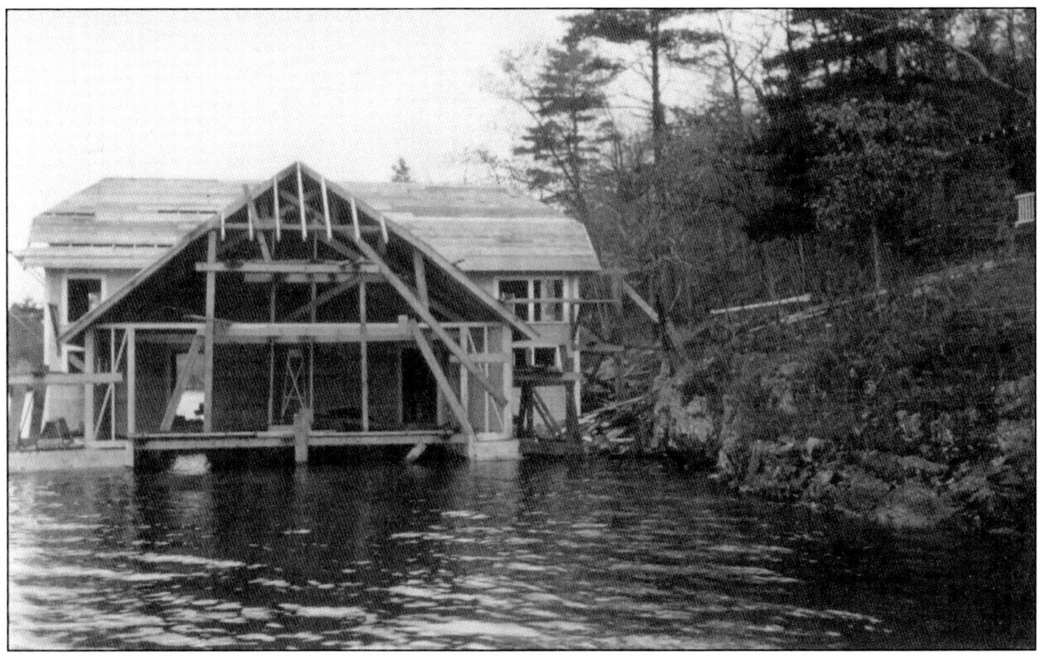

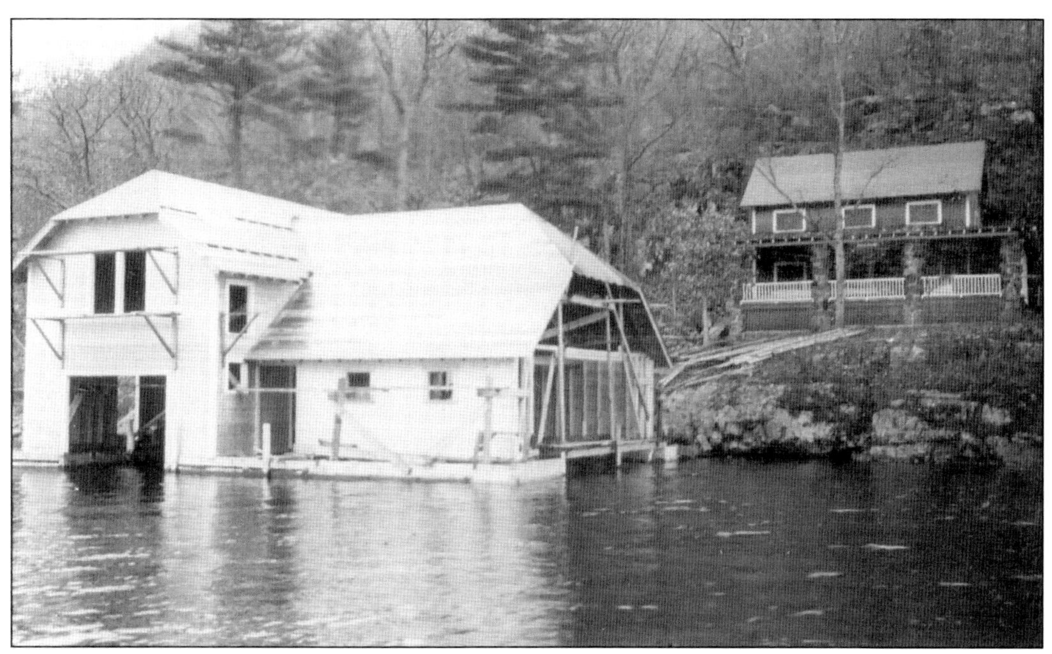

Once completed, the boathouse could accommodate several overnight guests. This raised concerns about sanitation. Of course, more than anything, Apperson hated to think that other boathouses would spring up everywhere. He raised his concerns to the officers of the Lake George Association but got an unsatisfactory response. Below is a view of Turtle Bay several years later with the controversial boathouse in the background, completely dwarfing the traditionally sized boathouse to its left. Apperson never found a way to get the boathouse removed but at least stirred up a lively debate. (Both, courtesy of KARC.)

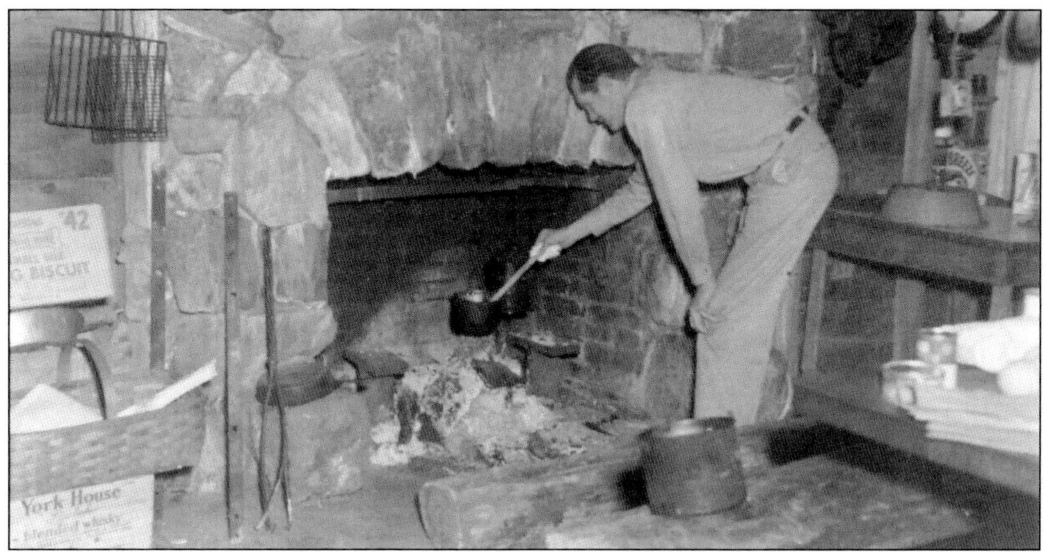

In 1958, a few of Apperson's friends, knowing how anxious he was to preserve his legacy in Turtle Bay, offered to purchase his camp, signing an agreement to maintain it just as he had been doing for 30 years. They officially formed a Turtle Bay Association, led by another GE engineer, John Newkirk. Here, Newkirk cooks over the fire in the 1950s. (Courtesy of KARC.)

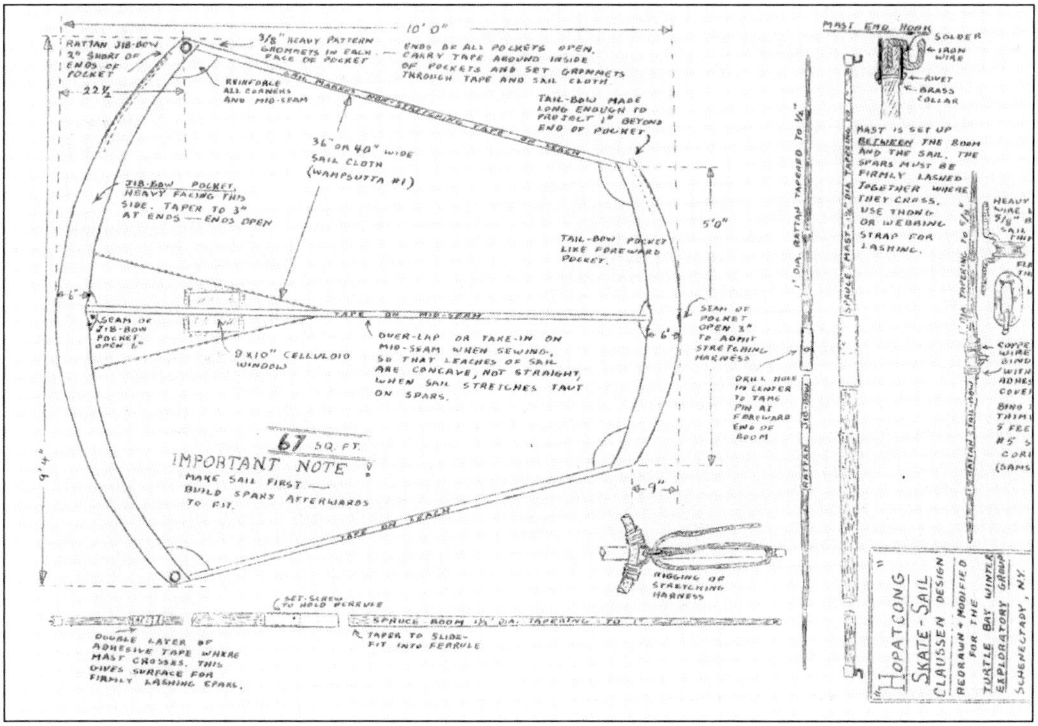

Also during the 1950s, Apperson's nephew John Apperson III tried to launch a business manufacturing skate sails. Here is a blueprint from the archives for the "Hopatcong Skate Sail, Claussen design, redrawn and modified for the Turtle Bay Winter Exploratory Group, Schenectady, New York." The business never got off the ground, primarily because so many of its partners were reassigned to work in other parts of the country. (Courtesy of KARC.)

Eight

Family Ties

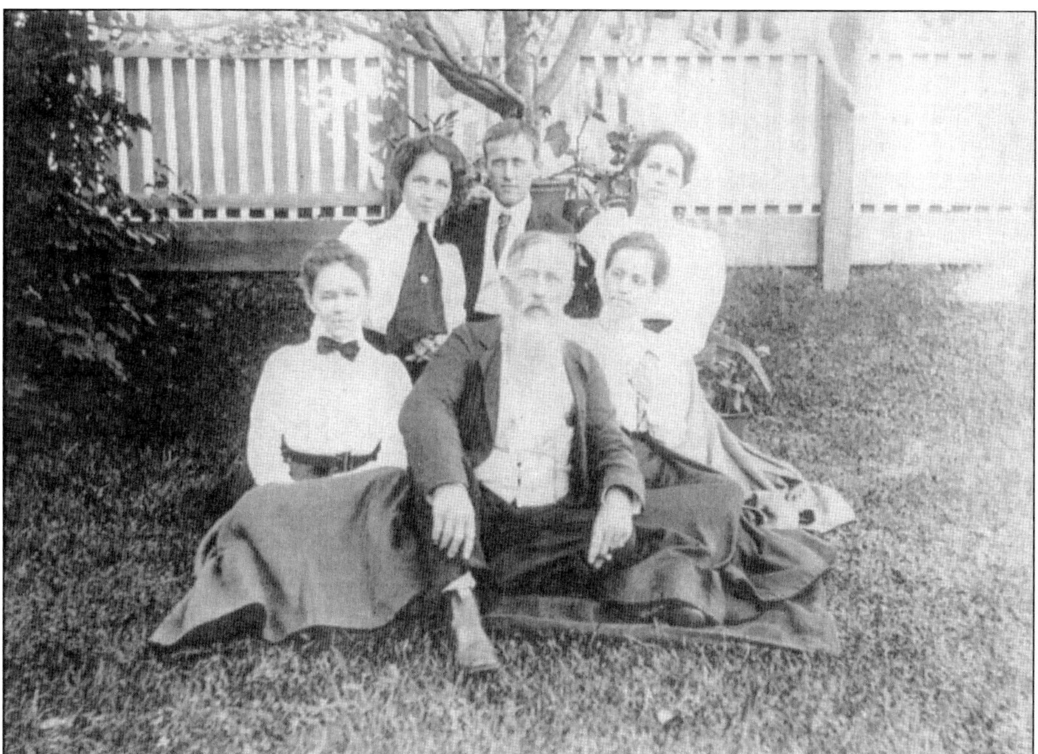

People have heard of John Muir and his battle to prevent construction of a dam in Yosemite National Park. A similar battle took place in New York State. At the center of this battle was Lake George, in all its natural beauty, which was threatened by a host of commercial interests. Like Muir, John Apperson was passionate and determined. This chapter looks back to his childhood and education, to try to find out how he became such an effective activist, and why he cared. In 1899, John Apperson was ready to leave home and head out into the world, so someone took a photograph of the children of Ellen Victoria Hull Apperson. Seated around their father clockwise from left are Ellen, Nancy, John, Sallie, and Georgia Apperson. Their other sibling, Hull Apperson, had already moved away from Marion—perhaps to Schenectady, New York. (Author's collection.)

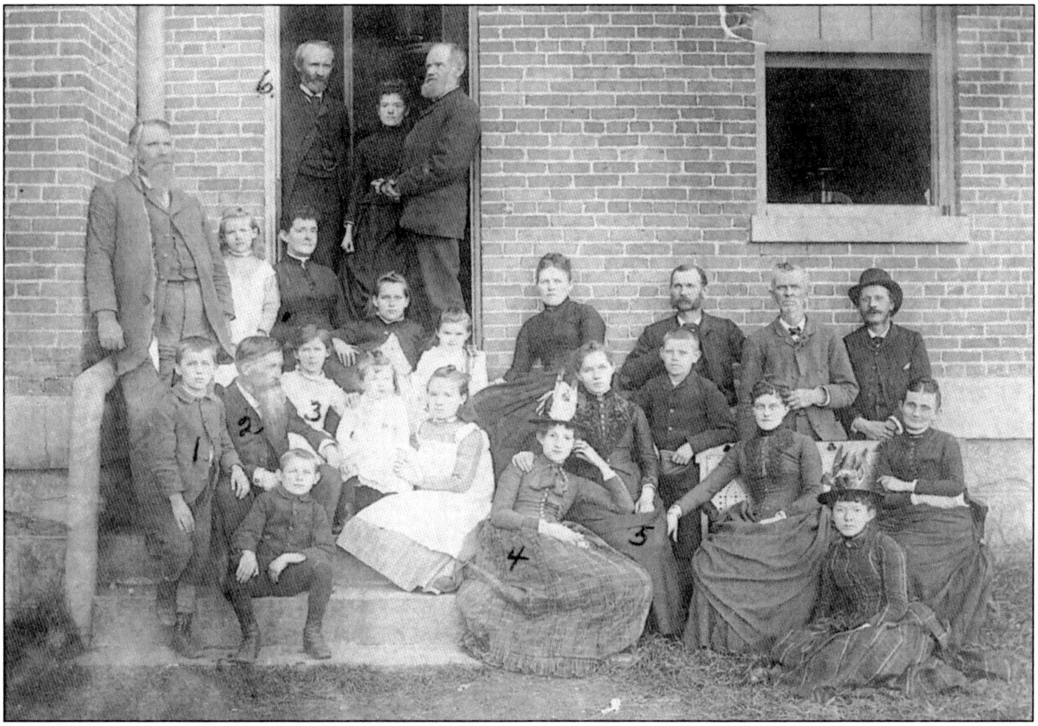

In 1887, Dr. John Apperson had to relocate his family from the village of Chilhowie in southwest Virginia, about 10 miles away from the larger town of Marion, where he was employed as an assistant physician at the Southwest Virginia Lunatic Asylum. The Apperson family was going through a hard time, as the oldest daughter, Mary, had died from typhoid just a few weeks before this photograph was taken. The mother, Ellen Victoria Hull Apperson, exhausted and in poor health, died within a few days, leaving behind two sons and four daughters. Dr. Apperson (No. 2) is seated on the steps between Nancy (No. 3) and John Jr. (No. 1). (Courtesy of the Smyth County Historical Society.)

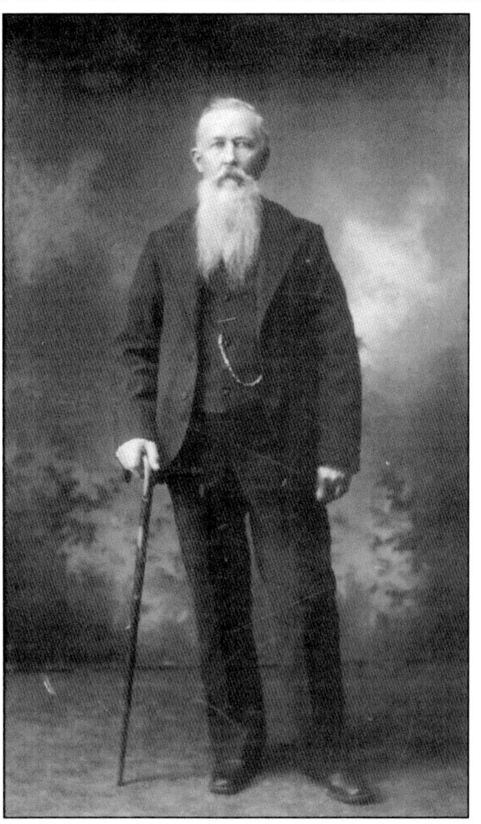

By 1893, Dr. Apperson had remarried Elizabeth Black and fathered four more children (Harvey, Kent, Alex, and Mary). Leaving behind his former profession as country doctor, Dr. Apperson branched out, becoming manager for the Marion and Rye Valley Railroad, the Marion Foundry, and the Staley's Creek Manganese and Iron Company. This photograph was taken in 1894 when he was appointed commissioner from Virginia to the Chicago World's Fair. (Courtesy of the Smyth County Historical Society.)

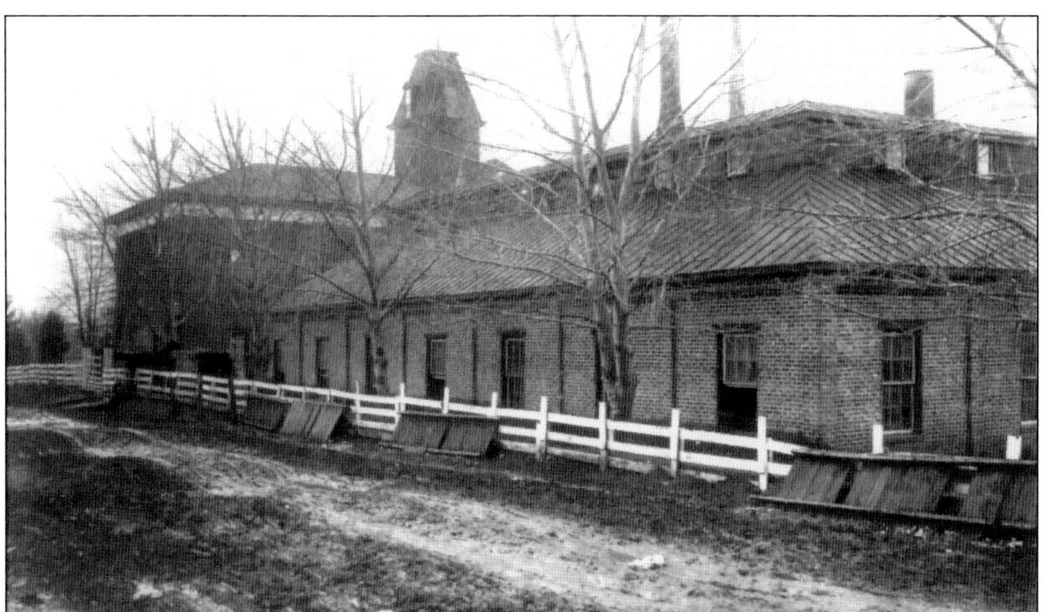

Options for higher education in the South were limited, but the Virginia Agricultural and Mechanical Institute, a land-grant college, had been founded in Blacksburg in 1874. By 1894, Hull Apperson had completed a bachelor's degree and was enrolling in a graduate program in electrical engineering. His younger brother, John, now age 16, was also enrolled in the Blacksburg school, as a sub-freshman. This photograph of the shops in 1893 gives an idea of the limited educational offerings in the young institution. (Courtesy of the Harry Downing Temple Jr. Papers, Special Collections, University Libraries, Virginia Polytechnic Institute and State University.)

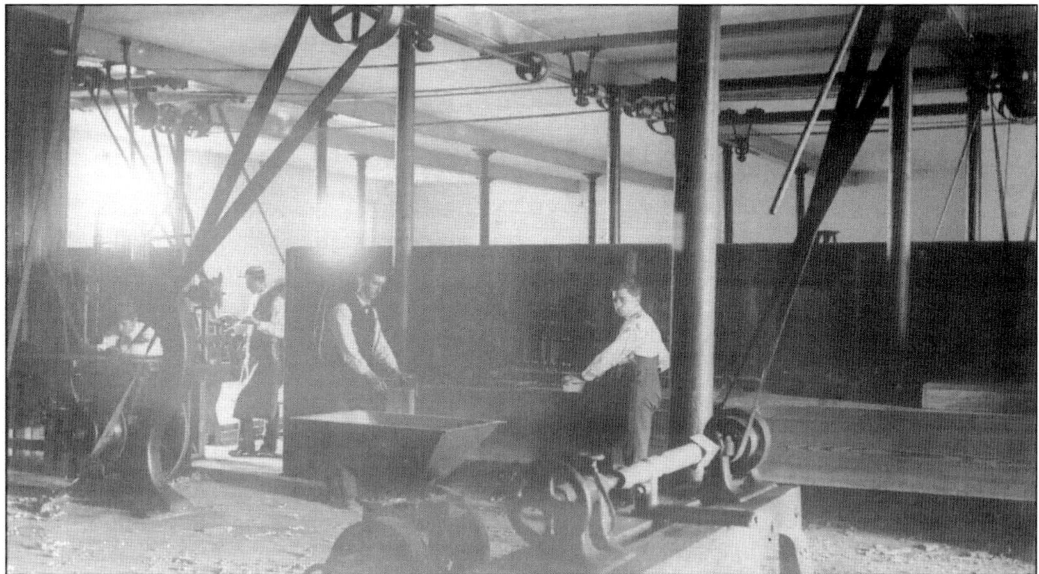

Hull Apperson apparently enjoyed spending time in the woodworking shops and later made furniture as a hobby. While a graduate student in electrical engineering, he was responsible for installing wiring to the new buildings on campus. His younger brother John, still a rebellious and independent sort, got into trouble with demerits and poor grades. (Courtesy of Special Collections, University Libraries, Virginia Polytechnic Institute and State University.)

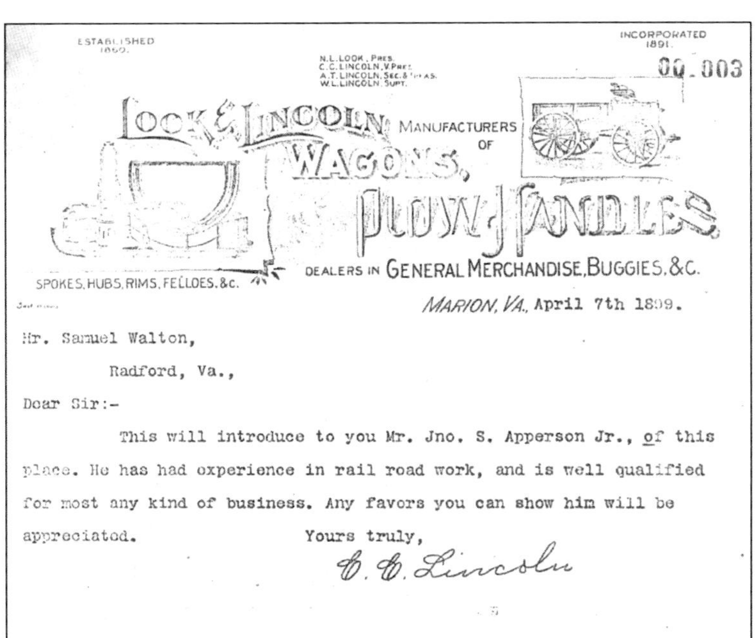

ESTABLISHED 1869.

INCORPORATED 1891.

N.L. LOOK, PRES.
C.C. LINCOLN, V.PRES.
A.T. LINCOLN, SEC.& TREAS.
W.L. LINCOLN, SUPT.

LOOK & LINCOLN, MANUFACTURERS OF WAGONS, PLOW HANDLES

SPOKES, HUBS, RIMS, FELLOES, &c.

DEALERS IN GENERAL MERCHANDISE, BUGGIES, &C.

MARION, VA., April 7th 1899.

Mr. Samuel Walton,

Radford, Va.,

Dear Sir:-

This will introduce to you Mr. Jno. S. Apperson Jr., of this place. He has had experience in rail road work, and is well qualified for most any kind of business. Any favors you can show him will be appreciated.

Yours truly,

C. C. Lincoln

John Apperson did not stay in Blacksburg long enough to finish his degree. His father decided to stop paying his tuition and fees but then helped him find a job instead. So, at age 18, he became a surveyor for the Marion and Rye Valley Railroad, eventually having charge over several hundred men as they laid down tracks for a branch railroad. By 1899, as this letter attests, the South seemed to offer him little in the way of gainful employment. (Author's collection.)

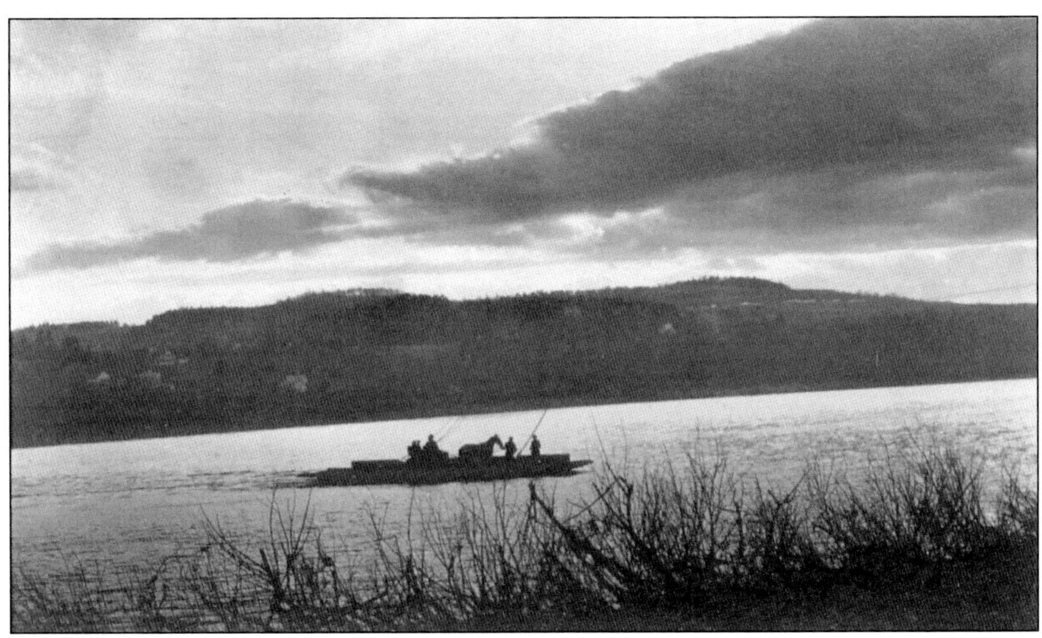

John Apperson arrived in Schenectady in January 1900, where his older brother Hull was already employed at GE. In one story, John first started working in construction, doing manual labor, but got into a physical altercation with his boss, who was arrogant and incompetent. Instead of being fired for his temper, he was rewarded for his courage and spirit and sent over to the engineering training program. He took this interesting photograph of Hoffman's Ferry in 1903. (Author's collection.)

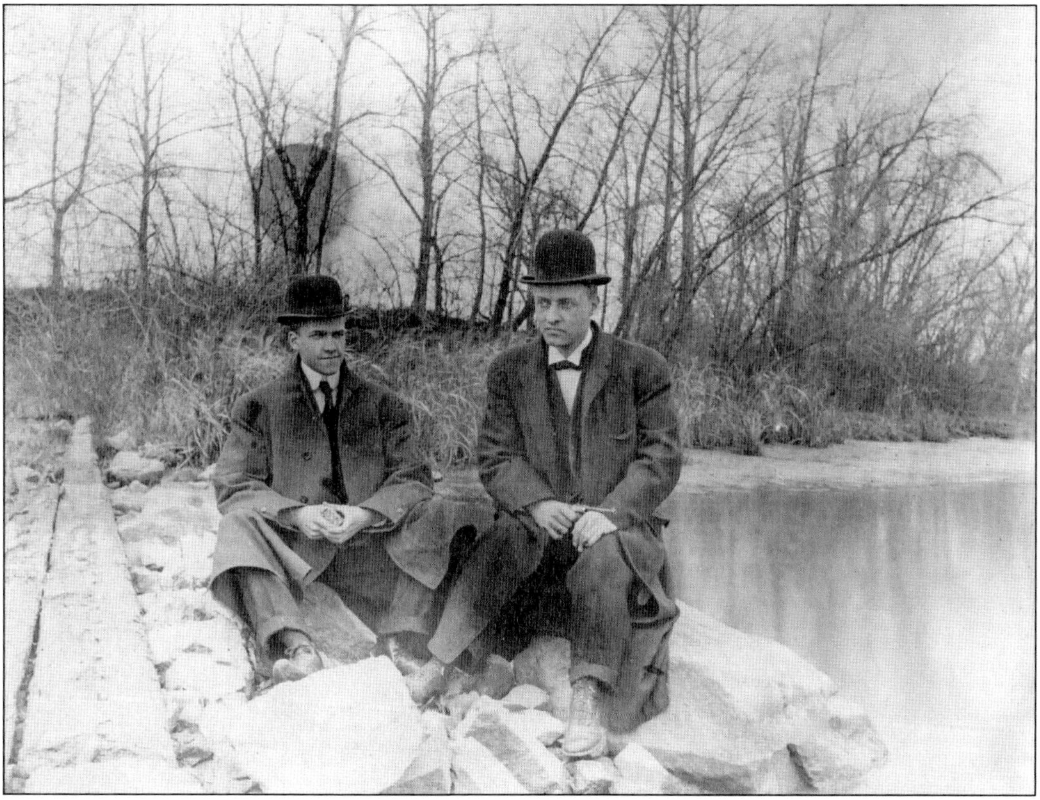

For the two brothers, nine years apart in age, the chance to be in the North and working for such a big industrial firm must have been exciting. However, when they ventured out of the city one day wearing bowler hats, neck ties, and freshly ironed collars, they looked rather anxious and uncomfortable. Notice that John (left) is holding a large rock, and Hull holds a revolver. John soon acquired more suitable clothing and gear, as seen at right in a picture of him wearing baggy trousers and putting on a pair of socks. Beside him is a fishing pole and a creel full of the day's catch. The image is unusual too, since it has been double exposed, showing a lake and forest in the background. It is unknown who took the picture or what they had in mind. (Both, author's collection.)

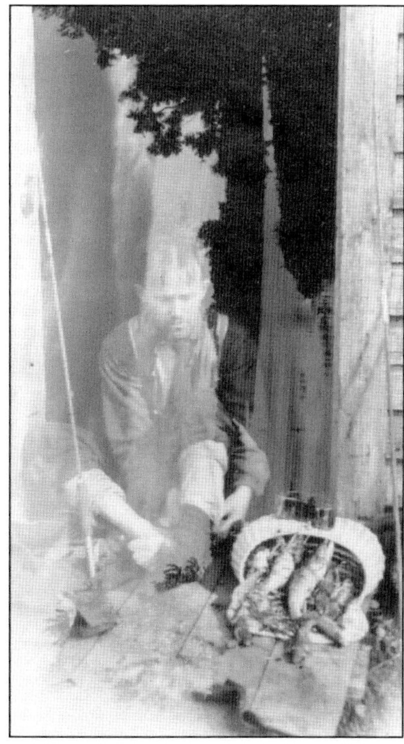

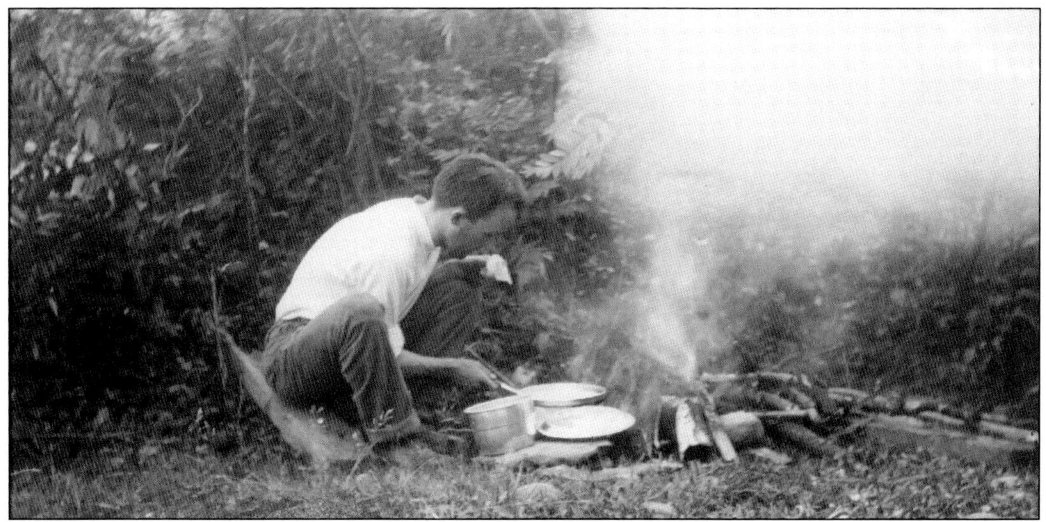

Apperson seemed perfectly at home in the outdoors, shown here cooking breakfast over an open fire. It did not take long before he had become a sort of pied piper, luring other test engineers to come along on camping trips in the vast playground near Schenectady. (Author's collection.)

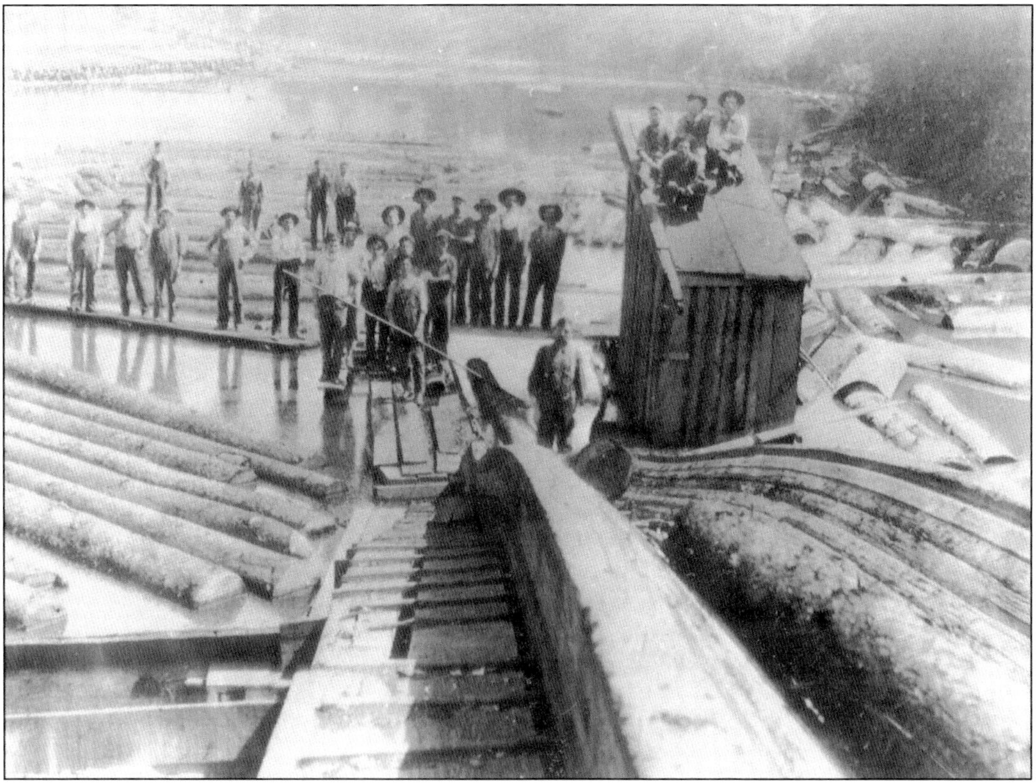

Despite all the distractions of his new life, Apperson must have felt concern about forest fires and illegal lumber operations in the Adirondacks. He was also aware of the damage being done to the forests back in Virginia. This photograph, taken around 1905, shows a log dam at the United Spruce Lumber Company's band mill on Staley's Creek. (Courtesy of the Smyth County Historical Society.)

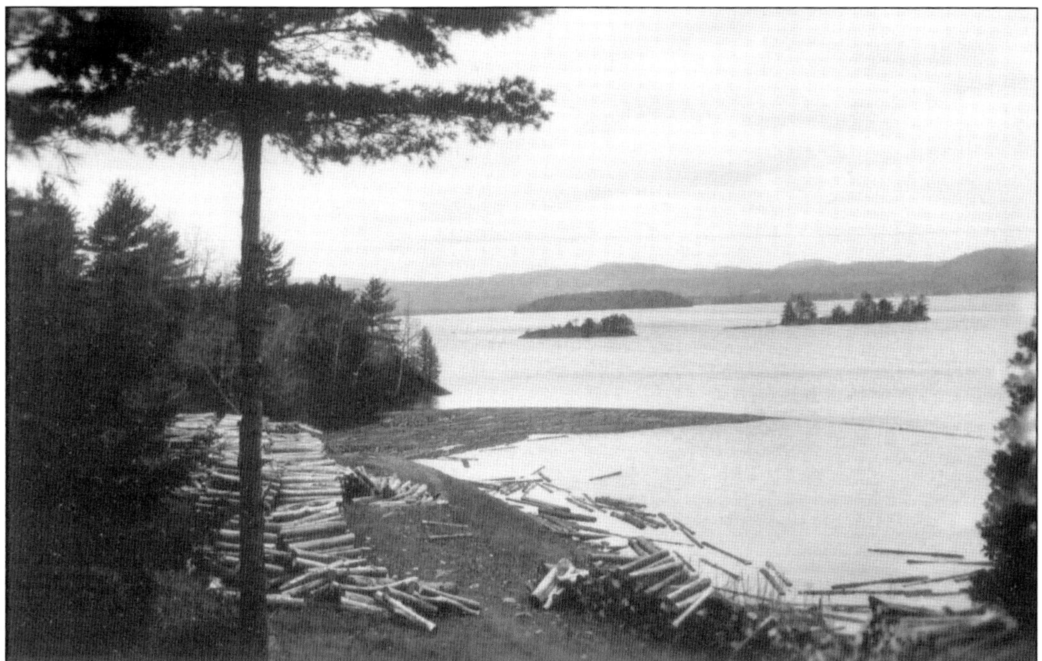

On one of Apperson's first trips to Lake George, he could have seen this disturbing sight of a log-strewn bay with Dome Island in the background. Surely, it would have stirred his curiosity, if not his anger, to see logging operations right on the edge of such a beautiful lake. (Courtesy of KARC.)

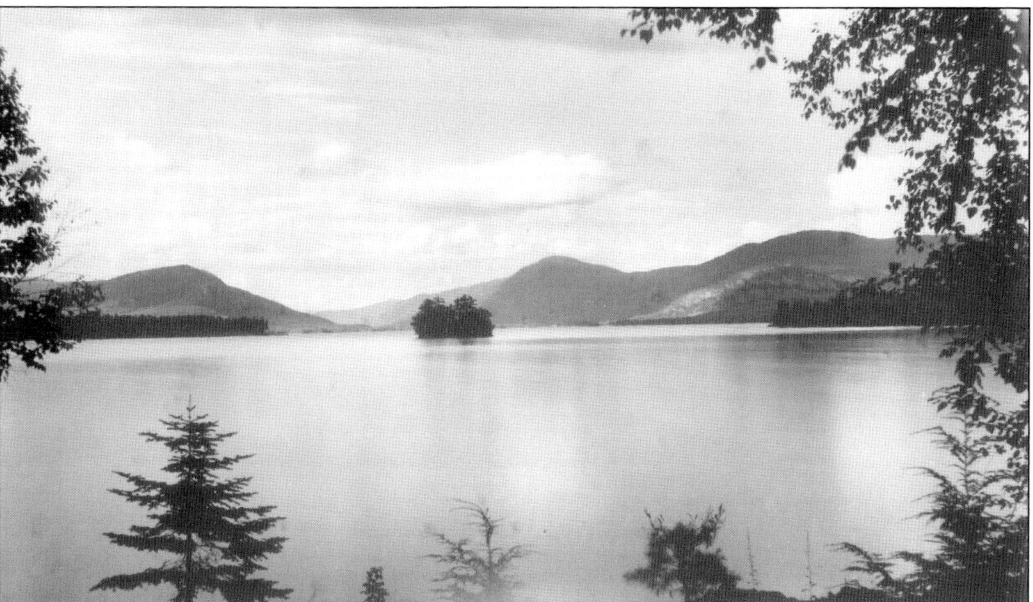

As Apperson made repeated visits to the lake, he started thinking about boats, tents, and the best campsites. With an engineer's methodical mind, he began planning his trips, recruiting friends to join in on the fun, and compiling a long list of items he hoped to purchase, including a camera. He had a good eye and started taking photographs of the incredible scenery, like this one looking north toward Black Mountain. (Author's collection.)

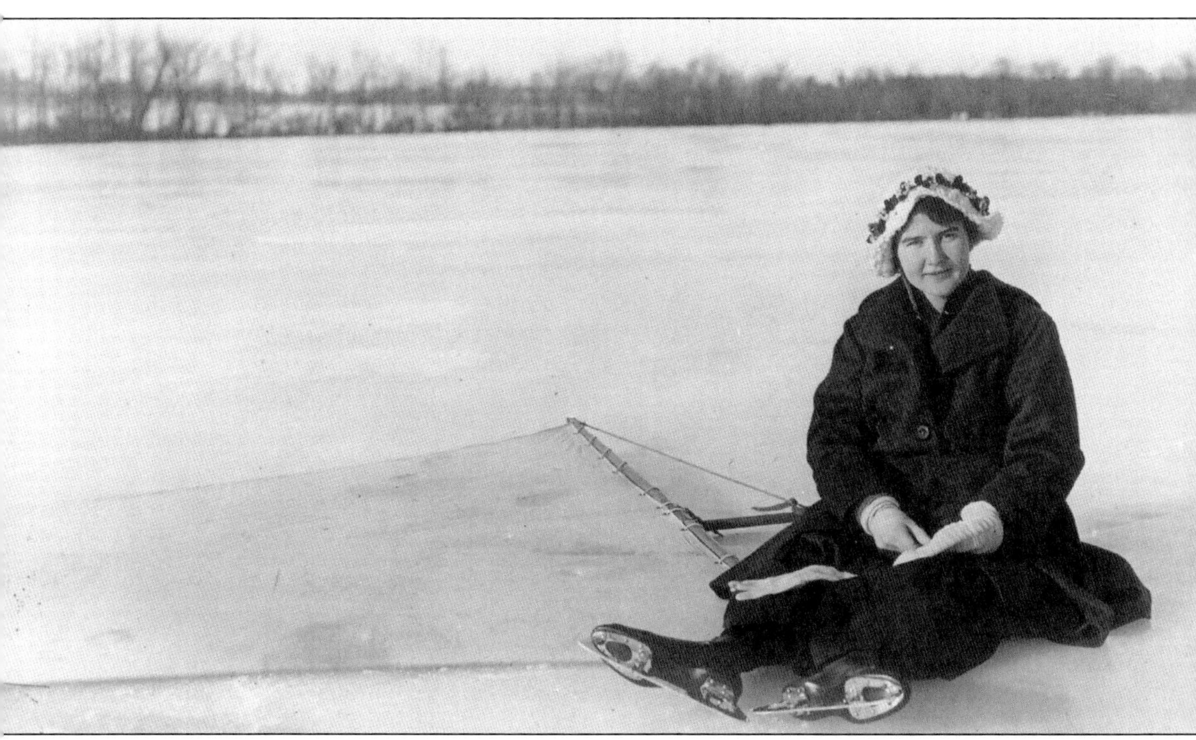

Apperson was a romantic at heart and fell in love with skate sailing, braving the freezing cold temperatures, and the possibilities for sharing these wonderful experiences with others. He may have pursued one or more romantic relationships during those years, but he did not leave much of a paper trail. This young woman, wearing a white hat, shows up repeatedly. (Courtesy of KARC.)

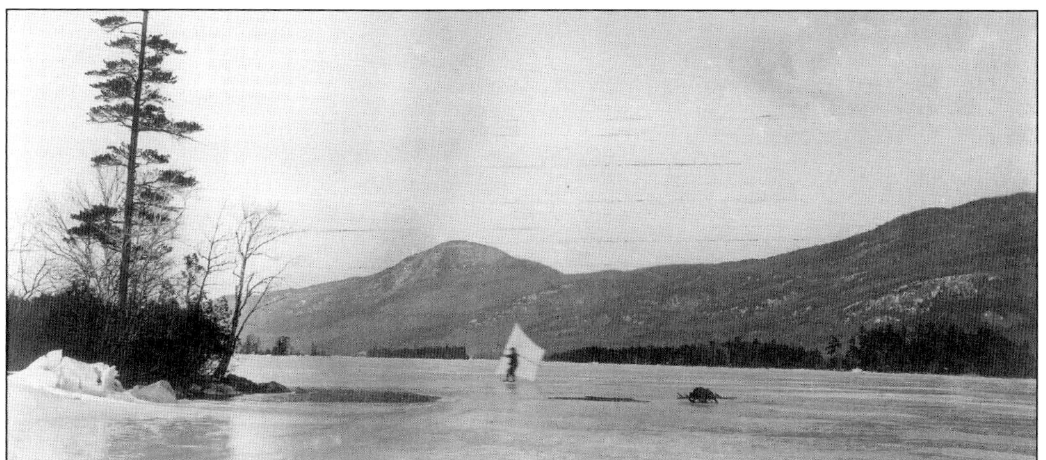

There was a special appeal to skate sailing since it was so effortless and silent, yet fast. Not usually a competitive sport like sailing, it could be enjoyed by an individual or in the company of several friends. It did not require much in the way of equipment and was thus affordable to the average working man or woman. That is why Apperson loved it so. (Courtesy of KARC.)

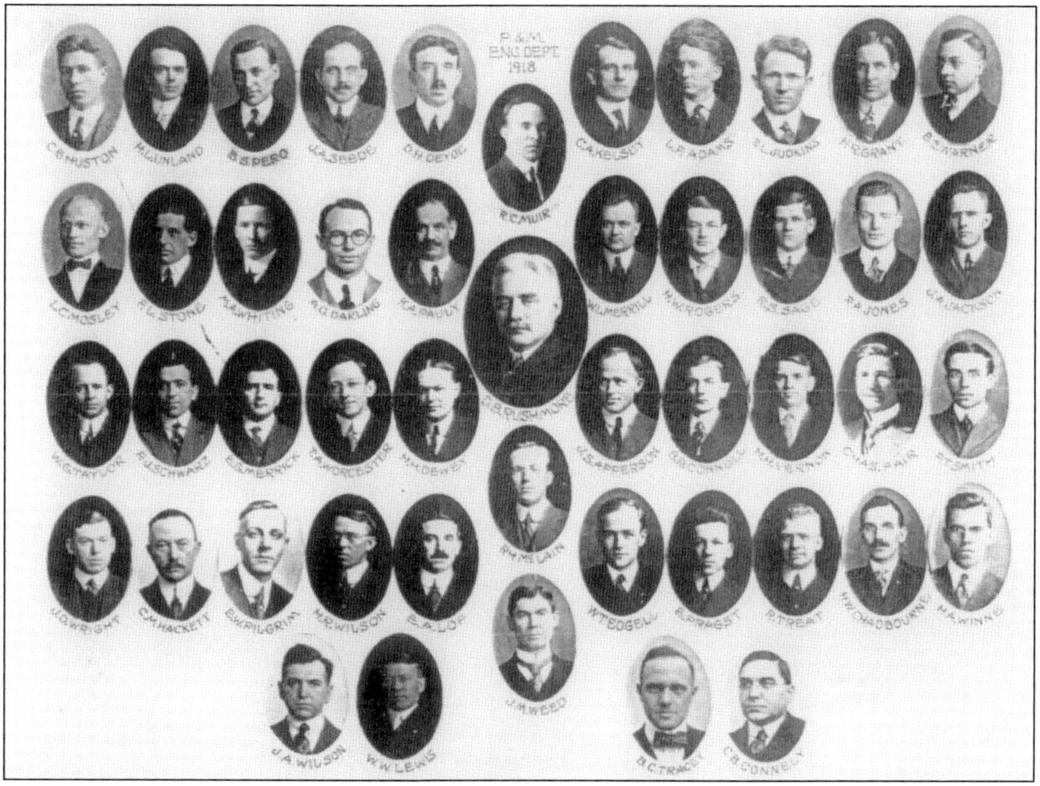

Here is a page out of a GE newsletter providing names and photographs of the engineers in the power and mining department in 1918. John Apperson appears close to center, just to the right of David Rushmore, the top man in the department. While Apperson was hauling rocks and planning excursions to Lake George, he was also earning the respect of his peers and contributing significantly to the company's success. Rushmore, his boss, was very supportive of Apperson's work as an engineer and his enthusiasm for Lake George. (Author's collection.)

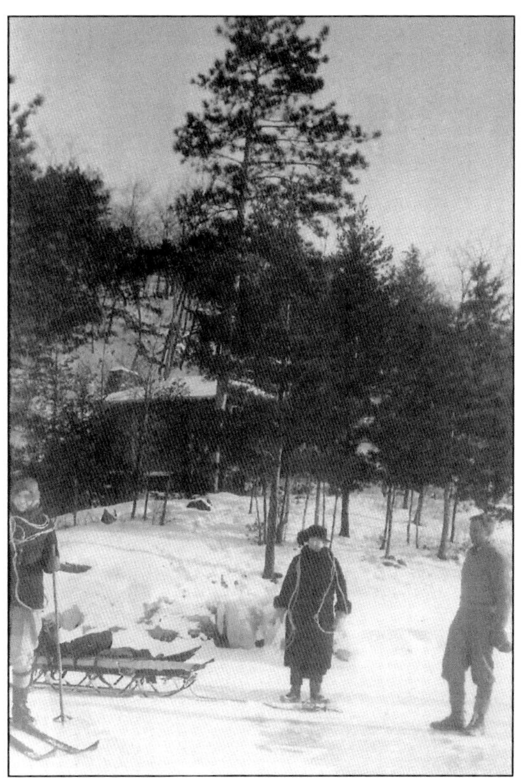

Apperson had a certain charm with the ladies, many of them college graduates, who appreciated his joyful embrace of exciting new sports. They enjoyed helping him fight political battles. These women were pleased with their new voting privileges and used their connections to help get out the vote and influence their peers. This photograph may have been taken in Northwest Bay on the Loines property. (Author's collection.)

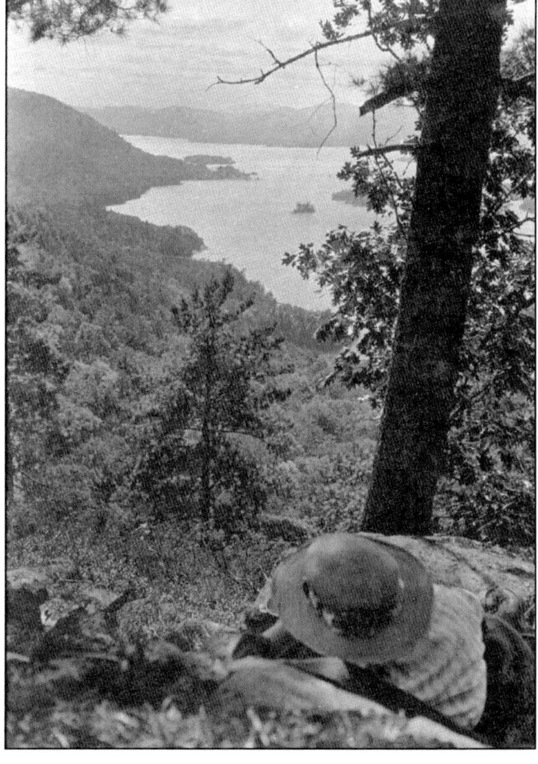

Here is a photograph of an unidentified woman wearing a straw hat while taking a hike on Black Mountain. Apperson wanted to be sure that hikers could explore all the mountains and shores around this lake and not be greeted with signs saying, "Private Property, No Trespassing." (Author's collection.)

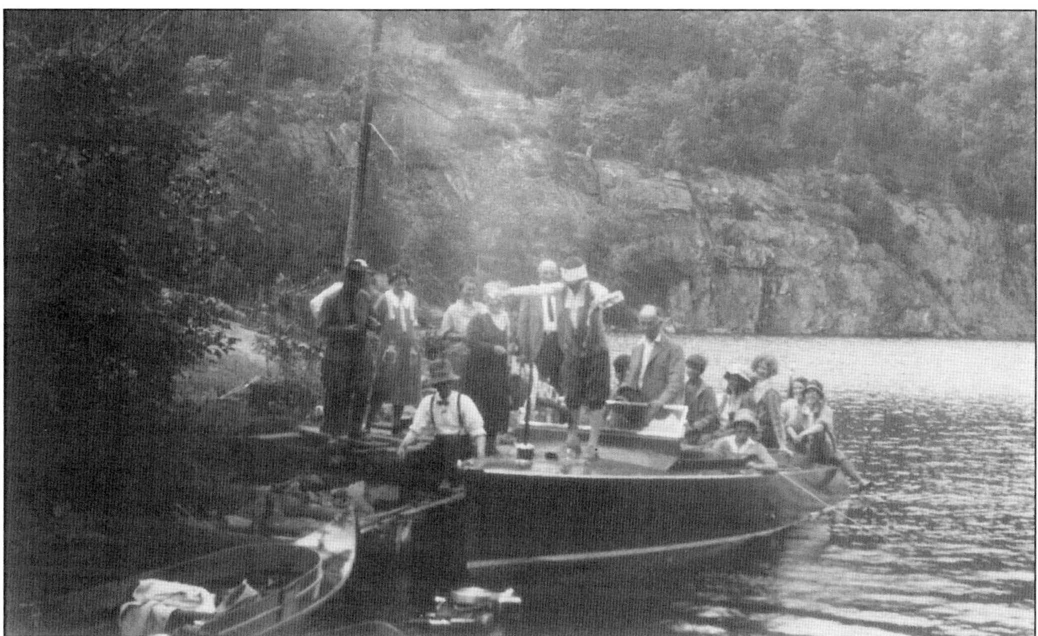

Perhaps the pinnacle of Apperson's success came in the summer of 1927, when he purchased a Chris-Craft Cadet and invited all his family from Virginia to come for a visit. His sister Nancy brought up bottles of water from Staley's Creek, and they had a little christening ceremony near Dollar Island. It was a festive occasion, and the women wore fancy hats as if they were attending a social event in a big city. Below is another photograph taken during the big family reunion. Hull Apperson is seated at the wheel, with his wife, Duncan, directly behind him, holding pillows in her lap. Their five children are there, with Hull Jr. on the left, Jim looking impish and half hidden behind his sister, Ellen. John III is getting a hug from one of his aunts, and the oldest child, Martha, is wearing a white blouse. (Both, author's collection.)

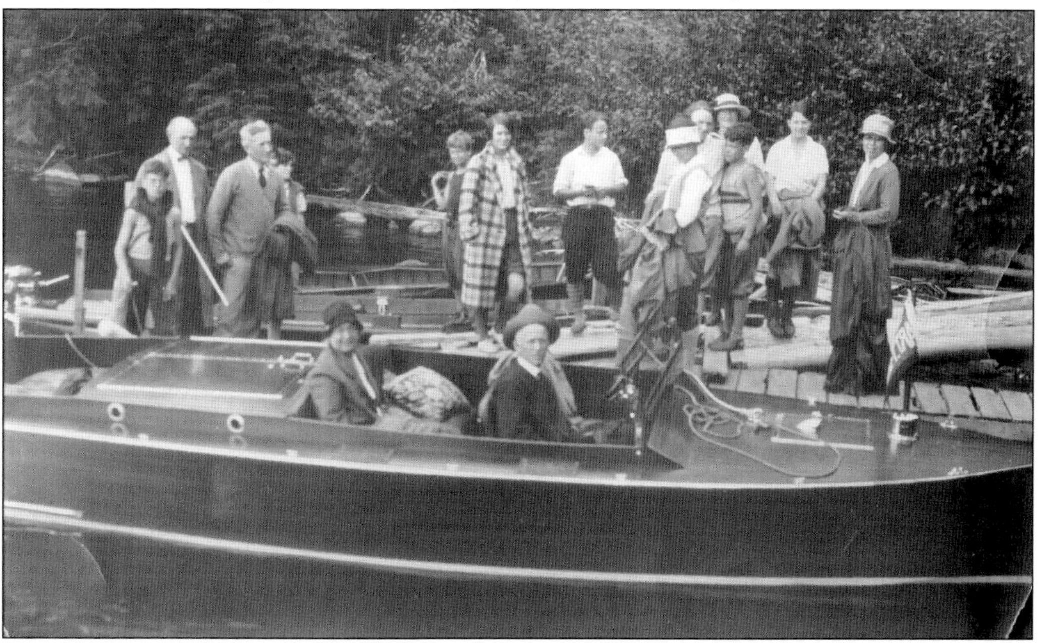

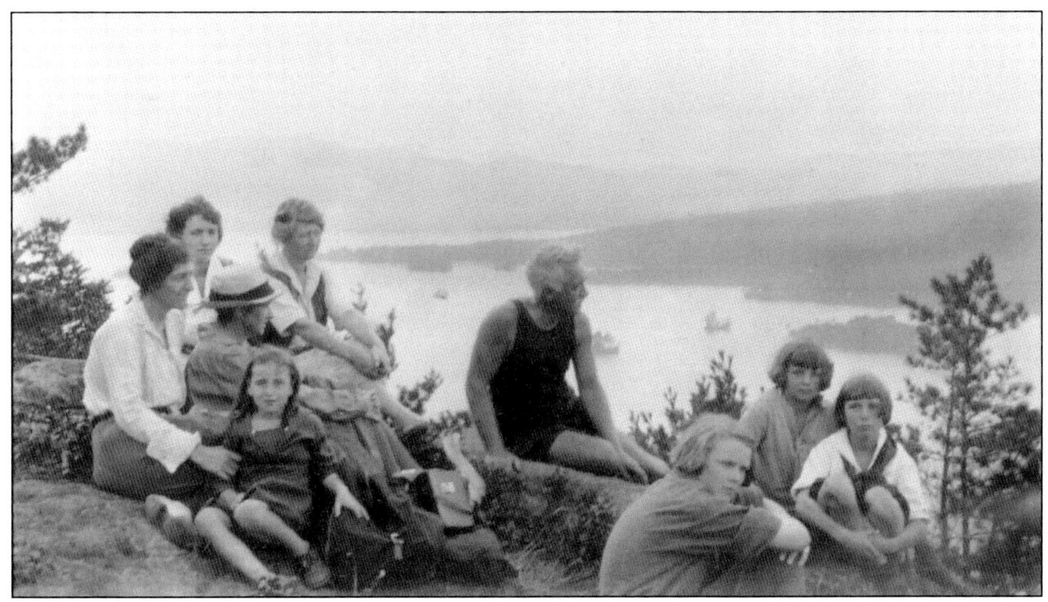

The following summer, another crowd of Virginians made the trip to visit their uncle John's slice of paradise at Lake George. This photograph was taken from the eastern side of the lake, probably during a hike up Black Mountain, looking down on Turtle Bay and Tongue Mountain. (Courtesy of KARC.)

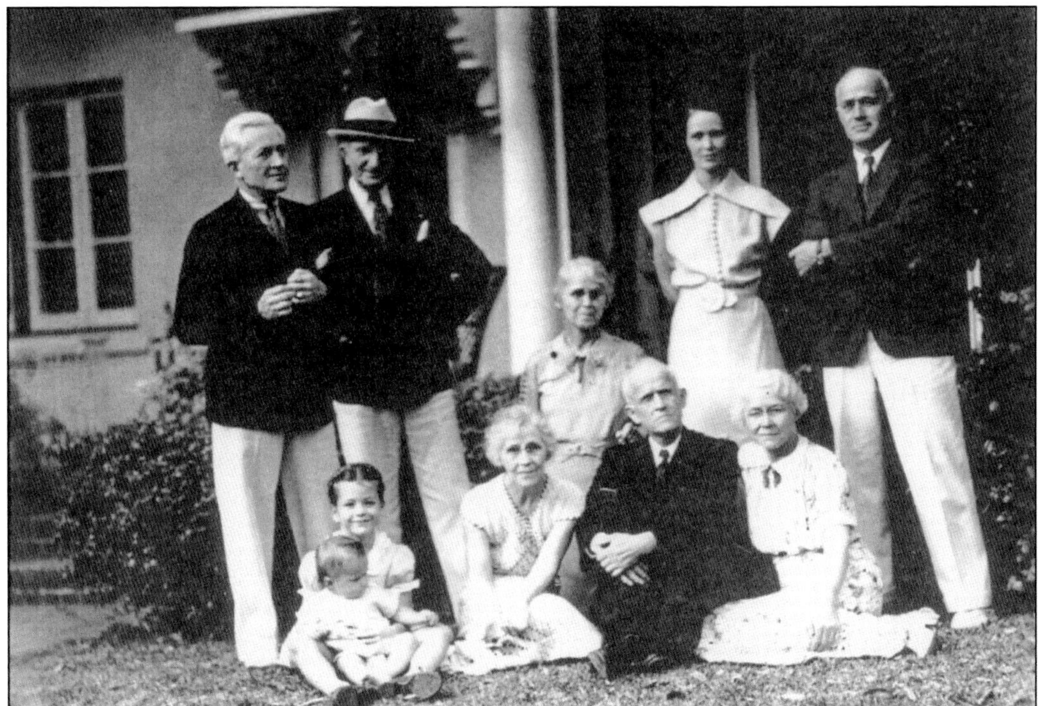

About 10 years later, the Apperson siblings and their spouses spent Christmas vacation in Florida. From left to right are (first row) Nancy and Barbara Fought, Nancy Dickinson, Hull Apperson, and Ellen Apperson; (second row) Ralph Dickinson, Lacey Tynes, Georgia Tynes, Sarah Fought, and John Apperson. (Author's collection.)

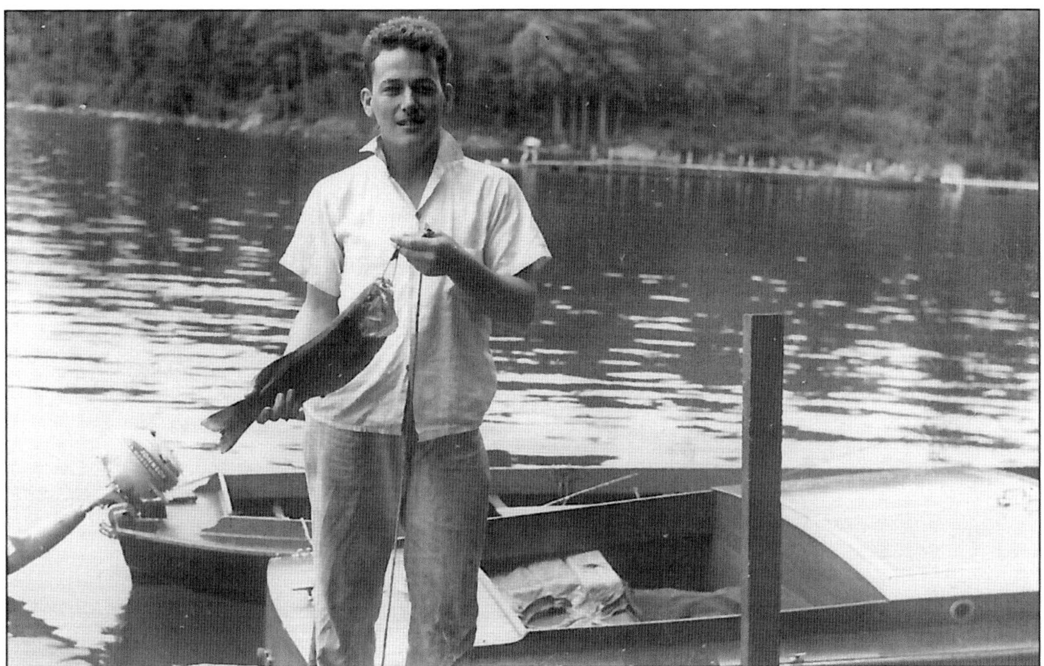

By 1942, Apperson's namesake, John Apperson III, had graduated from Virginia Polytechnic Institute with a degree in mechanical engineering and found a job working for GE in Schenectady. His uncle must have been delighted. Below, it was not long before young Apperson began courting a girl from Virginia, Katharine Hill, and invited her for a visit to Lake George. More accustomed to dancing than skating, she made a gracious attempt to participate in the unfamiliar sports then popular in Huddle Bay. (Both, author's collection.)

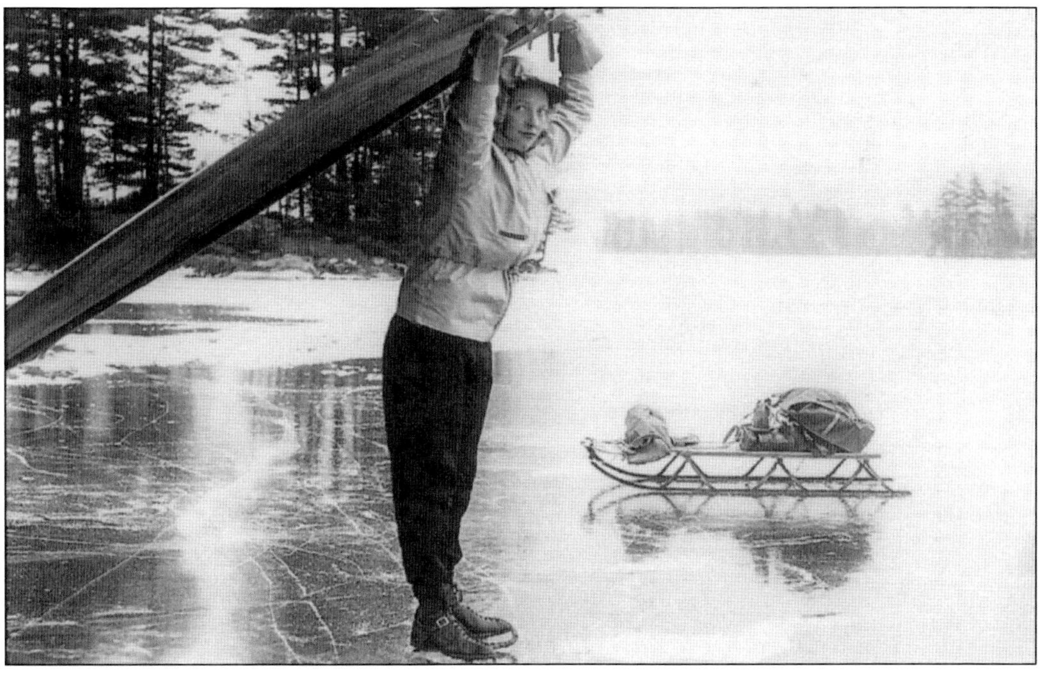

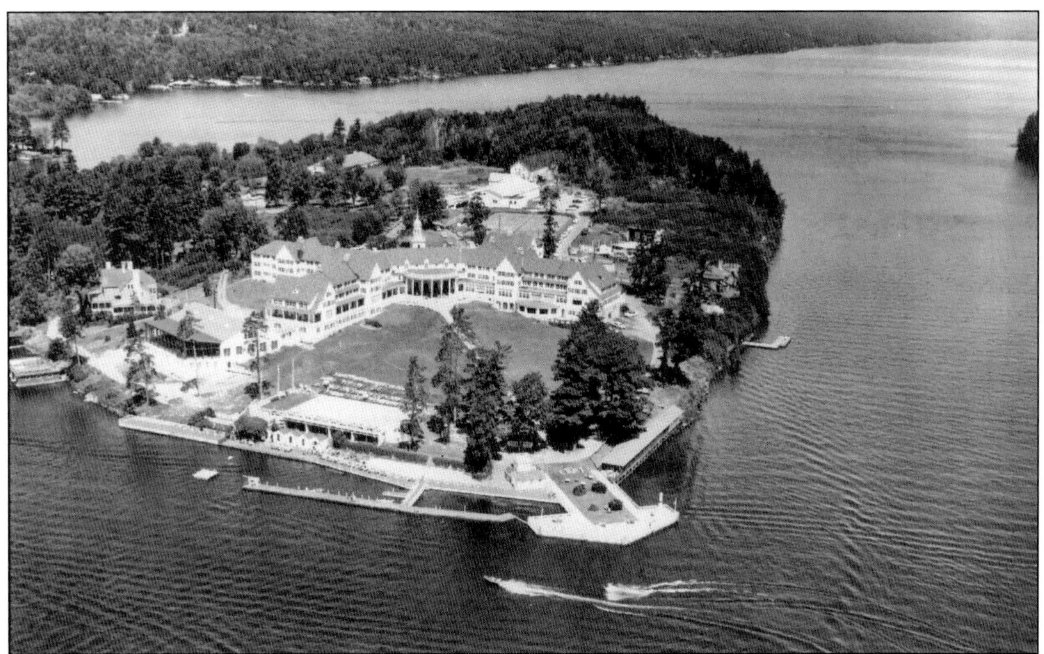

Katharine and John III spent their honeymoon at Lake George in September 1942. They spent a few nights at the Sagamore Hotel, and she often remarked about the luxurious accommodations. Otherwise, they stayed at John Apperson's camp in Huddle Bay. Katharine had never learned to cook, so her new husband had to teach her how to boil water over a wood stove. (Author's collection.)

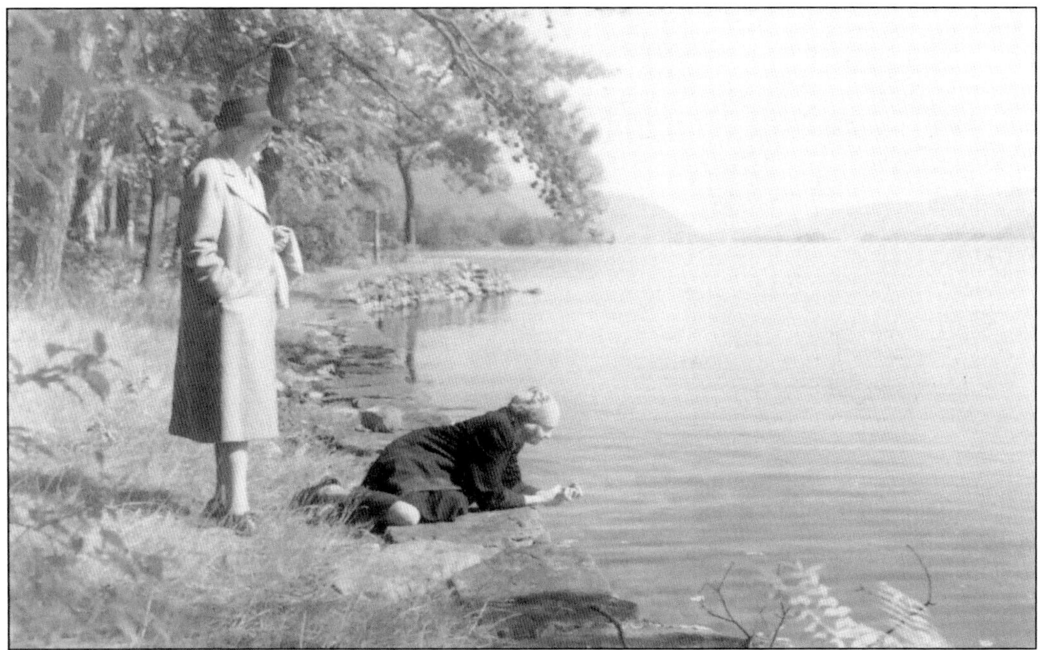

In the early 1950s, Katharine Apperson's mother, Katherine Hill (right) and her mother-in-law, Duncan Apperson, made a joint trip to Schenectady and Lake George to visit their grandchildren. John Apperson took them out for a ride in his boat, and they enjoyed the beautiful view of the lake from French Point. (Author's collection.)

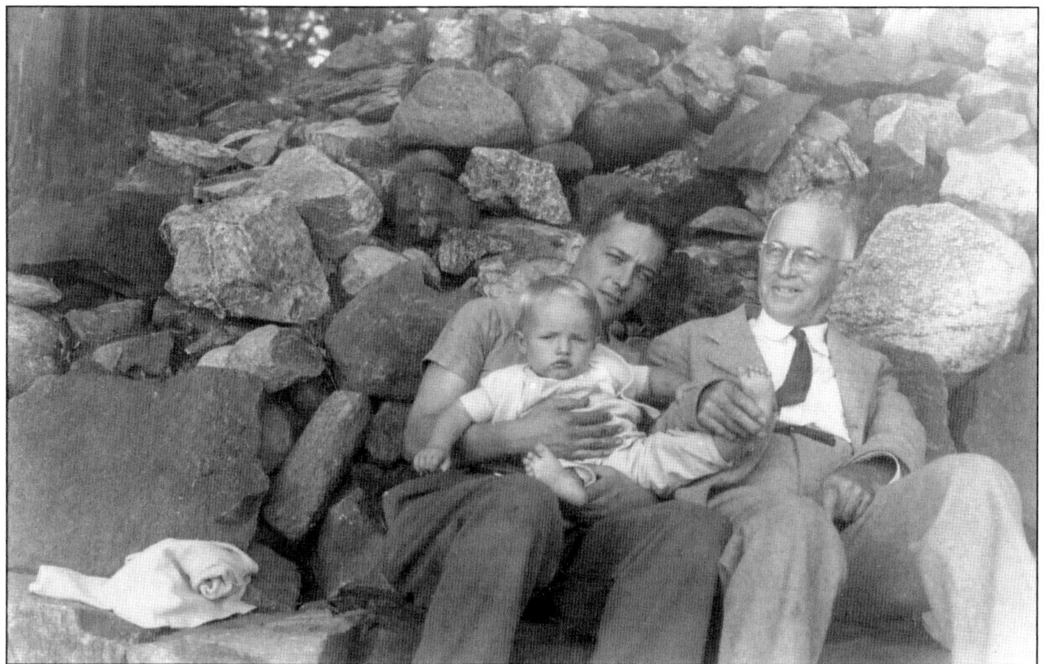

By 1944, John Apperson IV was born to Katharine and John. A friend had the good sense to capture this photograph of the three generations. (Author's collection.)

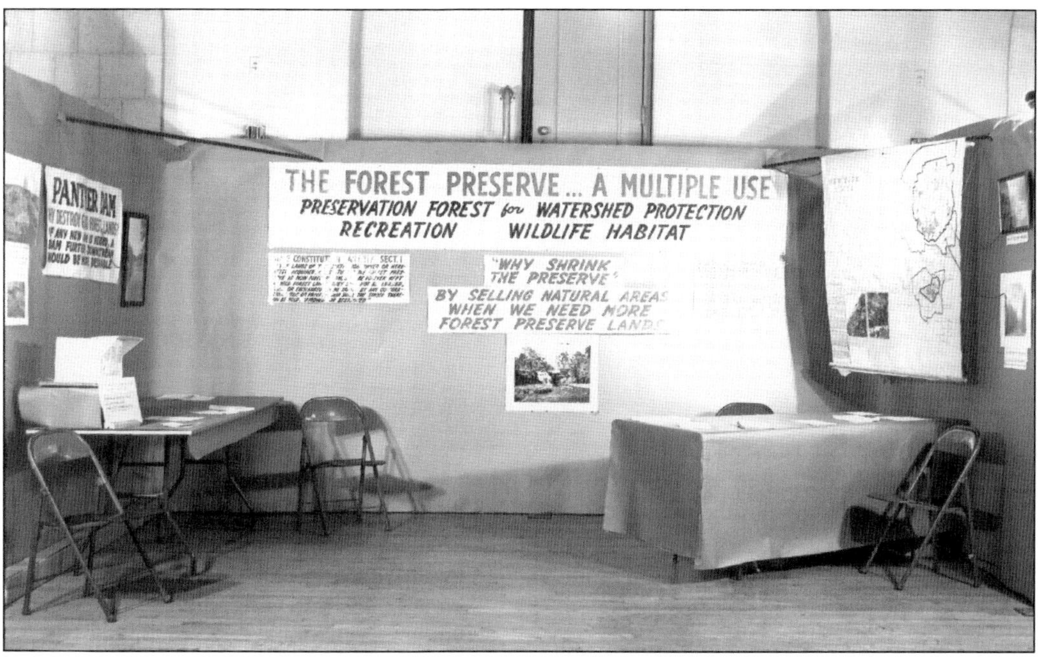

During the 1940s, Apperson turned over the leadership of many battles to his friend and protégé, Paul Schaefer, but helped provide educational materials and moral support. Here is an exhibit Apperson helped design as part of the important battle known as the Black River Dam War. (Author's collection.)

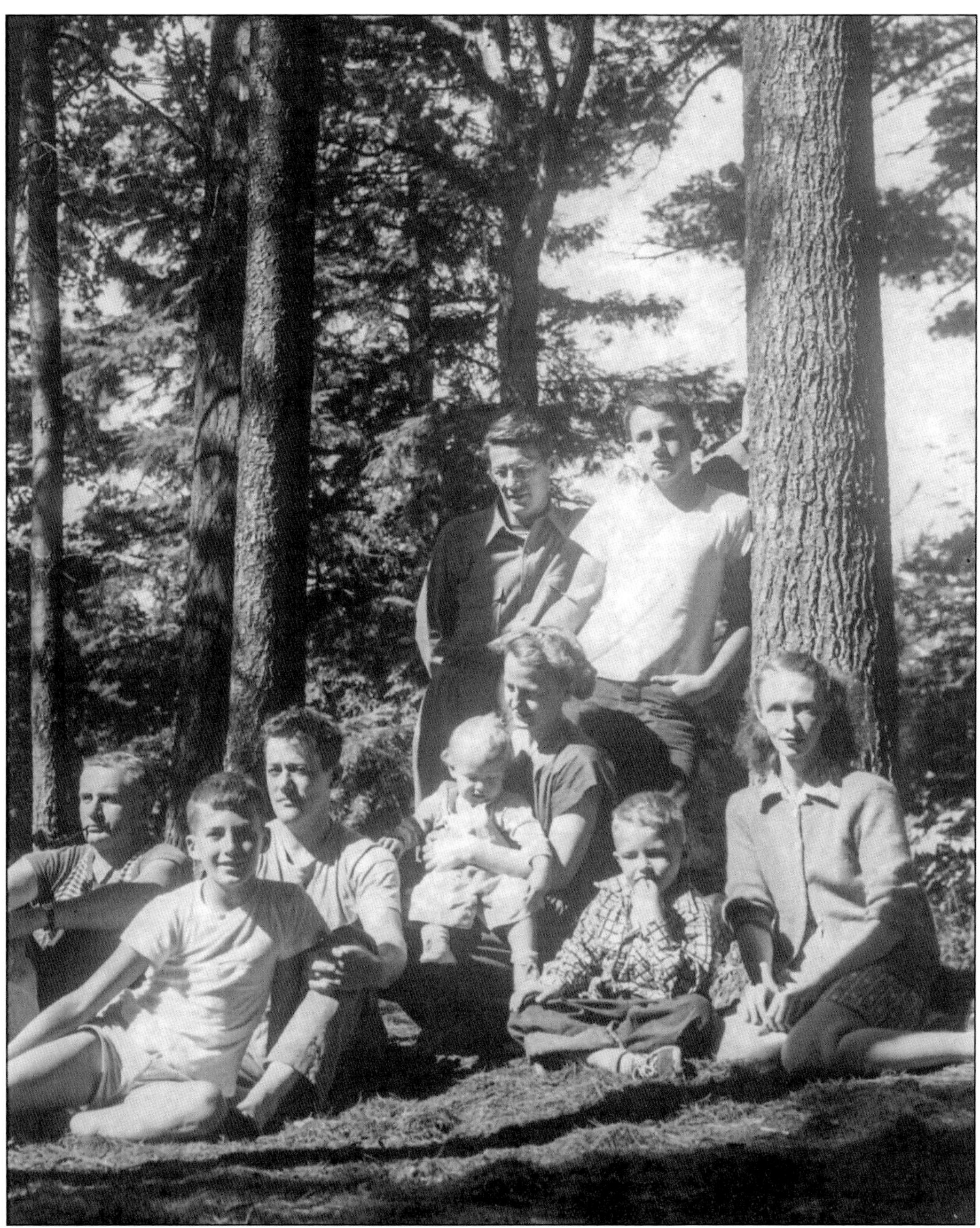

In the summer of 1950, Ellen Apperson DeVoe, one of Apperson's nieces, came up with her husband and two boys, Garner and Jimmy, to spend a vacation at the lake. From left to right are (seated) Garner DeVoe Sr., Jimmy DeVoe, John Apperson III, Tommy Apperson, Ellen DeVoe, John Apperson IV, and Katharine Apperson; (standing) Jim Apperson and Garner DeVoe Jr. These trees blew down in a storm in December of that year. (Author's collection.)

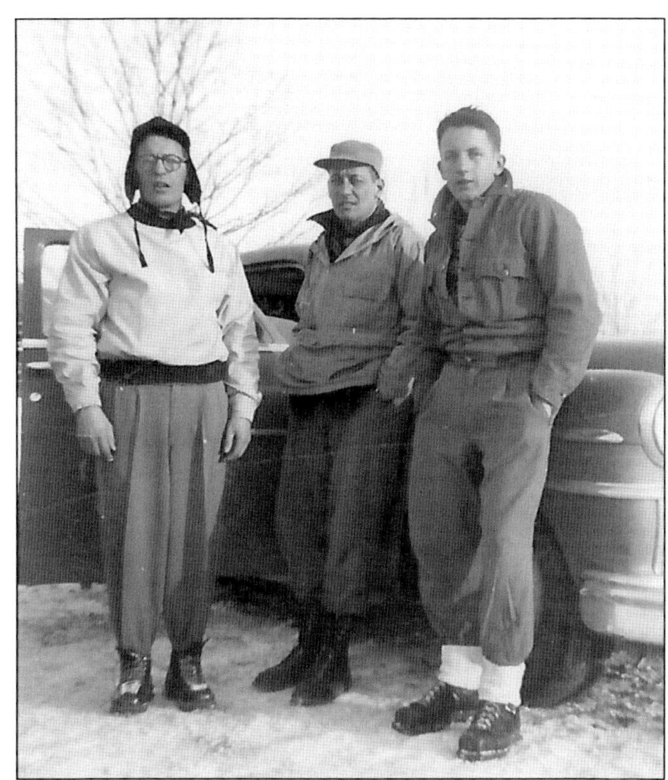

Apperson's nephews John III and Jim both enjoyed skiing and were happy to try out commercial ski slopes whenever possible. Their uncle still insisted on winter sports the old-fashioned way. At right, in the 1950s, Apperson's nephews invited their nephew, Garner DeVoe, who was serving in the Air Force in Plattsburg, New York, to spend a weekend at the lake. Below are the three again, standing in front of the Main Camp with Uncle John, preparing to climb Appie Top. (Both, author's collection.)

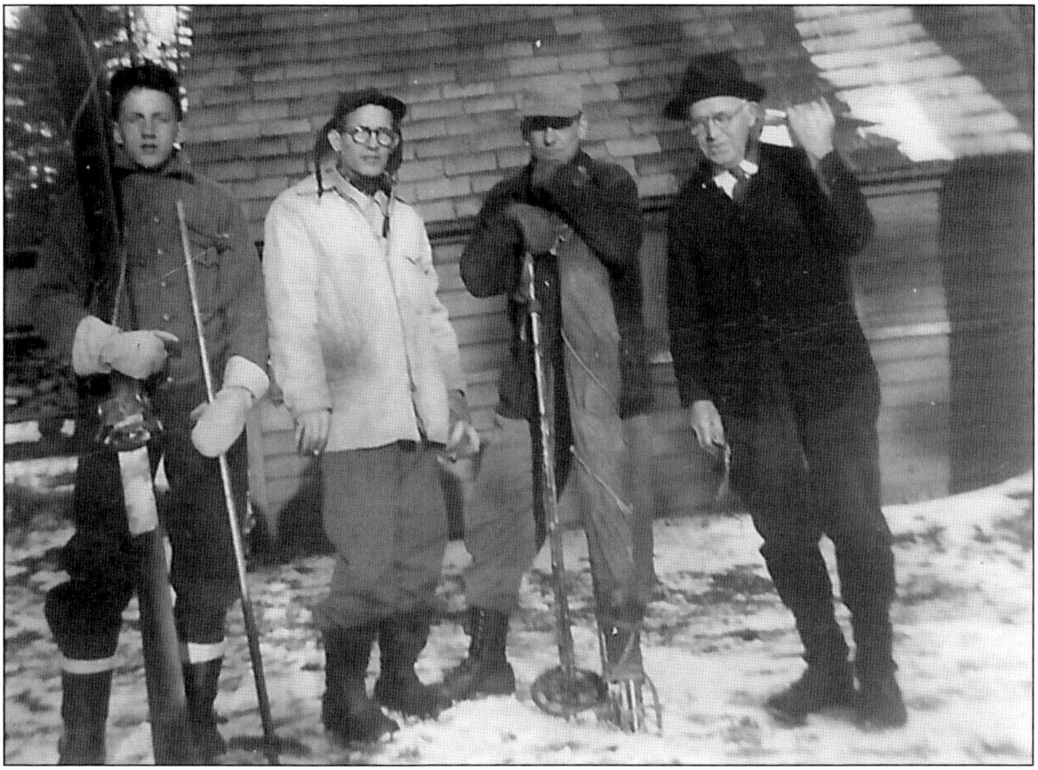

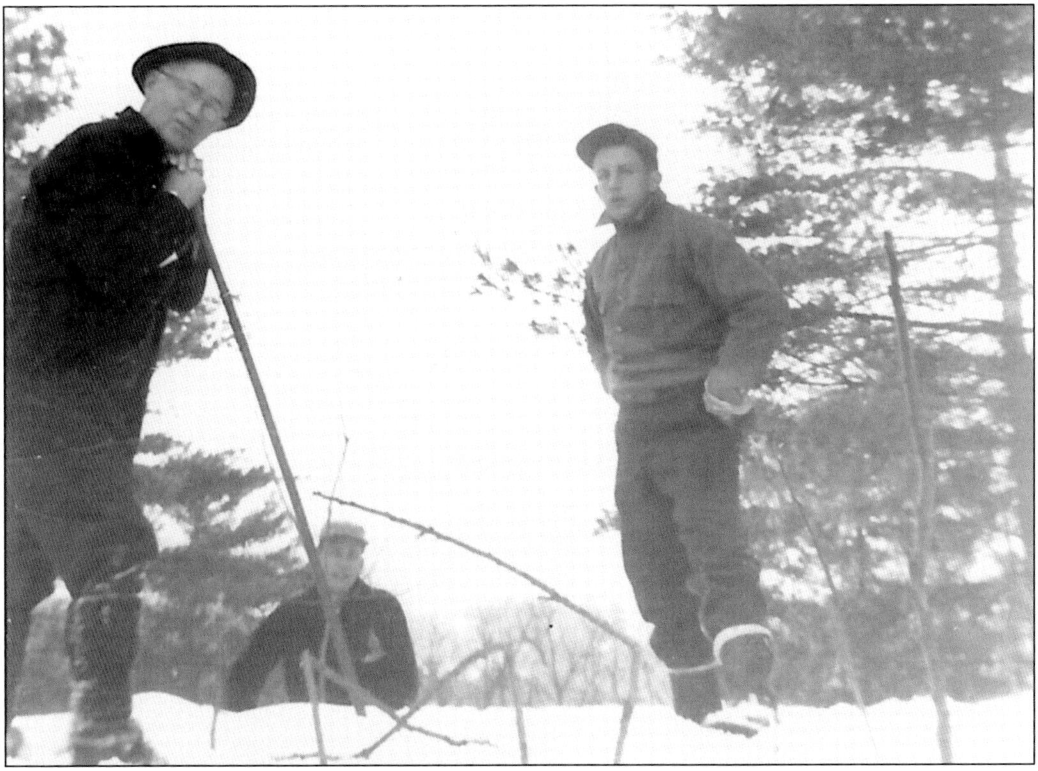

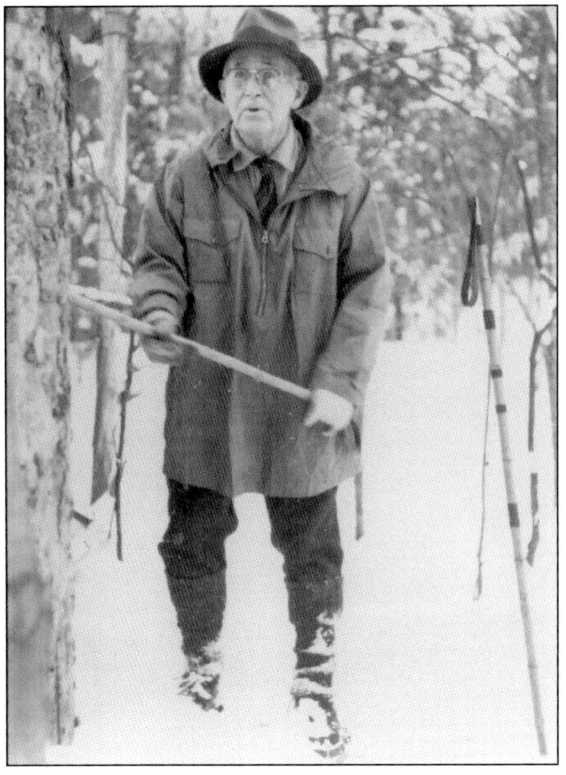

Apperson, now about 75 years old, is pictured here on the climb to Appie Top leaning on a long hiking stick. At left is another photograph of him from about the same time, measuring the growth of trees he had planted. In 1956, John Apperson III moved to Erie, Pennsylvania, so Jim Apperson, who had been working as a metallurgist for GE in Lynn, Maine, transferred to Schenectady and moved into his uncle's house on Teviot Road. He looked out for his uncle and spent time with Florence Christie by playing card games, eating her home-cooked meals, and keeping her laughing with his teasing ways. By the time his uncle John died, Jim had already purchased back the deed to Christie's property for $1, the same price she and Kilgore had paid in 1928. (Both, courtesy of KARC.)

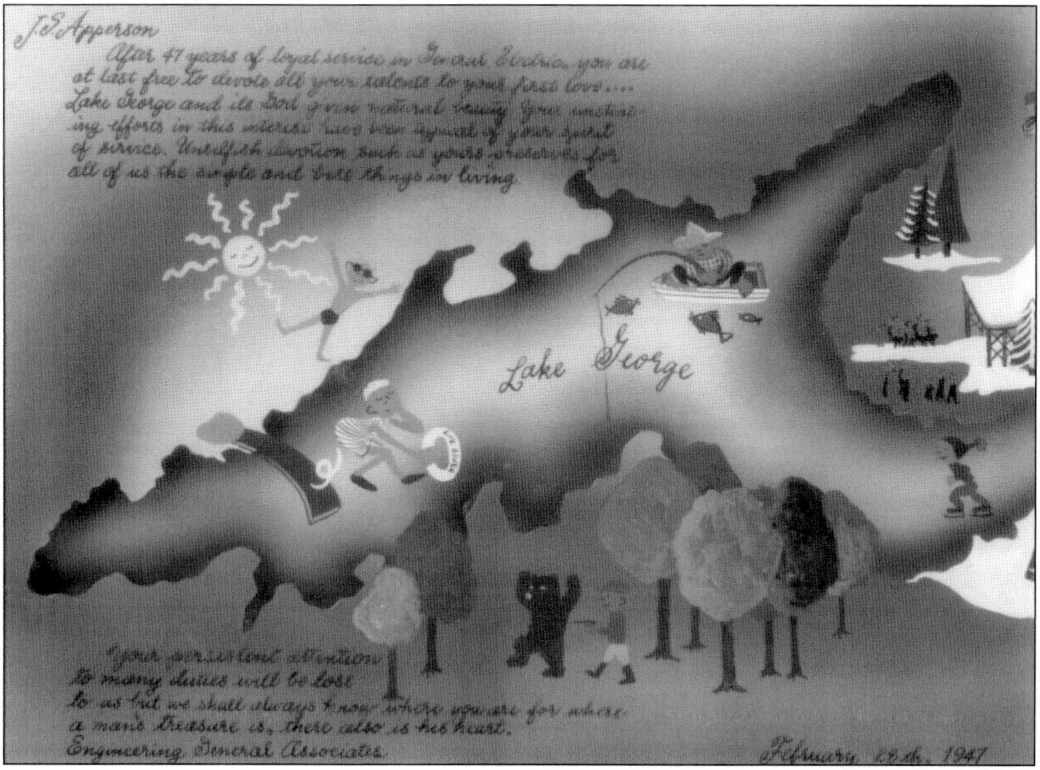

Despite all the enemies Apperson may have made over the span of more than 50 years, he had earned the sincere respect and gratitude from his colleagues at GE. This artwork was presented to him in 1947 as a tribute to his 47-year career and in recognition of all his accomplishments at Lake George. (Author's collection.)

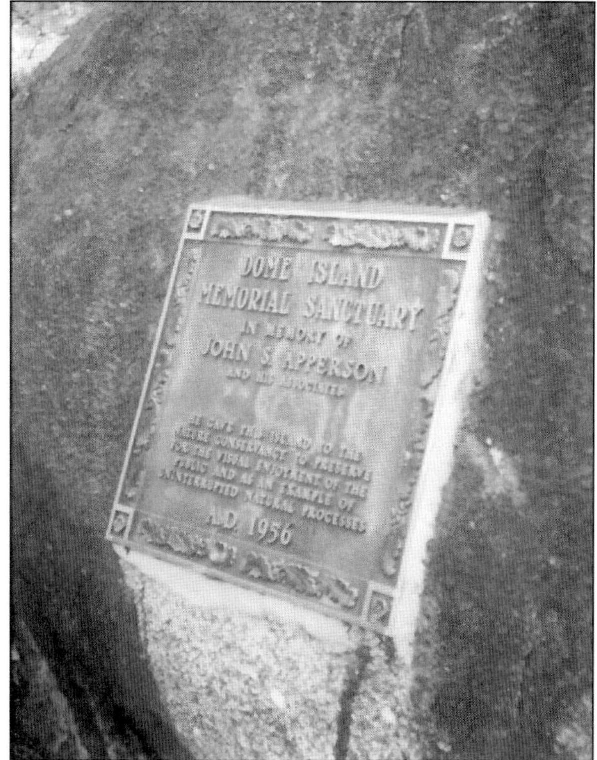

When John Apperson gave Dome Island to the Nature Conservancy in 1956, his friends raised $20,000 as a sort of endowment, and a special committee was formed to watch over the island in perpetuity. The Eastern New York chapter of the Nature Conservancy still maintains a special Dome Island fund, and a committee still meets several times a year to talk about problems and concerns. Apperson's friends also raised money to erect a bronze plaque on the island. The author took this photograph of the plaque about 20 years ago. (Author's collection.)

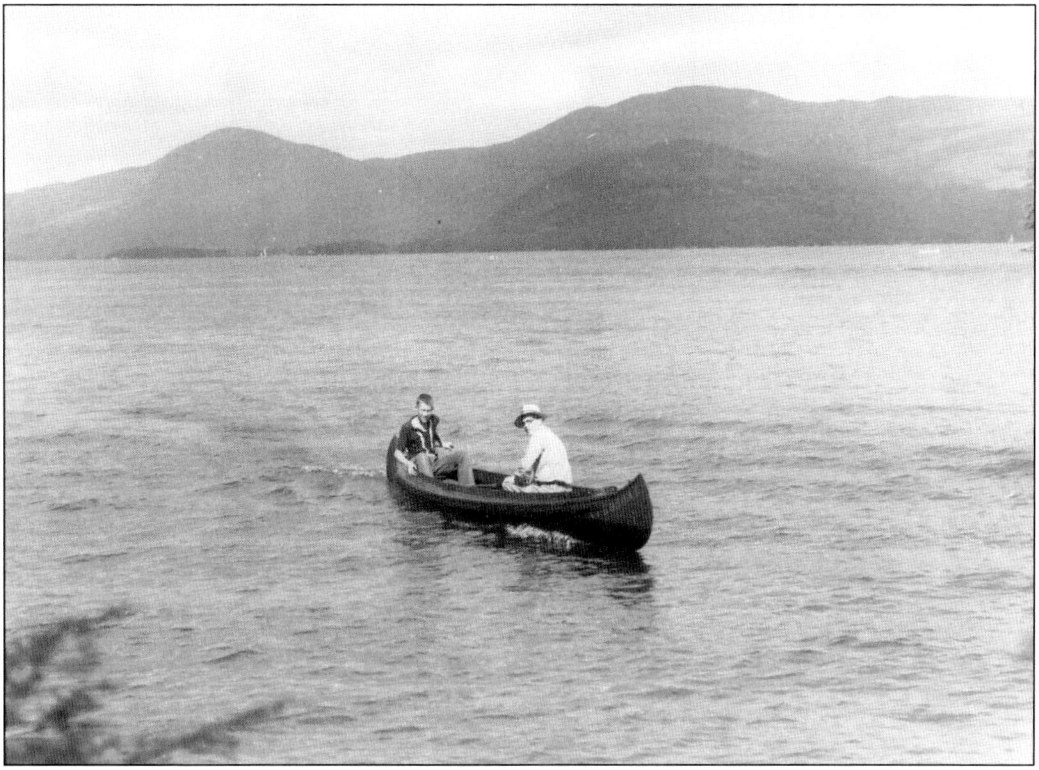

In the summer of 1962, great nephew Tom Apperson had a chance to spend a month or so at Lake George, listening to all the stories and learning how to do things properly. He is seen here, out in the old canvas canoe with his uncle Jim. His great uncle John Apperson Jr. died the following January 31, 1963. (Author's collection.)

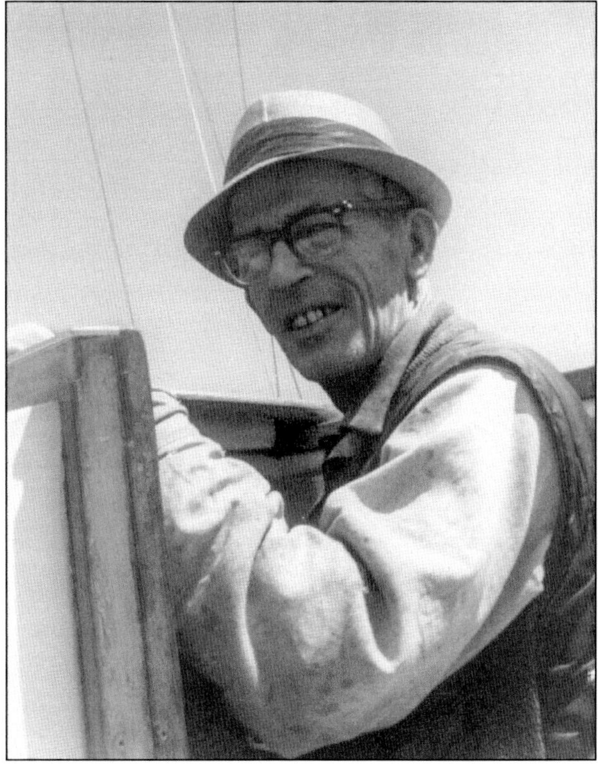

Jim Apperson always enjoyed wearing work clothes, but he had a remarkable mind and heart. At least four couples named their sons after him, including Ellen and Garner DeVoe. When his brother's wife, Katharine, was diagnosed with tuberculosis in 1952 and had to be sent off to a special sanitarium, Jim came over from Lynn, Massachusetts, almost every weekend to help his brother take care of the three children. (Author's collection.)

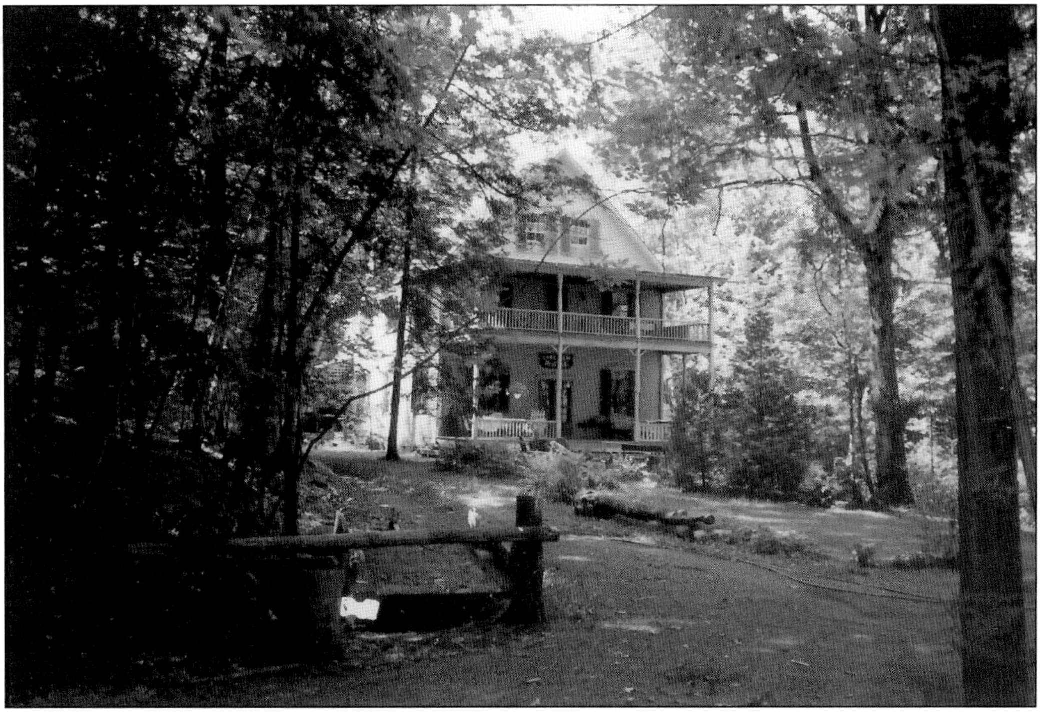

Florence Christie came to the lake every summer, even after she could no longer drive, with lots of help from Jim Apperson. She will be remembered for her peanut butter cookies and her warm hospitality. This is the way her annex looked in 1994. Below is a view of the side entrance to Lake View House. There was a large ballroom immediately to the right. (Both, author's collection.)

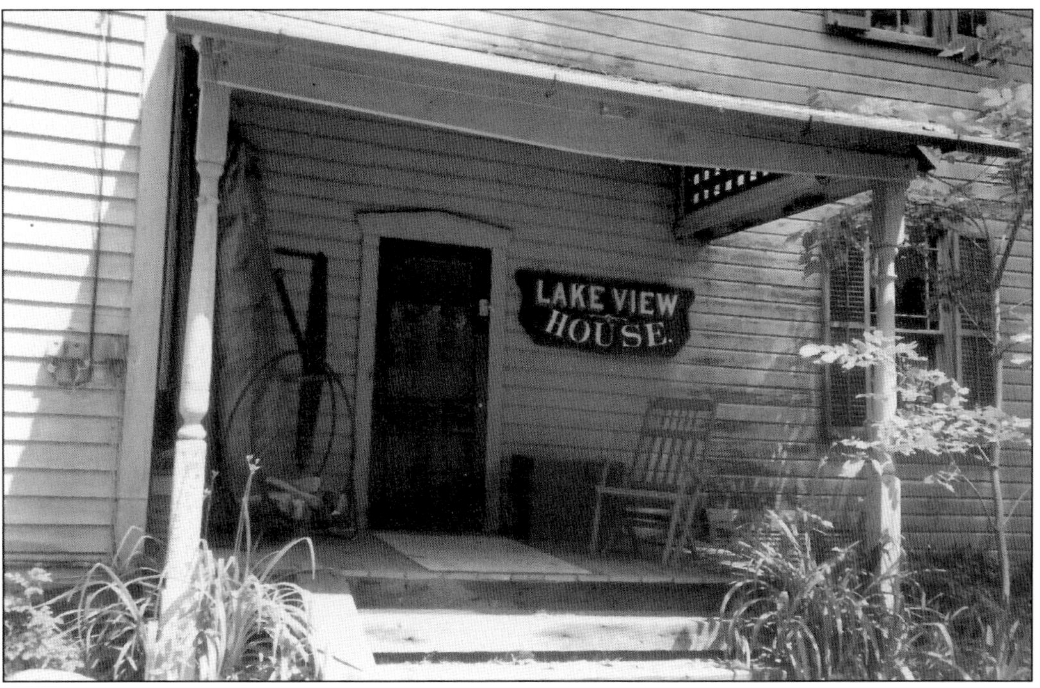

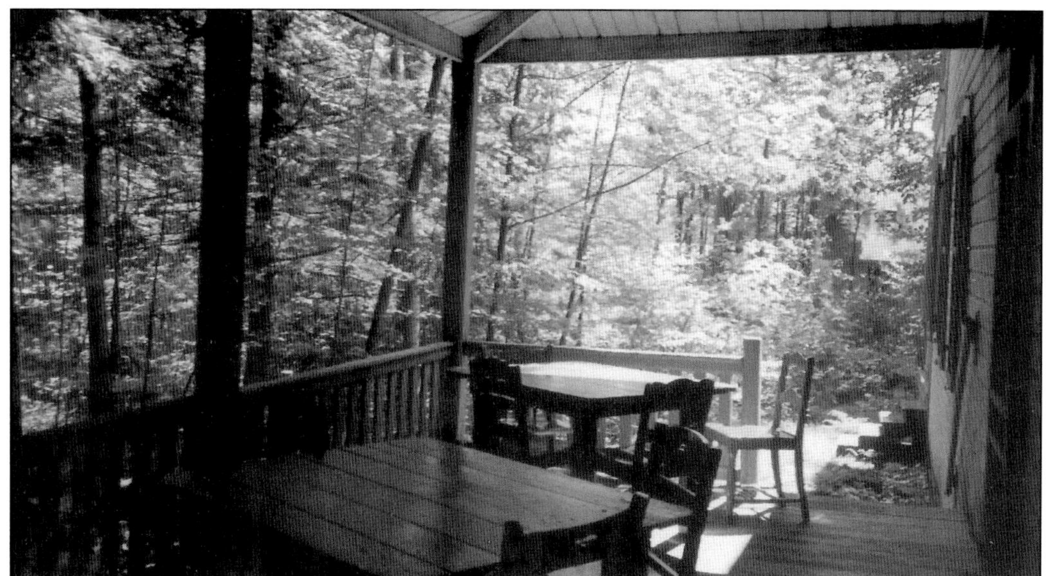

This porch is where Florence Christie would serve meals in the summertime. She expected her guests to wear shoes and for girls to wear dresses, not pants. She taught her guests about the traditions of serving a five-course meal. Often, the Appersons brought her a Smithfield ham from Virginia, to her delight. (Author's collection.)

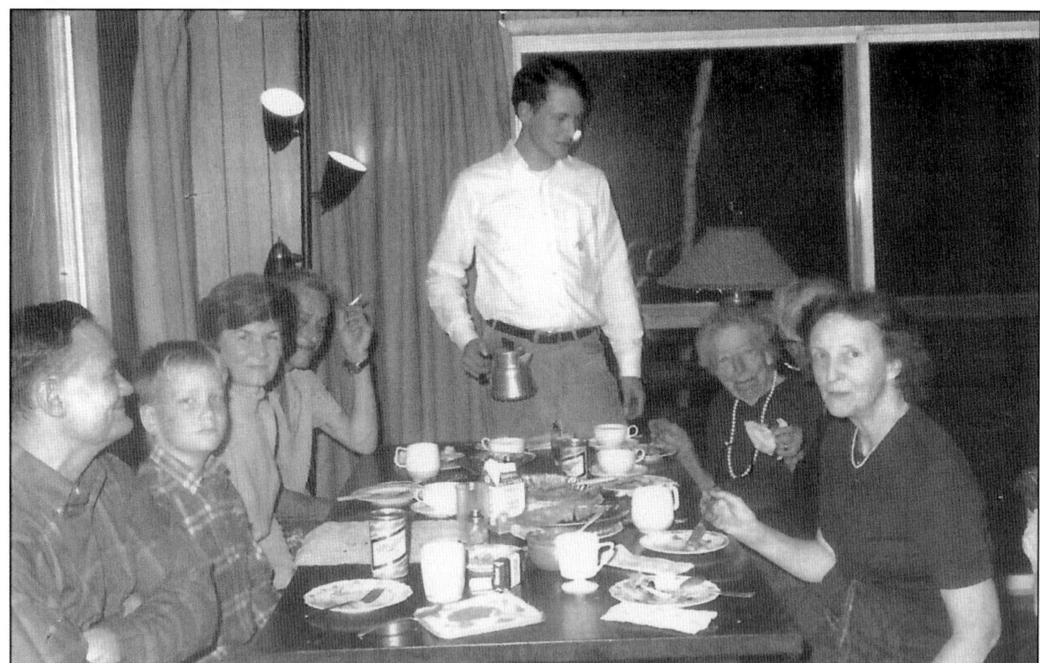

In the fall of 1971, John Apperson III was diagnosed with cancer. He and Katharine stayed a month or so at the lake, spending the daytime hours at Camp Chilhowie but the nights at the neighbor's winterized camp, the home of Doug and Arlene Langdon. This is a poignant record of a special meal they had together. From left to right are Doug Langdon, Christopher Langdon, Roberta Luce, John Apperson III, Tom Apperson (standing), Florence Christie, Jim Apperson, and Katharine Apperson. (Author's collection)

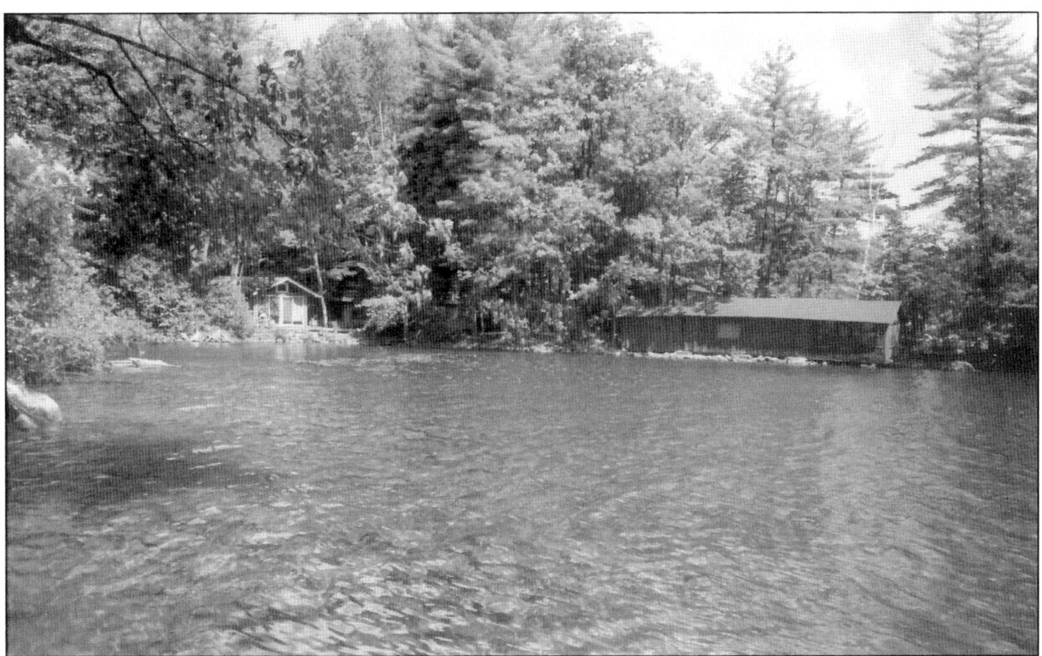

The Langdons have been good neighbors to the Appersons. They now own this camp, built in 1928 or so in Huddle Bay, which belonged to Douglas's aunt Katie, or Dr. Katharine Blodgett, a famous scientist at GE. (Author's collection.)

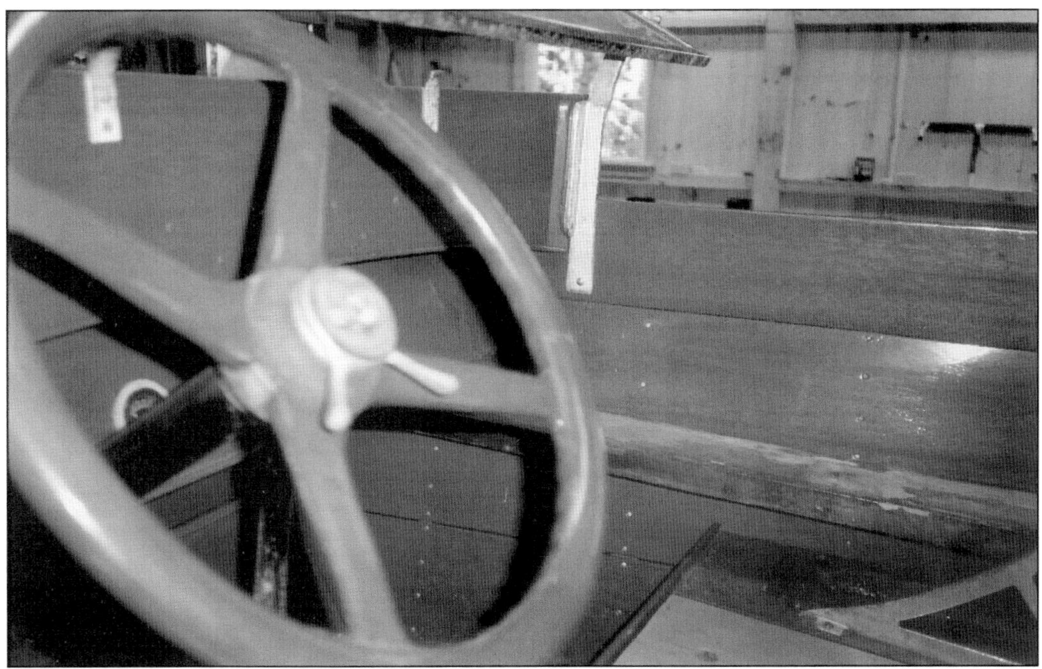

John Apperson's Chris-Craft Cadet now belongs to Chris Langdon, son of Douglas and Arlene Langdon. It has been fully restored and can be seen again on Lake George. (Author's collection.)

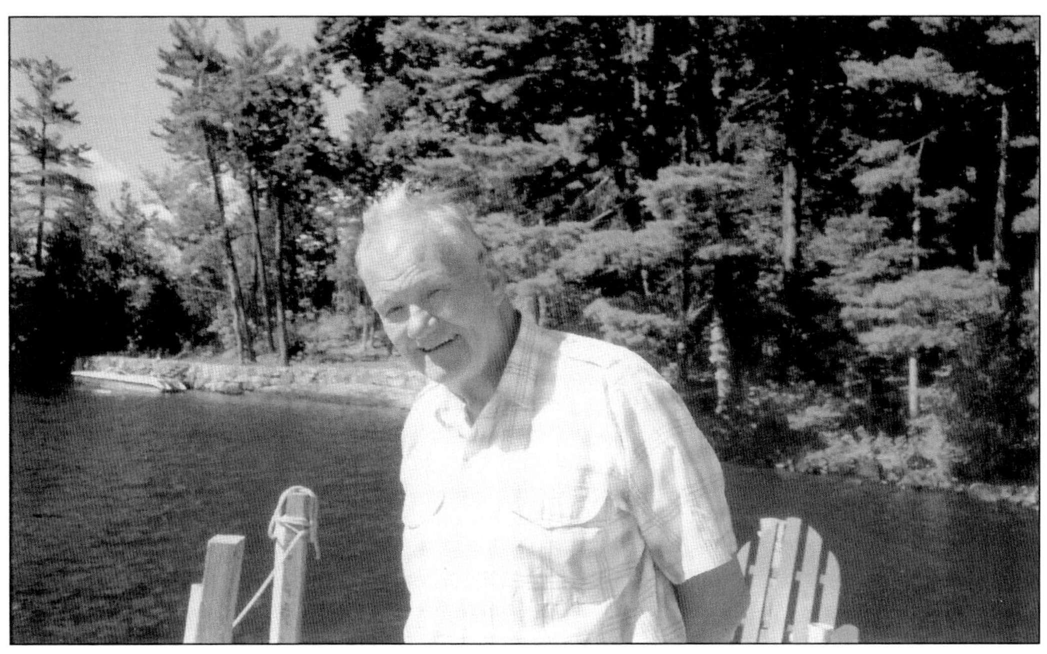

The author had the pleasure of riding out to Dome Island with Doug Langdon on their way to a meeting of the Dome Island Committee. Langdon continues to offer hospitality to members of the Apperson family and remind them of their mutual affection. Below, Roger Summerhayes joined the boat ride in 1999 or so. He is the grandson of Irving Langmuir and maintains a beautiful summer home on Crown Island. He has made a documentary film about the famous scientist and serves faithfully on the Dome Island Committee. (Both, author's collection.)

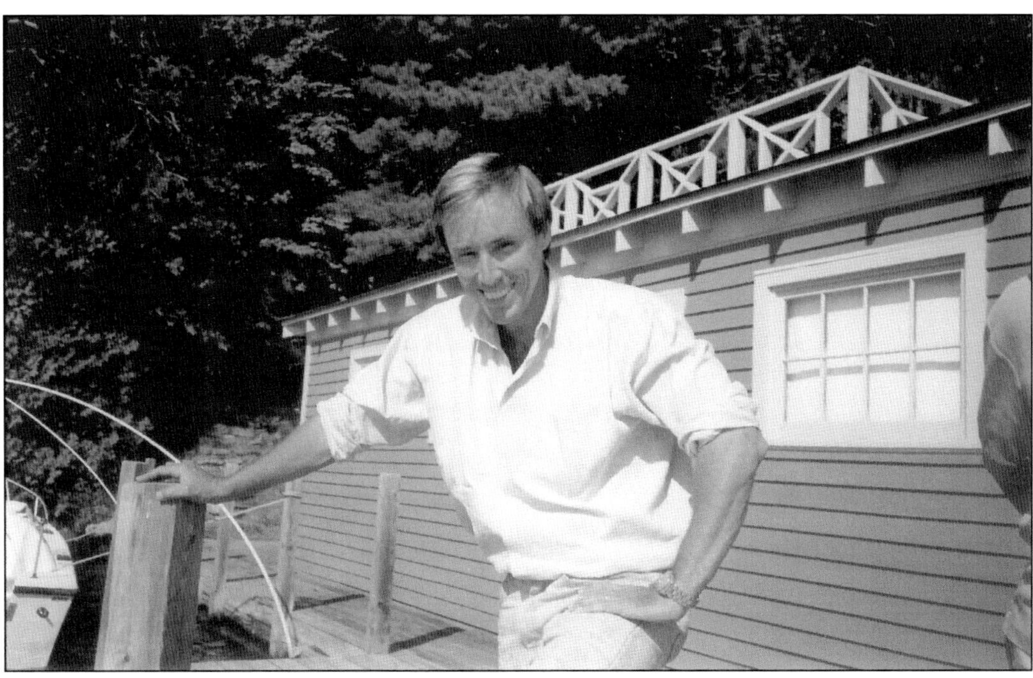

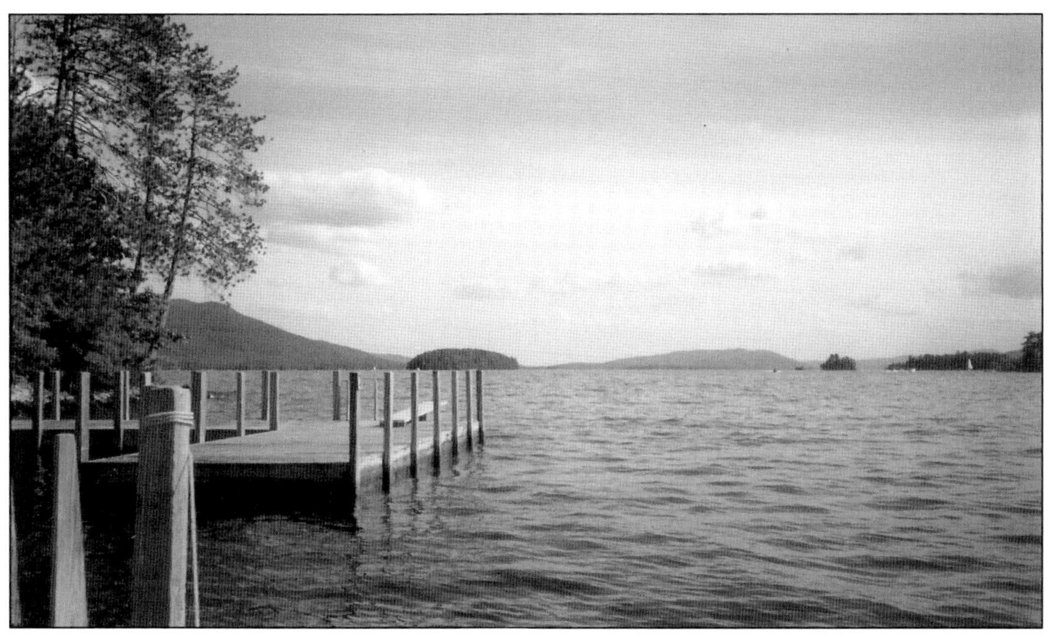

Seen above is the view of Dome Island from Roger Summerhayes's dock on Crown Island. Below is the view of Dome Island from Bill White's camp near Bolton. (Both, author's collection.)

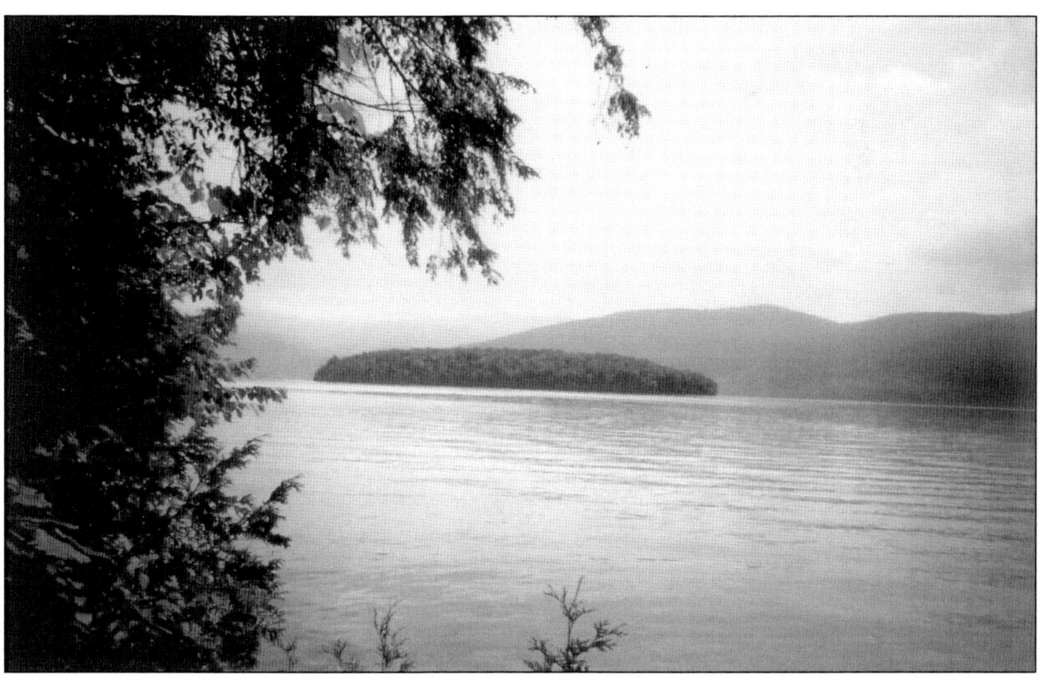

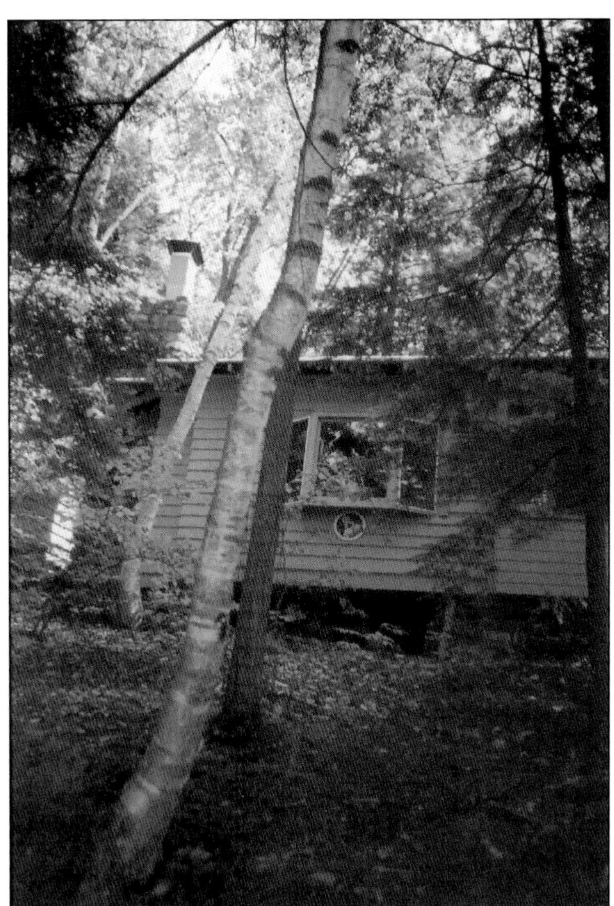

Bill White was a volunteer at the Adirondack Research Library for many years and probably did more research in the Apperson papers than anyone else. He purchased a camp that once belonged to John Apperson on the west side of Tongue Mountain and took the author out to see it in 1999. It was called "the Playhouse." Below is a photograph of Bill White sitting in front of the Playhouse in 1999. (Both, author's collection.)

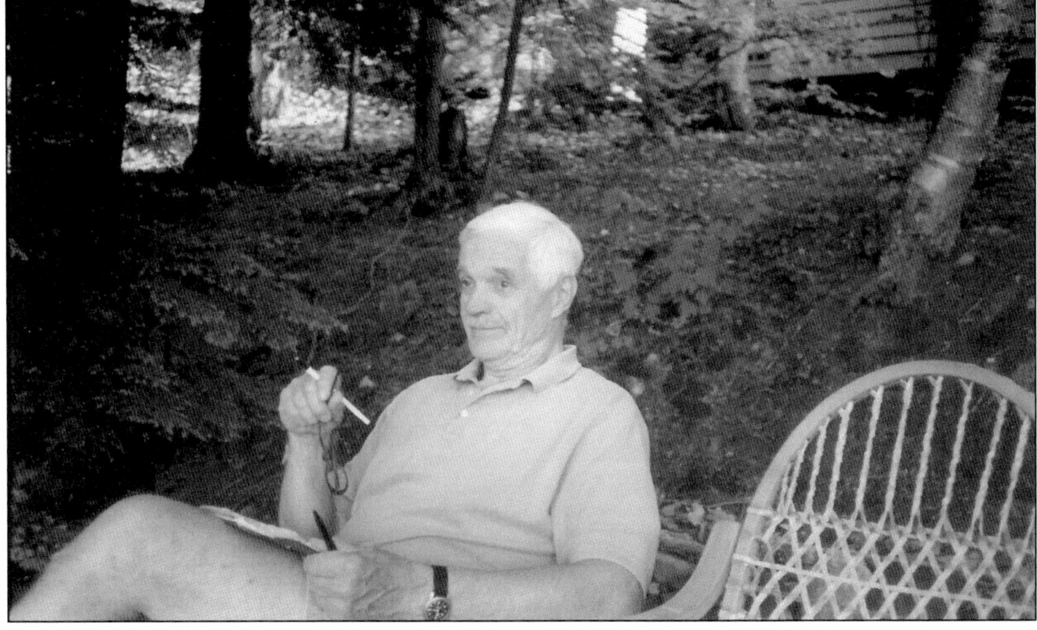

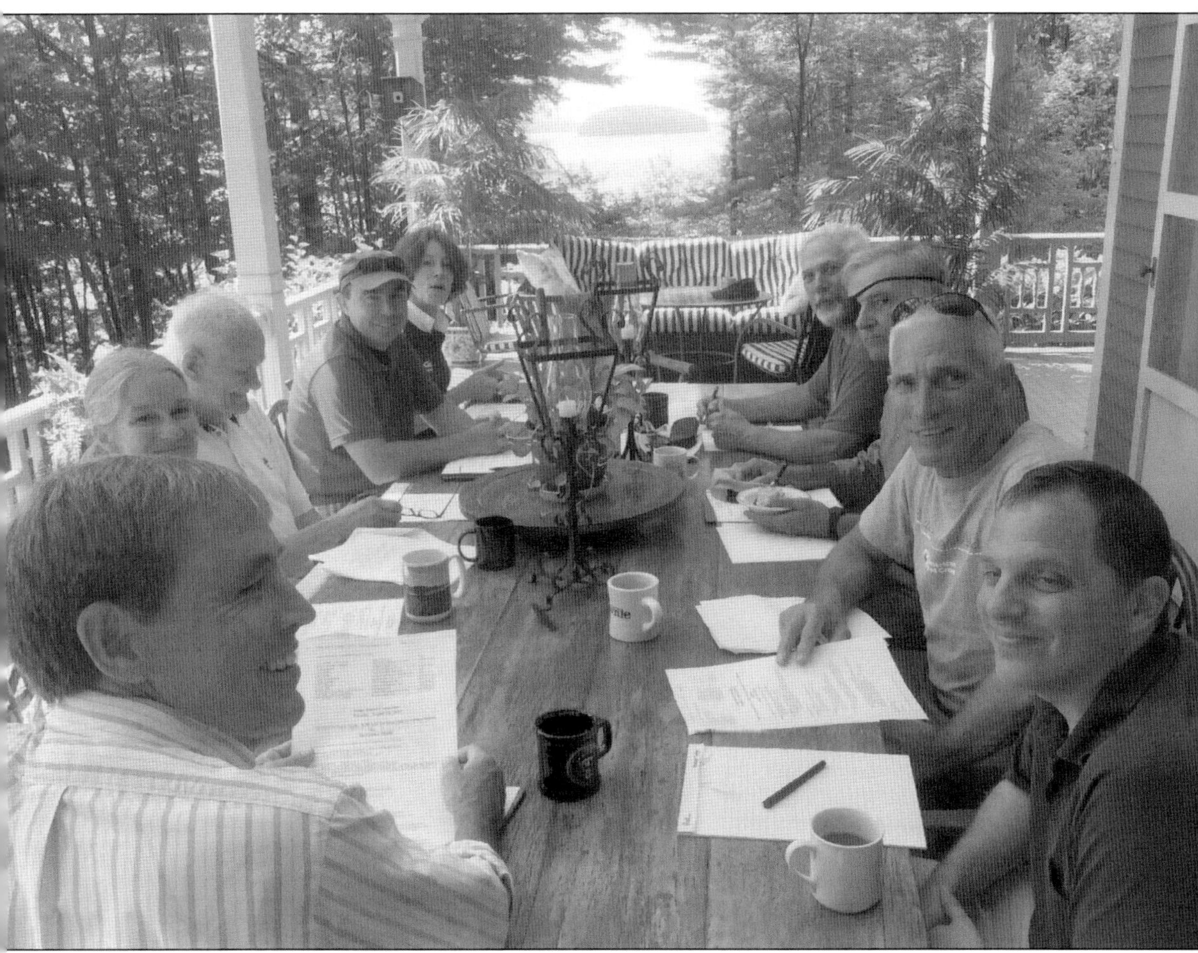

In the summer of 2016, the Dome Island Committee held its annual meeting on Crown Island. Here, looking out from the porch, is a perfect view of Dome Island. Seated clockwise from left to right are Roger Summerhayes, Emily Van Dyke, Doug Langdon, Troy Weldy (of the Nature Conservancy), Laura Finley, Peter White, Alexander Gabriels, John Gaddy, and Jamie Brown (of the Lake George Land Conservancy.) (Courtesy of Henry Caldwell.)

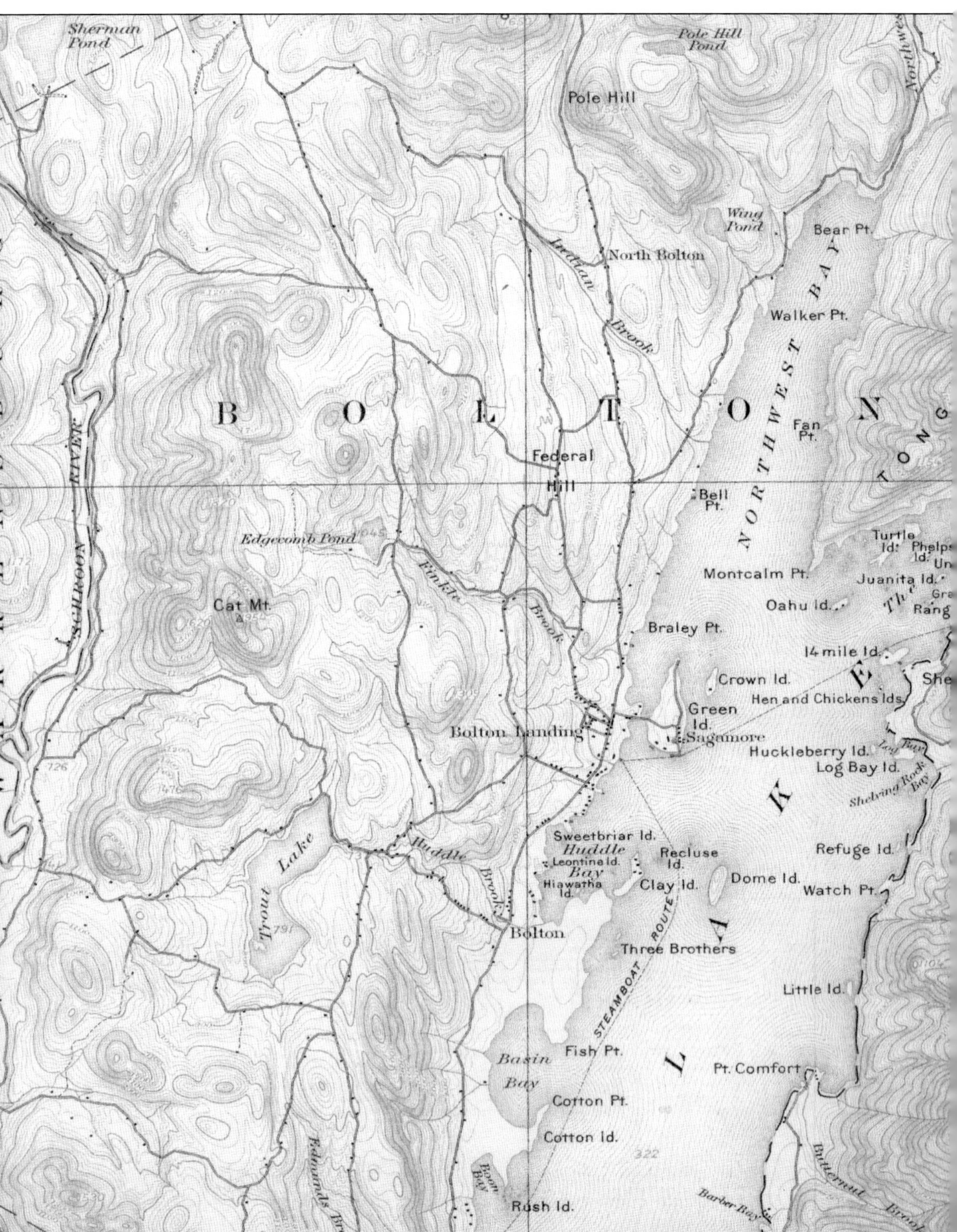
Sherman Pond
Pole Hill Pond
Pole Hill
Wing Pond
Bear Pt.
North Bolton
Indian Brook
Walker Pt.
NORTHWEST BAY
B O L T O N
Fan Pt.
Federal Hill
Bell Pt.
SCHROON RIVER
Edgecomb Pond
Finkle Brook
Turtle Id.
Montcalm Pt.
Juanita Id.
Cat Mt.
Oahu Id.
Braley Pt.
14 mile Id.
Crown Id.
Hen and Chickens Ids.
Green Id.
Bolton Landing
Sagamore
Huckleberry Id.
Log Bay
Log Bay Id.
Shelving Rock Bay
L A K E
Trout Lake
Huddle Brook
Sweetbriar Id.
Huddle Bay
Leontina Id.
Hiawatha Id.
Recluse Id.
Clay Id.
Dome Id.
Refuge Id.
Watch Pt.
Bolton
Three Brothers
STEAMBOAT ROUTE
Little Id.
Basin Bay
Fish Pt.
Pt. Comfort
Cotton Pt.
Cotton Id.
Edmunds Brook
Rush Id.
Barber Bay
Butternut Brook

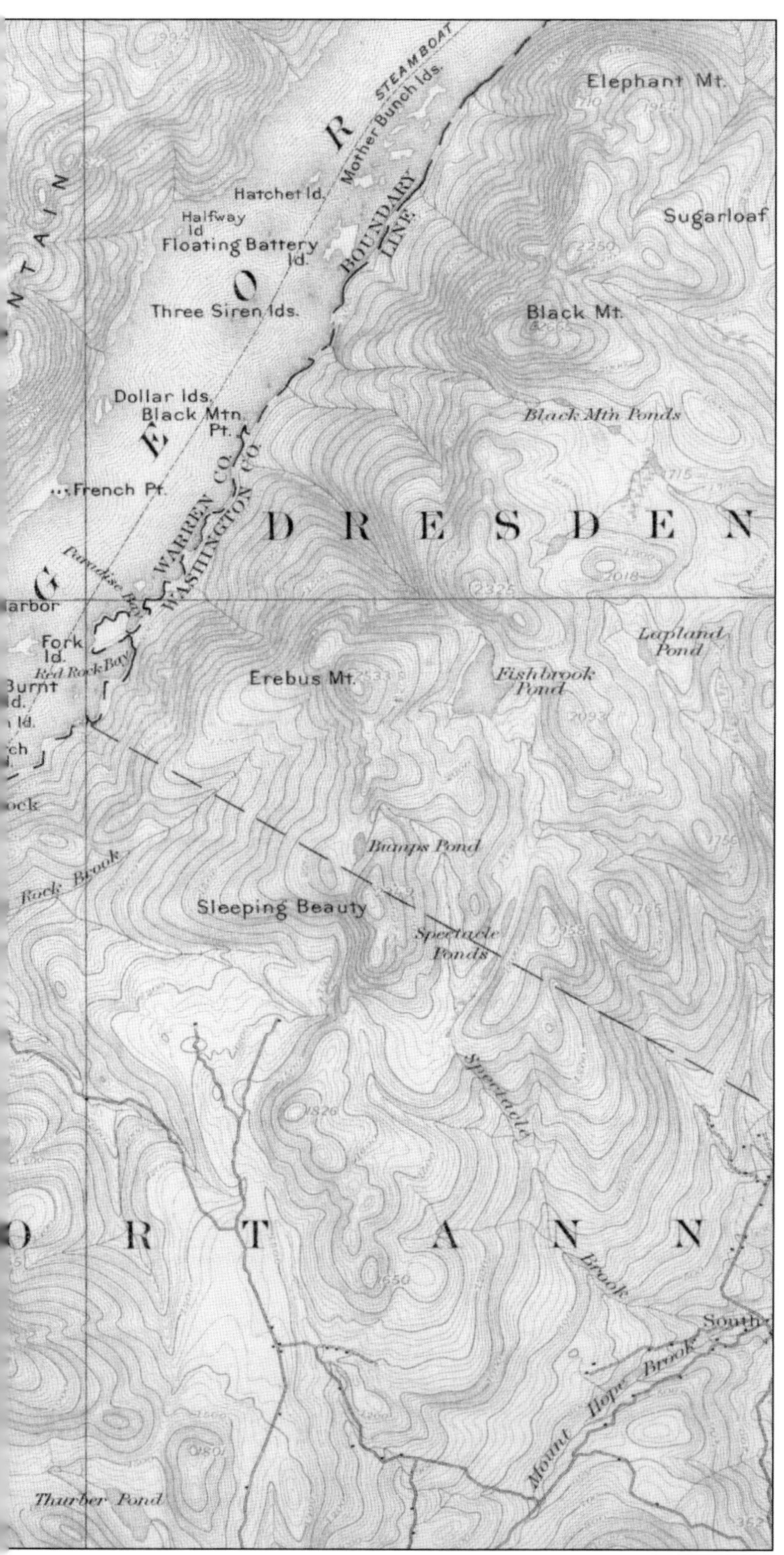

Here is an early map of Lake George from a book published by a local philanthropist in 1913 entitled *Mohican Point on Lake George: The Summer Home of Mr. and Mrs. William K. Bixby, of St. Louis, Mo.* Apperson must have been delighted to own a copy, especially since it represented such a detailed topographical record of all the islands and other points of interest. Apperson spent the rest of his life trying to preserve all the natural scenery represented here, and succeeded in bringing almost all of it under state ownership or some sort of conservation easement. (Courtesy of KARC.)

Consistent with our mission to preserve history on a local level, this book was printed in South Carolina on American-made paper and manufactured entirely in the United States. Products carrying the accredited Forest Stewardship Council (FSC) label are printed on 100 percent FSC-certified paper.

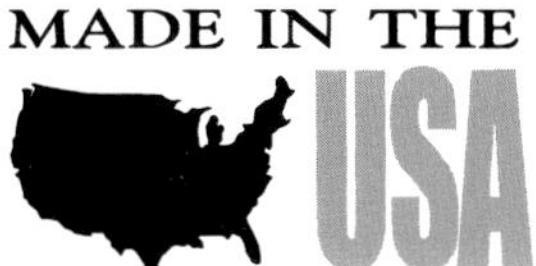